T0201721

Computational Analysis of Storylines

Event structures are central in linguistics and artificial intelligence research: People can easily refer to changes in the world, identify their participants, distinguish relevant information, and have expectations of what can happen next. Part of this process is based on mechanisms similar to narratives, which are at the heart of information sharing. But it remains difficult to automatically detect events or automatically construct stories from such event representations. This book explores how to handle today's massive news streams and provides multidimensional, multimodal, and distributed approaches, like automated deep learning, to capture events and narrative structures involved in a "story." This overview of the current state-of-the-art on event extraction, temporal and casual relations, and storyline extraction aims to establish a new multidisciplinary research community with a common terminology and research agenda. Graduate students and researchers in natural language processing, computational linguistics, and media studies will benefit from this book.

TOMMASO CASELLI is an Assistant Professor in Computational Semantics at the University of Groningen. He received his PhD in computational linguistics on temporal processing of texts from the University of Pisa. His main research areas are in discourse processing, event extraction, and (event) sentiment analysis. He is one of the founders of the "Event and Stories in the News" workshop series and is currently working on developing computational models and natural language processing tools to extract plot structures from news. He took part in organizing semantic evaluation campaigns in natural language processing for English and Italian.

EDUARD HOVY is a Research Professor at the Language Technology Institute at Carnegie Mellon University. He was awarded honorary doctorates from the National Distance Education University (UNED) in Madrid in 2013 and the University of Antwerp in 2015. He is one of the initial 17 Fellows of the Association for Computational Linguistics (ACL). His research contributions include the co-development of the ROUGE text summarization evaluation method, the BLANC coreference evaluation method, the Omega ontology, the Webclopedia QA Typology, the FEMTI machine translation evaluation classification, the DAP text harvesting method, the OntoNotes corpus, and a model of structured distributional semantics.

MARTHA PALMER is a Professor at the University of Colorado in Linguistics, Computer Science, and Cognitive Science. She is a AAAI Fellow and an ACL Fellow. She works on trying to capture elements of the meanings of words that can comprise automatic representations of complex sentences and documents. She is a co-editor of *Linguistic Issues in Language Technology* and has been on the CLJ Editorial Board and a co-editor of JNLE. She is a past President of the Association for Computational Linguistics, past Chair of SIGLEX and SIGHAN, and was the Director of the 2011 Linguistics Institute held in Boulder, Colorado.

PIEK VOSSEN is Professor at Vrije Universiteit Amsterdam. He is the co-founder and co-president of the Global Wordnet Association, organizing the international Wordnet conferences since 2002. In 2013, he received the Dutch Spinoza prize for his research. He used this prize to launch a series of projects that included the structuring of news streams using storylines and reader/writer perspectives. Vossen's current main research focuses on cross-document event co-reference and perspective modeling of multiple sources with respect to event data and modeling event implications, as well as event timelines and storylines.

Studies in Natural Language Processing

Series Editor:
Chu-Ren Huang, The Hong Kong Polytechnic University

Associate Series Editor:
Qi Su, Peking University

Editorial Board Members:
Nianwen Xue, Brandeis University
Maarten de Rijke, University of Amsterdam
Lori Levin, Carnegie Mellon University
Alessandro Lenci, Universita degli Studi, Pisa
Francis Bond, Nanyang Technological University

This series offers widely accessible accounts of the state of the art in natural language processing. Established on the foundations of formal language theory and statistical learning, natural language processing is burgeoning with the widespread use of large annotated corpora, rich models of linguistic structure, and rigorous evaluation methods. New multilingual and multimodal language technologies have been stimulated by the growth of the web and pervasive computing devices. The series strikes a balance between statistical versus symbolic methods; deep versus shallow processing; rationalism versus empiricism; and fundamental science versus engineering. Each volume sheds light on these pervasive themes, delving into theoretical foundations and current applications. The series is aimed at a broad audience who are directly or indirectly involved in natural language processing, from fields including corpus linguistics, psycholinguistics, information retrieval, machine learning, spoken language, human-computer interaction, robotics, language learning, ontologies, and databases.

Also in the series

Douglas E. Appelt, *Planning English Sentences*
Madeleine Bates and Ralph M. Weischedel (eds.), *Challenges in Natural Language Processing*
Steven Bird, *Computational Phonology*
Peter Bosch and Rob van der Sandt, *Focus*
The Language of Word Meaning: (editors) *Federica Busa and Pierrette Bouillon*
Inheritance, Defaults and the Lexicon: (editors) *Ted Briscoe, Valeria de Paiva, and Ann Copestake*

Computational Analysis of Storylines
Making Sense of Events

Edited by

TOMMASO CASELLI
University of Groningen

EDUARD HOVY
Carnegie Mellon University, Pennsylvania

MARTHA PALMER
University of Colorado at Boulder

PIEK VOSSEN
Vrije Universiteit, Amsterdam

CAMBRIDGE
UNIVERSITY PRESS

University Printing House, Cambridge CB2 8BS, United Kingdom

One Liberty Plaza, 20th Floor, New York, NY 10006, USA

477 Williamstown Road, Port Melbourne, VIC 3207, Australia

314–321, 3rd Floor, Plot 3, Splendor Forum, Jasola District Centre,
New Delhi – 110025, India

103 Penang Road, #05–06/07, Visioncrest Commercial, Singapore 238467

Cambridge University Press is part of the University of Cambridge.

It furthers the University's mission by disseminating knowledge in the pursuit of
education, learning, and research at the highest international levels of excellence.

www.cambridge.org
Information on this title: www.cambridge.org/9781108490573
DOI: 10.1017/9781108854221

© Cambridge University Press 2021

First published 2021

Printed in the United Kingdom by TJ Books Limited, Padstow Cornwall

A catalogue record for this publication is available from the British Library.

Library of Congress Cataloging-in-Publication Data
Names: Caselli, Tommaso, 1980– editor. | Palmer, Martha Stone, editor. |
Hovy, Eduard H., editor. | Vossen, Piek, editor.
Title: Computational analysis of storylines : making sense of events /
edited by Tommaso Caselli, Martha Palmer, Eduard Hovy, Piek Vossen.
Description: New York : Cambridge University Press, 2021. | Series: Studies
in natural language processing | Includes bibliographical references.
Identifiers: LCCN 2021024558 (print) | LCCN 2021024559 (ebook) |
ISBN 9781108490573 (hardback) | ISBN 9781108854221 (epub)
Subjects: LCSH: Discourse analysis, Narrative. | Narration (Rhetoric)–Data
processing. | Natural language processing (Computer science) |
BISAC: COMPUTERS / Artificial Intelligence / Natural Language Processing |
LCGFT: Essays.
Classification: LCC P302.7 .C656 2021 (print) | LCC P302.7 (ebook) |
DDC 401/.41–dc23
LC record available at https://lccn.loc.gov/2021024558
LC ebook record available at https://lccn.loc.gov/2021024559

ISBN 978-1-108-49057-3 Hardback

Contents

Contributors

André Schmidt
3pc Neue Kommunikation GmbH, Germany

Andres Cremisini
Florida International University, USA

Anthony R. Davis
Southern Oregon University, USA

Benjamin Miller
Emory University, USA

Claire Bonial
Army Research Lab, USA

Clare Voss
Army Research Lab, USA

Dan Simonson
BlackBoiler LLC, USA

Fredi Šarić
University of Zagreb, Croatia

Georg Rehm
DFKI GmbH, Germany

Ghazaleh Kazeminejad
University of Colorado Boulder, USA

Heng Ji
University of Illinois at Urbana–Champaign, USA

Jakub Piskorski
Joint Research Centre of the European Commission, Italy

James Pustejovsky
Brandeis University, USA

Jan Thomsen
Condat AG, Germany

Jens Rauenbusch
3pc Neue Kommunikation GmbH, Germany

Joachim Böttger
ART+COM AG, Germany

Joachim Quantz
ART+COM AG, Germany

Julián Moreno-Schneider
DFKI GmbH, Germany

Karolina Zaczynska
DFKI GmbH, Germany

Kristin Wright-Bettner
University of Colorado Boulder, USA

Malte Ostendorff
DFKI GmbH, Germany

Maria Berger
DFKI GmbH, Germany

Mark A. Finlayson
Florida International University, USA

Martha Palmer
University of Colorado Boulder, USA

Martin Atkinson
Joint Research Centre of the European Commission, Italy

Michael Regan
University of New Mexico, USA

Mikka Wild
3pc Neue Kommunikation GmbH, Germany

Mustafa Ocal
Florida International University, USA

Paramita Mirza
Max Planck Institute for Informatics, Germany

Pavlína Kalm
University of New Mexico, USA

Peter Bourgonje
DFKI GmbH, Germany

Piek Vossen
Vrije Universiteit Amsterdam, the Netherlands

Rolf Fricke
Condat AG, Germany

Roxane Segers
Vrije Universiteit Amsterdam, the Netherlands

Susan W. Brown
University of Colorado Boulder, USA

Tim O'Gorman
University of Massachusetts Amherst,USA

Tommaso Caselli
Rijksuniversiteit Groningen, the Netherlands

Vanni Zavarella
Joint Research Centre of the European Commission, Italy

William Croft
University of New Mexico, USA

Introduction and Overview

Introduction

Contemporary societies are exposed to a continuous flow of information, producing vast amounts of documents at different points in time. Assume that someone needs a comprehensive report of the *events* that occurred in the 2020 Minneapolis protests (e.g., When did they start? Why did they start? Who was involved? Who was in favor/against? How did they end?). An attentive reader will have to (1) collect documents from different sources over a period of time and order them chronologically; (2) select the relevant events and participants (i.e., who, what, and where), deduplicating repetitions at in- and cross-document level; (3) reconstruct the chronological order of the events (i.e., when); (4) connect the relevant events and participants in a coherent way (i.e., why and how); (5) distinguish between important and peripheral information; and (6) distinguish between reporting of events and perspectives on events (i.e., who thinks/feels what).

Available technologies struggle to solve these issues. News aggregation systems can easily monitor the burst and the development of a topic in terms of the quantity of documents published, but they fail in providing content-based analysis. People have to read the documents and a single, stand-alone coherent report manually.

Current natural language processing (NLP) systems also fail when documents' coherence and cross-document connections play a major role in the extraction of information, as in this case. They can identify complex information, but they lack a method combining it into a unitary and coherent message. Steps in this direction have been conducted with the development of entailment recognition tasks (Dagan et al., 2013; Bowman et al., 2015), end-of-story prediction tasks (Mostafazadeh et al., 2016, 2017), narrative

1

chains (Chambers and Jurafsky, 2008, 2009), and script embeddings (Regneri et al., 2010; Pichotta and Mooney, 2014; Rudinger et al., 2015; Modi, 2016; Bisk et al., 2019), but they are still limited and in their infancy.

It has been suggested that what actually makes us human is our ability to tell stories and create narratives (Boyd, 2009; Gottschall, 2012). Narratives represent an evolutionary asset of mankind that allows us to make sense of our experiences and reality, identify explanatory patterns, and build models for reasoning and decision making (Boyd, 2009). People can easily refer to changes in the world, identify their participants, distinguish relevant information, and have expectations of what can happen next. The human ability to find and create narratives allows us to deal with huge streams of fragmented information on a daily basis. Such narrative structures are at the heart of information sharing, as is exemplified by the structure of news articles. Developing systems and approaches that can represent, understand, and generate narratives would lead to more user-friendly and "intelligent" systems that could effectively help humans in their everyday navigation across information and contribute to the reduction of the negative effects of information overload.

Narrowing down the generic expression of "what happens in a narrative," we can see that at least three big notions are involved: events, representing the "what"; their participants, representing the "who and where"; and a set of relations that connect the previous elements together and contribute to the development and coherence of narratives, at both local and global levels.

A somewhat simplified picture that emerges is that of stories as sequences of events. This is actually true for many stories and in particular for stories emerging from news articles. An additional dimension highly connected to the production of stories is that of a moral compass. Many stories, regardless of the specific media that realize them (i.e., a painting, a novel, a play, a song, among others), contain a point or a moral. Aesop's *Fables*, a collection of fables from ancient Greece, were originally addressed to an adult public, covering different themes (e.g., religion, politics, societal issues), and all have an ethical dimension.[1] As a more provocative statement, all religious textbooks (e.g., the Bible, the Koran, the Vedas, among others) can be see as stories with a moral. Others include changes of fortune, insights and growth of personality, or depictions of personalities. Handling such aspects and dimensions of stories is an open challenge for NLP systems, because multiple complex aspects (e.g., coherence of the document, characters' intentions and personalities, moral insights) have to be modeled and dealt with at the same time.

---

[1] All stories end with an ethical summary (e.g., "This story teaches us that [. . .]") of what one learns from each story.

This volume, on the other hand, focuses on methods and approaches that address the "simple" event-sequence type of story. In the following paragraphs, we present a (short) overview of the components and notions that are involved in this type of story to help the readers to navigate through the upcoming chapters.

Event Structure: Microlevel of Analysis

Event structures have been at the heart of linguistics, philosophy, and artificial intelligence. The dialogue across these disciplines to better understand what events are and how to automatically work with them has been continuous and it is still ongoing. Much work has been conducted in this area, which we call microlevel of analysis of events, and consensus has been reached across disciplines and communities on some aspects.

From an ontological point of view, events are considered objects that can occupy portions of time and space. There is also a general consensus to define events as things that occur or happen or hold true. Using a more appropriate ontological terminology, and especially of upper ontologies (Niles and Pease, 2001; Gangemi et al., 2002), events are "perdurants"; i.e., concepts that must be defined dependent on time. An entity's continuity of existence in time has a pivotal role in conceptual classification of human knowledge systems (Huang, 2016).

Human perception, action, language, and thought manifest a commitment to events. It is quite easy to refer to events, either directly (example (1a)) or by means of anaphoric pronouns (example (1b)); to quantify over them; or to modify them through adverbial phrases (example (1c)).

(1) a. *John had a **walk**.*

   b. *John **walked**$_i$. **It**$_i$ was nice.*

   c. *John **walked**$_i$ in the park with Mary.*

The investigation of adverbial modification has led to the formulation of a program to systematically capture and account for appropriate entailment and representation of propositions involving event expressions. From example (1c) it is quite intuitive to infer that the complex event of John walking in the park with Mary entails the simpler event of John walking. Because events can be represented as predicates expressing a, n-ary relation between entities, it becomes very difficult to explain why example (1c) that expresses a ternary relation (*John, in the park, with Mary*) also entails a different unary relation (*John*; Kenny, 2003). The solution of this "riddle" impinges on three subjects (logic, linguistics, and ontology) and has been presented (not without problems) by Davidson (1969). It requires a reification process (i.e., the introduction of new entities in the domain of discourse) of the events as if they were individuals, thus allowing quantification and reference. Predicates of natural language predicate denote events; thus, they require an additional event argument as part of their argument structures (Bach, 1986; Dowty, 1989; Parsons, 1990). This operation has opened new perspectives in the treatment of events and the study of event semantics. For instance, it strengthens the ontological analysis of events as spatiotemporal entities and, at the same time, allows the extension of the event argument to any predicate (Higginbotham, 1985).

When it comes to the linguistic realizations of events, the introduction of the event argument allows a comprehensive analysis of events without being restricted to any specific parts of speech. Verbs, of course, represent the preferred and unmarked realization of events, but any other part of speech that instantiates a predicate may be considered an event. An interesting applicative case of this vision is represented by the TimeML Annotation Guidelines for English (Saurí et al., 2006), which exhaustively illustrates all possible linguistic realizations of events, ranging from verbs to nouns, adjectives, and predicative constructions with prepositional phrases.

As events pertain to reality, it has been noted that their linguistic realizations convey meaning about the temporal properties of events. Work in this area has investigated both when events happen (Reichenbach, 1947) and their intrinsic temporal properties.[2] These matters focus on the lexical semantic properties of events and are also known as "lexical aspect" or *aktionsarten* (German for "kinds of action").

The seminal work of Vendler (1967) focused on verbs and laid down a four-class typology of types of actions: activities, states, accomplishments, and achievements. The distinctions across these classes is based on a set of parameters involving the change undergone during the time the event occurs (dynamicity), the presence of a natural ending point for the event (telicity), and the temporal span the event occupies (duration). States have no internal structure or change during the time span in which they hold (or are true). In a sentence like "*Marc knows English*" there is no difference between the knowing of English by Marc at different moments in time, nor must the knowing of English reach a natural ending point for it to be valid. Activities are events that consist of successive actions over a period of time; they have

---

[2] Very recently, attention has also been focused on a more neglected aspect of events: space. Interested readers are referred to Pustejovsky (2013)

an internal change and a duration but no natural end point. In *"John walks in the park,"* the event is perceived as valid whether John walks for 10 minutes or an hour. Accomplishments are events with a duration and a necessary end point. In *"John drew a circle"* the event requires some time in order to reach a "climax," or its natural end point. Failure to do so will result in a nonvalid event: *"John is drawing a circle,"* pictures John in the act of drawing a circle and it entails that the circle has not been finished yet. Achievements are events with an instantaneous end point and no duration. In *"John arrived,"* the event is valid only when John is actually at his destination; i.e., the event has reached its climax but there is no extension of the event over time.

The validity of this classification has been proved by means of batteries of linguistic tests (e.g., compatibility with temporal adverbials introduced by *for* or *in*; compatibility with progressive form, among others). Furthermore, different organizations and refinements have been proposed over time by different authors (Pustejovsky, 1991; Krifka, 1992; Tenny, 1994; Lenci and Bertinetto, 2000; Verkuyl, 2013). Overall, following Bach (1986), we can characterize a global class of *eventualities* whose major distinction is along the dynamicity parameter, differentiating between states and events, with the latter further distinguished by different subtypes.

Recent work in computational linguistics (Setzer, 2001; Pustejovsky et al., 2003a; Linguistic Data Consortium [LDC], 2005) has adopted the term "event" as a general umbrella expression to include both states and events. At the same time, different classifications of events have been proposed. An extensive overview of the different annotation schemes for events shows that none of them adopts a typology based on the temporal properties of events. Event classes are based on either semantic descriptions of the events (e.g., "Attack"; "Transportation", among others) as in LDC (2005) and Mitamura et al. (2015) or on syntactic-semantic properties of the events that can be further used for reasoning (Pustejovsky et al., 2003a) or dealing with temporal relations (O'Gorman et al., 2016).

A challenging aspect of events concerns how their meaning must be represented to account for their internal structure. A large body of literature has developed the idea that event meaning can be analyzed into its structural components. Decompositional models (Jackendoff, 1983; Dowty, 1989; Levin and Rappaport Hovav, 1995) have promoted an analysis of event meaning in their compositional primitive elements. An accomplishment event such as *"John drew a circle"* could be decomposed into a fixed set of semantic primitives: CAUSE(John, BECOME(DRAWN(y))). In these works, there is a consensus around the idea that complex events, such as accomplishments, are composed of an inner and an outer event, where the outer event expresses causation and agency and the inner event expresses telicity and change of state. Limitations of primitive-based approaches are known and correspond to a risk of proliferation of the primitives themselves. A different approach was proposed by Pustejovsky (1991): rather than decomposing event structures into primitives, events are decomposed into subevents (i.e., substructure of events), each with predicative content, together with rules that govern event composition (see also Chapter 1).

Because events can be represented as predicates, one of their functions is that of expressing a relation with respect to the elements to which they apply. Elements to which event predicates apply are referred to as event participants, and they contribute to the definition of event structures. Different proposals and approaches to effectively modeling event structures have been made in the literature. Besides some inherent differences, theses models are largely concerned not only with identifying the event participants but also in assigning roles to the participants within the event. In other words, the (linguistic) investigation of event structures aims at understanding the "meanings of arguments (e.g., subjects and objects) in the linguistic coding of events and their structural expressions in sentences" (Marantz, 2013, p. 152).

Most meaning representations use a lexically based approach that assumes that the lexical semantics of a verb determines the complements that occur with it in a clause. Recent developments in the generative semantics tradition place the construction of meaning at the interface between syntax and semantic interpretation, with the syntactic configurations determining event structure interpretations.

Access to the event structure has important consequences from a computational linguistics (CL)/NLP perspective. On the one hand, it appears that CL/NLP has used the patterns mapping the semantic arguments of events into syntactic structures for both the creation of language resources (e.g., VerbNet, PropBank, among others) and the development of systems. On the other hand, access to the event structure represents a first step for the development of more advanced systems for understanding narratives. Knowing the actors involved in an event and, most important, their roles and the semantics associated with them may help the development of systems that will allow some form of reasoning and (possibly) prevent wrong inferences.

Finally, recent work has started to investigate "*where do events come from?*" By introducing refinements on the interplay between events and relationships, Guarino and Guizzardi (2016) proposed to distinguish events from scenes. Scenes are described as things that happen in a specific spatiotemporal region; i.e., perdurants that are the object of a unitary perception act.[3] A scene always has some time duration and it occurs in a certain place. In this analysis, events are described as relationships emerging from scenes through a *focusing process*. The focus here is to be interpreted as the relationships that the different participants have with respect to the event (i.e., the event structure): "[s]o we can distinguish some *core participants*, and others that are not involved at all in the event, except in a very indirect way" (Guarino and Guizzardi, 2016, p. 246). By refining the individuation principle that applies to these notions, different scenes must have different spatiotemporal locations, whereas different events may share the same spatiotemporal location.

Connecting Events: Macrolevel of Analysis

As soon as we move outside the boundaries of single sentence analysis of events and their structures, it becomes even more evident how events are complex hubs of information. As a matter of fact, sentences hardly exist or are interpreted in isolation. Context, being the actual context of utterance or the previous discourse history, plays a major role.

When investigating events in discourse, multiple aspects are at play. For instance, the event structure may be influenced or modified by the context of occurrence. In this section, we will overview three aspects that involve event–event relations and that play a crucial role for the development of robust narrative understanding systems: coreference relations, temporal relations, and finally, causal relations.

Davidson (1969) already used anaphoric relations in support of his proposal of an event argument. However, being able to exactly identify when two events are coreferential – i.e., they denote the same event mention – is not an easy task. Strict definitions of event coreference will require an exact match across different features, such as (i) the event description; i.e., what has happened; (ii) the event participants; i.e., who is involved and their roles; and (iii) the spatiotemporal location; i.e., when and where the event mention occurred. As Lu and Ng (2018) clearly illustrated, an end-to-end system for event coreference resolution requires addressing the following subtasks: (1) extract the event mentions (event trigger) and their associated participants, (2) extract the entity mentions (including time and place) and determine

---

[3] It is easy to draw parallels between this definition of scene and frames in frame semantics (Fillmore, 1968, 1982) or that of scripts (Schank and Abelson, 1977).

those that are coreferential, and (3) determine which events are coreferential by matching event triggers and event participants. A challenging aspect of event coreference is the potentially high variation of linguistic realizations of an event (i.e., verbs, nouns, adjectives, prepositional phrases, pronouns). In addition to cross–part of speech relations, challenges are represented by lexical semantic relations such as similarity, hyperonymy/hyponymy, among others, that can be used to refer to event mentions. This variability of realizations combined with the fact that events can relate to each other in different ways makes the task of event coreference even more difficult. In particular, this means that events can corefer fully (identity) or partially (quasi-identity; Poesio et al., 2004; Hovy et al., 2013). Among the set of relations that give rise to semi-identity is the subevent relation (Araki et al., 2014; Araki and Mitamura, 2015).[4] Event coreference resolution is an important building block for properly understanding narratives and extracting storylines both from a single document and when combining multiple documents.

Temporal relation extraction, more than event coreference, is an essential task for the extraction and generation of storylines. When reading a text, we interpret sentences in succession, and at the same time we fit them into a temporal structure. This temporal structure is responsible for allowing us to make inferences on the chronological order of events (i.e., a timeline reflecting the actual temporal order in which events might have occurred), even in the absence of explicit information in the text. In this case, the set of devices that natural languages have at their disposal is varied and larger than those used to express events. These include grammatical devices such as tense and aspect (grammatical aspect), use of discourse connectives such as prepositions and conjunctions, the structure of the discourse itself, and, finally, our own event knowledge. Their combination is responsible for generating what we perceive as a temporal structure of events.

An important aspect concerns the distinction between the actual temporal structure, the chronological order of events as they happen in the world, and the narrative conventions that different text genres adopt when presenting a story. For instance, in the case of news articles, the order of presentation of events is influenced by their perceived news value, which can actually be independent of their chronology. This makes the extraction of such relations from these types of texts even more complex. Additional relevant aspects concern the granularity of the temporal relations used to chronologically connect events. TimeML (Pustejovsky et al., 2003b) qualifies as the most advanced proposal

---

[4] For a recent overview of corpora and systems on this topic, readers are referred to Lu and Ng (2018).

for annotating temporal relations in texts and subsequently using the annotated data to train systems to extract timelines. The task is far from being solved due to numerous pending issues, including the number and types of temporal relations to be used and the sparseness of the annotation between potential event pairs. A more comprehensive overview of the task and solutions in the perspective of storyline extraction is presented in Chapter 4.

Causality plays a central role in the making of stories. Sequences of events ordered in time do not make up a story per se unless there is some sort of "explanation" or logical connections among them. To clarify, consider the tradition of the annals (*annales*), a literary genre very popular in ancient Rome and in the Middle Ages, devoted to chronological records of events. These, like any other timeline, present events exactly in the order in which they happened but do not make connections or infer explanations as to the reasons why an event happened. Causality, on the other hand, is the essential glue that explains why certain things happened and contributes to the making of a coherent story. The addition of causal relations across pairs of events can be envisioned as an aiding cleaning process of timelines in the generation of storylines: only events that are coherently connected will be maintained and presented to the users. Chapter 5 introduces an overview of the role of causal relations for storyline extraction, showing shortcomings of existing approaches and suggesting directions for future work.

One of the goals of this short overview is to show how much of the attention of scholars in linguistics, NLP, and artificial intelligence has mainly focused on the microlevels of analysis of events. Although there is an abundance of work on analysis of language outside the sentence boundary and in the context of larger and more complex units, such as text or discourse, when it comes to events the macrolevel of analysis appears still in its infancy. The complexity of the phenomena at stake (coreference, chronological order, causal inference, commonsense knowledge) are such that available systems as well as theoretical frameworks all present inadequate solutions. It is the goal of this volume to present both a perspective and the state-of-the-art viable approaches that aim at connecting into a homogeneous framework these two levels of analysis. Only by this means can we move toward new and more viable solutions for improving automatic methods for narrative understanding.

Part One: The Foundational Components of Storylines

The first six chapters of this volume introduce the foundational elements of a storyline, as well as state-of-the-art solutions.

Pustejovsky's chapter (Chapter 1) provides an excellent entry point for one of the key components of stories, namely, events and their structure. The chapter offers a thorough overview of research conducted on event structure representations by taking into account different perspectives including linguistics, NLP, and artificial intelligence. The dialogue that it creates across these perspectives will help the reader to appreciate the complexity of the problem and the proposed solutions, highlighting differences and commonalities. It is exactly on the commonalities of the different approaches that a unifying perspective of event semantics is outlined and proposed. An innovative distinction is proposed between surface events, namely, denoted by verbal predicates, and latent event structures; i.e., the finer-grained subeventual representations of events. The chapter offers an example of how to integrate the subeventual event representations into a (lexical) resource designed to model atomic event representations (i.e., VerbNet; Kipper et al., 2008). The distinction between surface and latent (or deep) event structures of sentences and texts is a step forward toward the development of a general computational theory of event structure, with a common vocabulary for events and their relations that may enable reasoning at multiple levels.

Bonial and colleagues (Chapter 2) dive deep into existing ontologies and lexicons for representing atomic event structures. Different approaches and perspectives involved in the development of these useful tools are presented, allowing the reader to also become familiar with the different theoretical backgrounds that have informed such efforts (of particular interest is the section dedicated to semantic role labeling), but it also demonstrates the variety of ways and extents to which lexical resources and ontologies can be integrated and thus enrich each other. A result of this integration effort is the rich event ontology (REO). REO offers a a novel hierarchy of event concepts capable of linking resources for atomic event structure representations (e.g., VerbNet and FrameNet). An immediate advantage of this integration is the expansion of the conceptual coverage of atomic events, thus facilitating deeper reasoning about events. Additionally, REO extends event representations with typical temporal and causal relations between events, a key information that could be integrated as prior event knowledge in systems for the extraction of storylines.

Models of events structure are essential in order to develop a robust storyline extraction framework. By taking the participants in the stories (and thus in the events) as the organizing criterion for the identification of storylines, the required model of event structure needs to express exactly what participants do and what happens to each of them in an event mention. Such an approach is presented by Croft and colleagues (Chapter 3). They propose a model of event decomposition that takes into account time, causation, and qualitative state, where time is analyzed as grammatical aspect (i.e., the structure of events as they unfold over time) and qualitative states model change over the course of the event. Decomposing subevents per participant introduces a treatment of the event–participant relation other than standard semantic role labeling, providing the reader with a different perspective when compared to Bonial et al.'s contribution. A critical aspect of this contribution is the strict connection between the theoretical framework and its conversion into an annotation scheme. This allows testing the framework on actual language data over texts of different genres, thus showing its potential.

The last three chapters of this part of the volume shift the focus from the microlevel of analysis of events to the macrolevel, targeting the temporal and causal relations and storylines.

Finlayson and colleagues (Chapter 4) open their overview with a rigorous analysis of the challenges of automatically anchoring and ordering events in time; i.e., extracting timelines. Timeline extraction has been an active research topic for the past 40 years, with a renewed interest since the availability of the English TimeBank Corpus (Pustejovsky, Hanks et al., 2003). Temporal relations represent a core component (necessary though not sufficient) of narratives and narrative structure. Correctly identifying timelines is a prerequisite to the understanding of stories. Some of the most interesting and challenging aspects of this task concern the sparseness of explicit cues/markers of temporal relations and that component events of a story may be scattered across multiple documents, either repeated or in fragments. Thus, two major ways of approaching this task can be distinguished: in-document and cross-document timeline extraction. In-document timelines can be obtained from temporal graphs through a temporal representation language (e.g., TimeML). Once timelines have been extracted from individual documents, their alignment across documents requires addressing a different problem, namely, cross-document event coreference. This chapter not only provides an overview of previous approaches to in-document timeline extraction and their alignment across documents but it introduces a new state-of-the-art system (TLEX; see Chapter 4) that addresses some of the pending challenges. Several new possible lines of research are highlighted and presented to the readers, each showing the complexity of the task and the limits of existing approaches, especially with the perspective of being able to extract a global, corpus-wide timeline alignment.

Mirza's chapter (Chapter 5) focuses on the other necessary component of narratives: causal relations. Causal relations have a special status because they are responsible for logically and purposefully connecting events. They explain why certain things happened and their contribution to making a story coherent. Similar to temporal relations, causality may be explicitly realized in most natural language documents, and this is especially valid for news articles. The chapter opens with an overview of three different models of causation grounded in psychology and psycholinguistics (the counterfactual model, the probabilistic model, and the dynamics model) and then shifts to discuss annotation efforts. Different corpora are presented and discussed according to the units of discourse – i.e., text spans or lexical units – that are taken into account to identify the causal links between events in the story. Research efforts in the automatic extraction of causal relations are presented and discussed for both annotation approaches (i.e., text spans and lexical units), showing advantages and limitations. An additional aspect that is discussed and presented concerns the acquisition of implicit causal relations from texts. This refers to a line of work grounded on the use of causal potential (Beamer and Girju, 2009), an association measure that exploits discourse structure and co-occurrence patterns across lexical items. Finally, the broadness of this contribution allows readers to appreciate the different layers and levels of analysis and approaches that target causality in natural language, showing advantages and limitations that need to be overcome.

Vossen and colleagues (Chapter 6) conclude this first part by describing a computational approach for storyline extraction. The authors provide a reference definition for storylines and introduce a computational model. The model is grounded in narratology theories. A further relevant aspect of the contribution is the introduction of a parallelism between properties of narratives and data structures. Chronological order, logical connections, and narrative arcs find their correspondences in timelines, causelines, and storylines. The contribution mainly focuses on the description of causelines and storylines, showing how to integrate commonsense knowledge in an event ontology and presenting two complementary annotation schemes that result in two new benchmark corpora for causelines and storylines. Finally, a series of experiments for storyline extraction based on different approaches is presented and discussed. The results highlight the complexity of the task at stake and show peculiarities related to the discourse structure of news articles.

Part Two: Resources, Tools, and Representations for Storylines

The second part of the volume is more focused on presenting resources (e.g., annotation schemes and corpora), systems, and data representations for storylines or for any of its subcomponents (e.g., events, temporal relations, among others).

The first three chapters are centered on events, each targeting a relevant aspect. The opening chapter (Chapter 7), by O'Gorman and colleagues, provides an extensive and systematic comparison of different approaches for annotating events and temporal information in written texts. The RED corpus is introduced, as well as its corresponding annotation scheme, and used as a pivot for comparing annotations of events and how modeling decisions have affected the representation of temporal, causal, and coreference relations of events. The contribution highlights that there is a wide consensus among scholars regarding what constitutes an event and when it should be annotated or not. Interestingly, there is also a consensus on the features with which those events might be annotated. On the contrary, disagreements and differences mainly affect the annotation of event–event relations. A distinguishing feature of numerous event–event relations corpora concern the strategies that have been adopted to define and annotate such relations. A major contribution of this chapter is the presentation of a case study on timeline annotation and comparisons across corpora. This chapter actually represents a snapshot of the status of current annotation efforts in this area, and it also suggests possible future directions for annotation to better distinguish informative *vs.* noninformative annotations.

Ji and Voss (Chapter 8) depict an application-oriented picture. The chapter is a deep dive into the so-called third wave of systems for event detection that embrace symbolic and distributional knowledge resources and propose a common semantic space across types, languages, and data modalities. The major challenges in event extraction are the identification of the different forms in which an event may be expressed, the classification of events into different types, and the identification of the participants. Systems based on this new paradigm, also known as a *share-and-transfer* framework, attempt to address these challenges as well as to improve the portability of systems to low-resource settings by reducing the need for annotated data. Three such settings are presented in this contribution: (i) a new domain, (ii) a new language, and (iii) a new data modality. Besides describing a state-of-the-art framework, the authors highlight current challenges and pending issues connected to event extraction in a call for action to the event extraction community to pay attention to these long tail phenomena.

Miller (Chapter 9) concludes this first set of application-oriented contributions on events by introducing a further aspect, namely, event factuality. In this context, factuality profiling of events is not to be confused with other phenomena such as misinformation or fake news. On the other hand, event factuality corresponds to the commitment of the relevant source (e.g., author of the article or any other relevant participants in a text) to the factual status of the events in a text. In other words, it characterizes whether an event is presented as a fact, a probability, a possibility, or even something that did not happen or a situation that did not hold. Factuality touches on two notions that have been widely discussed in linguistics and in philosophy: modality and evidentiality. From an NLP perspective, factuality plays a critical role in numerous tasks, among which are timeline and storyline extraction. Factuality is a necessary component for reasoning about eventualities in discourse. Miller, in his contribution, investigates factuality in a particular type of narrative, namely, witness testimonies, with a particular focus on assessing a speaker's certainty about the reported events. The chapter presents a new annotation study based on crowdsourcing, addressing the perception of speaker certainty and exploring how readers think and interpret the certainty with which a witness makes their statements. Starting from existing annotation schemes for event factuality (Saurí and Pustejovsky, 2009; Wan and Zhang, 2014; Lee et al., 2015; Stanovsky et al., 2017), the analysis of his annotation experiments shows the benefits of a finer-grained annotation when it comes to the interpretation of real-world testimonies.

The last three chapters, on the other hand, provide a series of different approaches for the storyline extraction problem. Such differences concern the granularity levels of the representation of storylines, including entity-centered storylines, event-centered storylines, and document-centered storylines. These variations in storyline representations are good examples of the complexity of the phenomenon and of the different layers at which it can be addressed.

Simonson and Davis (Chapter 10) elaborate on the narrative schemas (Chambers and Jurafsky, 2008, 2009) by introducing a new task: narrative argument salience through entities annotated (NASTEA). Narrative schemas are a form of entity-centric storyline extraction whereby sequences of events in precedence temporal order are created by large-size corpora by aggregating events on the basis of a common participant. In this chapter, NASTEA is used to examine the distributional properties of narrative schemas. The goal of NASTEA is to investigate how well these storyline representation structures capture the events and stories: a good narrative schema is one that captures the most salient participants in the story. A further aspect that is taken into account concerns the stability of the narrative schemas across documents of the same broad topic. Through a set of ablation experiments (at document level), the authors identify two sets of document categories in the corpus of news articles they took under consideration: *homogeneous* and *heterogeneous*. The first set of documents indicates news stories with a consistent and stable set of narrative schemas, with repeating events and participant roles. The second set of documents aggregates news stories with new combinations of events or circumstances, leading to more varied and less stable narrative schemas. On the basis of the results of the NASTEA task and schema stability experiments, the authors identify a shortcoming of the narrative schema approach for storyline extraction, namely, that they may have limitations when used to extract these kind of data representations and fail to adequately understand and interpret the complex novelty that appears in more articulated news stories.

Moving away from entity-driven approaches to event-centered ones, Piskorski and colleagues (Chapter 11) reframe the storyline extraction task as temporally linking related event templates. In this approach, events are represented by means of predefined templates that have to be automatically filled with relevant and appropriate entities. Storylines are approximated by automatically linking related event templates from different documents over a period of time. The chapter illustrates a set of experiments to link automatically generated event templates from security-related news data (e.g., natural and man-made disasters, social and political unrest, military actions and crimes). Event linking requires access not only to the temporal ordering of the events but also to event coreference, as different templates of the same events should be merged together or excluded, to avoid redundancies in the potential storyline.

Rehm and colleagues (Chapter 12) conclude this part by providing a different set of experiments and approaches to automatically generate storylines. The chapter can be seen as composed of two parts: the first part is dedicated to the description of existing technologies for document-level storylines. This approach is labeled semantic storytelling and is based on the application of a series of text analytics components to large collections of documents. Interaction with the end-users is a key feature of this approach, implemented through a series of services orchestrated using a workflow manager. Successful examples of the application of the semantic storytelling approach are presented and described. The second part of the chapter, on the other hand, concerns reflections and suggestions on how to develop long-term and flexible solutions related to the application of the semantic storytelling approach. Three industry use cases are presented to identify shortcoming of the existing methods and solutions for improvement of semantic storytelling technologies. A key component of the proposed solution lies in the identification and use of discourse relations to connect different texts about the same topic in a meaningful way.

Acknowledgments This volume collects papers that originated in a series of workshops on events and storyline extraction that took place between 2013 and 2018. We thank the participants to the workshops who made the events a success and contributed to rich discussions on different aspects of the connection between events and storylines. Several people participated and gave presentations that are not included in this volume, and we thank them all. We also thank Professor Chu-Ren Huang for his input in the making of this volume.

Finally, this series of workshop on events and storylines would not have been possible without the help of sponsors (NewsEdge Inc.) and the project "Understanding of Language by Machines – an escape from the World of Language" financed through the NWO Spinoza Prize 2013 SPI 30-673 (2014–2019) awarded to Professor Piek Vossen.

References

Araki, Jun, Liu, Zhengzhong, Hovy, Eduard, and Mitamura, Teruko. 2014. Detecting Subevent Structure for Event Coreference Resolution. In: Calzolari, Nicoletta, Choukri, Khalid, Declerck, Thierry, et al. (eds.), *Proceedings of the Ninth International Conference on Language Resources and Evaluation (LREC'14)*. European Language Resources Association.

Araki, Jun, and Mitamura, Teruko. 2015. Joint Event Trigger Identification and Event Coreference Resolution with Structured Perceptron. Pages 2074–2080 of: Màrquez, Lluís, Callison-Burch, Chris, and Su, Jian (eds.), *Proceedings of the 2015 Conference on Empirical Methods in Natural Language Processing*. Lisbon: Association for Computational Linguistics.

Bach, Emmon. 1986. The Algebra of Events. *Linguistics and Philosophy*, **9**(1), 5–16.

Beamer, Brandon, and Girju, Roxana. 2009. Using a Bigram Event Model to Predict Causal Potential. Pages 430–441 of: Gelbukh, Alexander (ed.), *International Conference on Intelligent Text Processing and Computational Linguistics*. Springer.

Bisk, Yonatan, Buys, Jan, Pichotta, Karl, and Choi, Yejin. 2019. Benchmarking Hierarchical Script Knowledge. Pages 4077–4085 of: Burstein, Jill, Doran, Christy, and Solorio, Thamar (eds.), *Proceedings of the 2019 Conference of the North American Chapter of the Association for Computational Linguistics: Human Language Technologies, Volume 1 (Long and Short Papers)*. Minneapolis, MN: Association for Computational Linguistics.

Bowman, Samuel R., Angeli, Gabor, Potts, Christopher, and Manning, Christopher D. 2015. A Large Annotated Corpus for Learning Natural Language Inference. In: Màrquez, Lluís, Callison-Burch, Chris, and Su, Jian (eds.), *Proceedings of the 2015 Conference on Empirical Methods in Natural Language Processing (EMNLP)*. Association for Computational Linguistics.

Boyd, Brian. 2009. *On the Origin of Stories*. Harvard University Press.

Chambers, Nathanael, and Jurafsky, Dan. 2008. Unsupervised Learning of Narrative Event Chains. Pages 789–797 of: Moore, Johanna D., Teufel, Simone, Allan, James, and Furui, Sadaoki (eds.), *Proceedings of the Conference of the Association for Computational Linguistics (ACL)*. Association for Computational Linguistics.

Chambers, Nathanael, and Jurafsky, Dan. 2009. Unsupervised Learning of Narrative Schemas and Their Participants. Pages 602–610 of: Su, Keh-Yih, Su, Jian, Wiebe, Janyce, and Li, Haizhou (eds.), *Proceedings of the Joint Conference of the 47th*

Annual Meeting of the ACL and the 4th International Joint Conference on Natural Language Processing of the AFNLP. Volume 2. Association for Computational Linguistics.

Dagan, Ido, Roth, Dan, Sammons, Mark, and Zanzotto, Fabio Massimo. 2013. Recognizing Textual Entailment: Models and Applications. *Synthesis Lectures on Human Language Technologies*, **6**(4), 1–220.

Davidson, Donald. 1969. The Individuation of Events. Pages 216–234 of: Rescher, N. (ed.), *Essays in Honor of Carl G. Hempel.* Springer.

Dowty, David R. 1989. On the Semantic Content of the Notion of "Thematic Role." Pages 69–129 of: Chierchia, G., Partee, B. H., and Turner, R. (eds.), *Properties, Types and Meaning.* Springer.

Fillmore, Charles J. 1968. The Case for Case. Pages 1–25 of: Bach, E., and Harms, R. T. (eds.), *Universals in Linguistic Theory.* London: Holt, Rinehart and Winston.

Fillmore, Charles J. 1982. Frame Semantics. Pages 111–137 of: Korea, The Linguistic Society (ed.), *Linguistics in the Morning Calm.* Seoul: Hanshin.

Gangemi, Aldo, Guarino, Nicola, Masolo, Claudio, Oltramari, Alessandro, and Schneider, Luc. 2002. Sweetening Ontologies with DOLCE. Pages 166–181 of: Gómez-Pérez, Asunción, and Benjamins, Richard (eds.), *International Conference on Knowledge Engineering and Knowledge Management.* Springer.

Gottschall, Jonathan. 2012. *The Storytelling Animal: How Stories Make Us Human.* Houghton Mifflin Harcourt.

Guarino, Nicola, and Guizzardi, Giancarlo. 2016. Relationships and Events: Towards a General Theory of Reification and Truthmaking. Pages 237–249 of: Adorni, Giovanni, Cagnoni, Stefano, Gori, Marco, and Maratea, Marco (eds.), *AI*IA 2016 Advances in Artificial Intelligence: XVth International Conference of the Italian Association for Artificial Intelligence.* Springer.

Higginbotham, James. 1985. On Semantics. *Linguistic Inquiry*, **16**(4), 547–593.

Hovy, Eduard, Mitamura, Teruko, Verdejo, Felisa, Araki, Jun, and Philpot, Andrew. 2013. Events Are Not Simple: Identity, Non-identity, and Quasi-identity. Pages 21–28 of: Hovy, Eduard, Mitamura, Teruko, and Palmer, Martha (eds.), *Workshop on Events: Definition, Detection, Coreference, and Representation.* Atlanta: Association for Computational Linguistics.

Huang, Chu-Ren. 2016. Endurant vs Perdurant: Ontological Motivation for Language Variations. Pages 15–25 of: *Proceedings of the 30th Pacific Asia Conference on Language, Information and Computation: Keynote Speeches and Invited Talks.*

Jackendoff, Ray. 1983. *Semantics and Cognition.* MIT Press.

Kenny, Anthony. 2003. *Action, Emotion and Will.* Routledge.

Kipper, Karin, Korhonen, Anna, Ryant, Neville, and Palmer, Martha. 2008. A Large-Scale Classification of English Verbs. *Language Resources and Evaluation*, **42**(1), 21–40.

Krifka, Manfred. 1992. Thematic Relations as Links between Nominal Reference and Temporal Constitution. *Lexical Matters*, **2953**, 30–52.

Lee, Kenton, Artzi, Yoav, Choi, Yejin, and Zettlemoyer, Luke. 2015. Event Detection and Factuality Assessment with Non-expert Supervision. Pages 1643–1648 of: Màrquez, Lluís, Callison-Burch, Chris, and Su, Jian (eds.), *Proceedings of the 2015 Conference on Empirical Methods in Natural Language Processing.*

Lenci, Alessandro, and Bertinetto, Pier-Marco. 2000. Aspect, Adverbs, and Events. Pages 265–287 of: Higginbotham, James, Pianesi, Fabio, and Varzi, Achille C. (eds.), *Speaking of Events*.

Levin, Beth, and Rappaport Hovav, Malka. 1995. *Unaccusativity: At the Syntax–Lexical Semantics Interface*. Cambridge, MA: MIT Press.

Linguistic Data Consortium. 2005. *ACE (Automatic Content Extraction) English Annotation Guide-lines for Events* ver. 5.4.3 2005.07.01. Philadelphia: Linguistic Data Consortium.

Lu, Jing, and Ng, Vincent. 2018. Event Coreference Resolution: A Survey of Two Decades of Research. Pages 5479–5486 of: Lang, Jérôme (ed.), *Proceedings of the Twenty-Seventh International Joint Conference on Artificial Intelligence, IJCAI-18*. International Joint Conferences on Artificial Intelligence Organization.

Marantz, Alec. 2013. Verbal Argument Structure: Events and Participants. *Lingua*, **130**, 152–168.

Mitamura, Teruko, Liu, Zhengzhong, and Hovy, Eduard H. 2015. Overview of TAC KBP 2015 Event Nugget Track. In: *TAC 2015*.

Modi, Ashutosh. 2016. Event Embeddings for Semantic Script Modeling. In: Riezler, Stefan, and Goldberg, Yoav (eds.), *Proceedings of the Conference on Computational Natural Language Learning (CoNLL)*.

Mostafazadeh, Nasrin, Chambers, Nathanael, He, Xiaodong, et al. 2016. A Corpus and Cloze Evaluation for Deeper Understanding of Commonsense Stories. Pages 839–849 of: *Proceedings of the 2016 Conference of the North American Chapter of the Association for Computational Linguistics: Human Language Technologies*. San Diego: Association for Computational Linguistics.

Mostafazadeh, Nasrin, Roth, Michael, Louis, Annie, Chambers, Nathanael, and Allen, James. 2017. *LSDSem 2017 Shared Task: The Story Cloze Test*.

Niles, Ian, and Pease, Adam. 2001. Towards a Standard Upper Ontology. Page 2–9 of: *Proceedings of the International Conference on Formal Ontology in Information Systems. Volume 2001*. FOIS '01. New York: Association for Computing Machinery.

O'Gorman, Tim, Wright-Bettner, Kristin, and Palmer, Martha. 2016. Richer Event Description: Integrating event coreference with Temporal, Causal and Bridging Annotation. Pages 47–56 of: Caselli, Tommaso, Miller, Ben, van Erp, Marieke, Vossen, Piek, and Caswell, David (eds.), *Proceedings of the 2nd Workshop on Computing News Storylines (CNS 2016)*. Austin, TX: Association for Computational Linguistics.

Parsons, Terrence. 1990. *Events in the Semantics of English: A Study in Subatomic Semantics*. Cambridge, MA: MIT Press.

Pichotta, Karl, and Mooney, Raymond J. 2014. Statistical Script Learning with Multi-Argument Events. Pages 220–229 of: Wintner, Shuly, Goldwater, Sharon, and Riezler, Stefan (eds.), *Proceedings of the 14th Conference of the European Chapter of the Association for Computational Linguistics*, Vol. 14. Gothenburg, Sweden: Association for Computational Linguistics.

Poesio, Massimo, Mehta, Rahul, Maroudas, Axel, and Hitzeman, Janet. 2004. Learning to Resolve Bridging References. Pages 143–150 of: *Proceedings of the 42nd Annual Meeting of the Association for Computational Linguistics (ACL-04)*.

Pustejovsky, James. 1991. The Syntax of Event Structure. *Cognition*, **41**(1), 47–81.

Pustejovsky, James. 2013. Where Things Happen: On the Semantics of Event Localization. Pages 29–39 of: Kelleher, John, Ross, Robert, and Dobnik, Simon (eds.), *Proceedings of the IWCS 2013 Workshop on Computational Models of Spatial Language Interpretation and Generation (CoSLI-3)*. Potsdam, Germany: Association for Computational Linguistics.

Pustejovsky, James, Castano, José M., Ingria, Robert, et al. 2003a. TimeML: Robust Specification of Event and Temporal Expressions in Text. *New Directions in Question Answering*, **3**, 28–34.

Pustejovsky, James, Castano, José, Ingria, Robert, et al. 2003. TimeML: Robust Specification of Event and Temporal Expressions in Text. In: Bos, Johan, and Koller, Alexander (eds.), *Fifth International Workshop on Computational Semantics (IWCS-5)*.

Pustejovsky, James, Hanks, Patrick, Saurí, Roser, et al. 2003. The TimeBank Corpus. Pages 647–656 of: Archer, Dawn, Rayson, Paul, Wilson, Andrew, and McEnery, Tony (eds.), *Proceedings of Corpus Linguistics Conference*. Lancaster, UK.

Pustejovsky, James. 2021. The Role of Event-Based Representations and Reasoning in Language. Pages 25–49 of: Caselli, Tommaso, Palmer, Martha, Hovy, Eduard, and Vossen, Piek (eds), *Computational Analysis of Storylines: Making Sense of Events*. Cambridge University Press.

Regneri, Michaela, Koller, Alexander, and Pinkal, Manfred. 2010. Learning Script Knowledge with Web Experiments. Pages 979–988 of: Hajič, Jan, Carberry, Sandra, Clark, Stephen, and Nivre, Joakim (eds.), *Proceedings of the 48th Annual Meeting of the Association for Computational Linguistics*. Association for Computational Linguistics.

Reichenbach, Hans. 1947. *Elements of Symbolic Logic*. London: Collier-Macmillan.

Rudinger, Rachel, Rastogi, Pushpendre, Ferraro, Francis, and Van Durme, Benjamin. 2015. Script Induction as Language Modeling. In: Màrquez, Lluís, Callison-Burch, Chris, and Su, Jian (eds.), *Proceedings of the 2015 Conference on Empirical Methods in Natural Language Processing (EMNLP-15)*.

Saurí, Roser, Littman, Jessica, Knippen, Bob, et al. 2006. TimeML Annotation Guidelines Version 1.2.1.

Saurí, Roser, and Pustejovsky, James. 2009. FactBank: A Corpus Annotated with Event Factuality. *Language Resources and Evaluation*, **43**(3), 227.

Schank, Roger, and Abelson, Robert P. 1977. *Scripts, Plans, Goals and Understanding: An Inquiry into Human Knowledge Structures*. Erlbaum.

Setzer, Andrea. 2001. *Temporal Information in Newswire Articles: An Annotation Scheme and Corpus Study*. Ph.D. Thesis, University of Sheffield.

Stanovsky, Gabriel, Eckle-Kohler, Judith, Puzikov, Yevgeniy, Dagan, Ido, and Gurevych, Iryna. 2017. Integrating Deep Linguistic Features in Factuality Prediction over Unified Datasets. Pages 352–357 of: Barzilay, Regina, and Kan, Min-Yen (eds.), *Proceedings of the 55th Annual Meeting of the Association for Computational Linguistics: Volume 2. Short Papers*.

Tenny, Carol L. 1994. *Aspectual Roles and the Syntax–Semantics Interface*. Dordrecht, the Netherlands: Kluwer.

Vendler, Z. 1967. *Linguistics in Philosophy*. Ithaca, NY: Cornell University Press.

Verkuyl, Hendrik Jacob. 2013. *On the Compositional Nature of the Aspects*. Vol. 15. Springer Science & Business Media.

Wan, Xiaojun, and Zhang, Jianmin. 2014. CTSUM: Extracting More Certain Summaries for News Articles. Pages 787–796 of: *Proceedings of the 37th International ACM SIGIR Conference on Research & Development in Information Retrieval*.

PART ONE

Foundational Components of Storylines

1

The Role of Event-Based Representations and Reasoning in Language

James Pustejovsky

Abstract. This chapter briefly reviews the research conducted on the representation of events, from the perspectives of natural language processing, artificial intelligence (AI), and linguistics. AI approaches to modeling change have traditionally focused on situations and state descriptions. Linguistic approaches start with the description of the propositional content of sentences (or natural language expressions generally). As a result, the focus in the two fields has been on different problems. Namely, linguistic theories try to maintain compositionality in the expressions associated with linguistic units, or what is known as *semantic compositionality*. In AI and in the planning community in particular the focus has been on maintaining compositionality in the way plans are constructed, as well as the correctness of the algorithm that searches and traverses the state space. This can be called *plan compositionality*. I argue that these approaches have common elements that can be drawn on to view event semantics from a unifying perspective, where we can distinguish between the surface events denoted by verbal predicates and what I refer to as the *latent event structure* of a sentence. Latent events within a text refer to the finer-grained subeventual representations of events denoted by verbs or nominal expressions, as well as to hidden events connoted by nouns. By clearly distinguishing between surface and latent event structures of sentences and texts, we move closer to a general computational theory of event structure, one permitting a common vocabulary for events and the relations between them, while enabling reasoning at multiple levels of interpretation.

1.1 Introduction

Reasoning about events and their temporal properties is a capability that all humans possess and a hallmark of intelligent behavior in any cognitive system. Our knowledge of actions and events in the world, as well as our thoughts, fears, and intentions in our mental lives, are essential for modeling causation, constructing complex plans, hypothesizing possible outcomes of actions, and almost any higher order cognitive task. It is not surprising, therefore, that temporal and event reasoning has been a central area of research in artificial intelligence (AI), linguistics, and natural language processing (NLP) for decades.

Event reasoning requires temporal reasoning, which is itself concerned with representing and reasoning about such anchoring and ordering relationships. This is not surprising, because one of the most difficult problems in reasoning about events is locating them temporally. Consider the following simple discourse illustrating this distinction.

(1)   a. Yesterday, John **fell** while **running**.
      b. He **broke** his leg.

Temporally situating the events in this example involves two independent strategies: establishing a *relative ordering* of the events to each other and a *temporal anchoring* of each event relative to a fixed time, such as the overt temporal expression, *yesterday*, or Reichenbach's speech time (Reichenbach, 1947). For this example, we may wish to temporally anchor the *falling*, *running*, and *breaking* events to the particular time (yesterday) or to the speech time (these are past events), as well as order the events relative to each other; e.g., the running precedes the falling, which precedes the breaking. Reasoning with even such a simple narrative requires identifying at least the three following temporal constraint sets, as shown in (2c).

(2)   a. **fall** $\subseteq$ *yesterday*, **run** $\subseteq$ *yesterday*, **break** $\subseteq$ *yesterday*
      b. **fall** $<$ *speech*, **run** $<$ *speech*, **break** $<$ *speech*
      c. **run** $<$ **fall** $<$ **break**

How these pairwise relations are identified and what constitutes the arguments of these relations, however, has been a major research problem for years, in both AI and linguistics, and is also addressed in detail in Chapter 7.

Using commonsense inference, for example, we would expect the falling event to occur before the breaking event, that the falling terminates the running, and that all three occurred yesterday. On the other hand, reasoning linguistically from the grammatical tense and aspect associated with the verbs, we can only conclude that the events are in the past relative to the speech time, that the falling overlapped the time of the running, and that the event of breaking is unordered relative to the others in the past. Further reasoning from the lexical aspect of the verbs could suggest that both falling and breaking are not compatible event types with running, but this would be a fairly sophisticated linguistic inference. Perhaps even more significant, these inferences already assume that appropriate events can be defined, identified, and packaged as input to subsequent inference procedures.

In the next section, I review what assumptions these fields have made with respect to the recognition of events and how to model them. We will identify two approaches that have figured prominently in event inferencing, the first from linguistics and the second from AI:

- Verbal predicates and some nominals in language are associated with individual events in the logical representation of a sentence.
- Verbal predicates are associated with fluents occupying begin and end states that are formally linked in a model to indicate change of state.

Which approach one adopts depends to a large extent on what kinds of inferences are being addressed; e.g., sentential semantics, discourse inferences, or reasoning about larger narratives and story understanding. The methodology employed in linguistics, where semantic compositionality is a prominent concern, has generally been a better fit for sentence-based event descriptions, and the approach taken in AI has some distinct advantages for narrative understanding and planning. I then discuss computational resources for event semantics, such as VerbNet, and how data structures reflect the linguistic approach to modeling events. Finally, I present some recent developments within event semantics from generative lexicon (GL), which can be seen as attempts to integrate these two methodologies, where the state-change model from AI is embedded within the compositional model of semantics adopted in the linguistic approach. We will see how this change-of-state (update semantics) model of events can be encoded in VerbNet, thereby providing a computational semantic resource to both the AI and NLP communities.

1.2 Introducing Situations and Events

In the simple narrative in (1b) above the verbs are identified as events, with the temporal orderings shown in (2c). Before we discuss how events are recognized and subsequently ordered, however, it is worth considering alternative strategies for temporally anchoring and ordering the content associated with our utterances, in both discourse and narratives.

There are essentially two major approaches to the problem of temporally anchoring the propositional content denoted by a sentence:

1. TENSE AS MODAL: treat the verbal tense as a temporal modal operator over the propositional content of the sentence; or
2. ARGUMENT REIFICATION: introduce a temporally interpreted argument to the expression denoting the propositional content.

In the TENSE AS MODAL approach, a sentence such as *John was hungry* is treated as a proposition scoped by a modal "past tense" operator, P (Prior, 1957; Kamp, 1968), shown in (3a) along with its interpretation.

(3) a. $\mathbf{P}(hungry(j))$
    b. $\exists t[t < \mathbf{now} \wedge M, t' \models hungry(j)]$

The interpretation function for this operator introduces a time, t', in the model, where $t' < \mathbf{now}$, and the sentence *John is hungry* is true at t'. Further examples of this logic in (4) demonstrate the interpretation of sentences with richer tense and aspect marking.

(4) a. John will have left Boston.
       $\mathbf{F}(\mathbf{P}(leave(j,b)))$
       $\exists t_1, t_2[\mathbf{now} < t_1 \wedge \mathbf{now} < t_2 < t_1 \wedge M, t_2 \models leave(j,b)]$
    b. John was going to leave Boston.
       $\mathbf{P}(\mathbf{F}(leave(j,b)))$
       $\exists t_1, t_2[t_1 < \mathbf{now} \wedge t_1 < t_2 \wedge M, t_2 \models leave(j,b)]$
    c. John had already left Boston.
       $\mathbf{P}(\mathbf{P}(leave(j,b)))$
       $\exists t_1, t_2[t_1 < \mathbf{now} \wedge t_2 < t_1 \wedge M, t_2 \models leave(j,b)]$

The model theory for a temporal modal logic does not include a domain of individuals denoting events; rather, the satisfaction conditions associated with what we might identify as an event occurring are actually operations over propositions navigating the accessibility relations in world valuations. As a result, it is impossible to refer to events as first-class objects for purposes of coreference and quantification.

Though this approach has been developed into a number of rich and very expressive languages for characterizing computational properties of systems – for example, Linear Temporal Logic (LTL; Pnueli, 1977) and Computation Tree Logic (CTL; Emerson and Sistla, 1984) – for even a simple discourse such as that in (2c), it is difficult to capture the temporal ordering constraints that present themselves, since neither events nor states are treated as individually quantified arguments in the logic.

The ARGUMENT REIFICATION method solves this problem by introducing an additional argument or index in the object language itself, which is used to anchor and identify the evaluation of the propositional content from the sentence in the model. There are two traditions associated with this method, one from the early days of AI and the other coming out of philosophical logic and formal semantics in linguistics. From the first tradition, in order to formalize the situations and actions associated with automated planning, McCarthy (1963) enriched the conventional domain of individuals in first-order logic to include *situations*. A situation is a snapshot of the world, containing the propositions holding at that state. The predicates associated with situations are called *propositional fluents*. Returning to the example in (3), this method reifies the situation encompassing the propositional content of "John being hungry" as *s* and anchors it to a temporal index, *t*.

(5) $\exists s, t[\text{hungry}(j, s) \land \text{time}(s) = t \land t < now]$

This method was adopted and enriched in McCarthy and Hayes (1969), where it became known as the *situation calculus*, one of the most influential event-based formalisms in logical approaches to AI and formal reasoning. By reifying the propositional content of John's hunger as a situation variable, it can be referenced for planning algorithms; for example, as one of the preconditions for someone eating food.

Addressing the same problem from the tradition of philosophical logic and language analysis, Davidson (1967) proposed a related but distinct representation for the interpretation of action sentences in natural language. Specifically, he proposed that events (but not states) should be included in the logical description of certain predicates (action verbs) as an additional argument, one that is associated with the verb rather than any overt syntactic argument. Hence, the sentence in (6a) is paraphrased in (6b) and has the logical form of (6c).

(6)   a. Brutus stabbed Caesar.

     b. "There was a stabbing event between Brutus and Caesar."

     c. $\exists e[\text{stab}(b, c, e)]$

Davidson argued that events are concrete entities that can be perceived, located in space and time, and, moreover, are linguistically real. In (7b), for example, both instances of the pronoun *it* refer to the event "Brutus stabbed Caesar," and the verb *witness* selects this event as one of its complements.

(7)   a. Brutus **stabbed** Caesar with a knife.

     b. He did **it** and everyone witnessed **it**.

In (7a), the prepositional phrase (PP) *with a knife* can be seen as modifying this event directly, as illustrated in (8).

(8)   a. Brutus stabbed Caesar with a knife.

    b. $\exists e, x[\text{stab}(b, c, e) \land \text{knife}(x) \land \text{with}(e, x)]$

After the adoption of Davidson's event variable in Parsons (1989), it became a standard method of interpretation for events in formal semantics and eventually in linguistics more broadly (Pustejovsky, 1991; Tenny and Pustejovsky, 2000). In neo-Davidsonian accounts, the event argument does not augment the valency of the verb but is linked to the event participants through semantic roles, such as AGENT (AG), PATIENT (PAT), LOCATION (LOC), and INSTRUMENT (INST), as in (9):

(9) $\exists e, x[\text{stab}(e) \land \text{AG}(e, b) \land \text{PAT}(e, c) \land \text{knife}(x) \land \text{INST}(e, x)]$

Parsons (1990) developed an interpretation of events that introduces a distinction between an event *culminating* (**Cul**) versus an event *holding* (**Hold**). This makes it possible to distinguish the telicity associated with a sentence. Hence, for an event, e, and a temporal interval, t, the following relations hold:

(10) a. TELIC EVENTS (achievements, accomplishments): **Cul**(e, t)

    b. ATELIC EVENTS (processes, states): **Hold**(e, t)

Returning to the sentence in (8a), we now modify the logical form in (9) to that in (11).

(11) $\exists e, t, x[\text{stab}(e) \land \text{AG}(e, b) \land \text{PAT}(e, c) \land \text{knife}(x) \land \text{INST}(e, x) \land Cul(e, t)]$

Though Davidson's approach appears similar if not identical to the situation calculus, there are significant differences in the way they approach the modeling and representation of events in language (and action or behavior). For Davidsonian models, an action or event in a natural language expression corresponds to an individuated event quantified in the meaning representation associated with that sentence (e.g., (8) and (12b)).

(12) a. John gave Mary a book.

    b. $\exists e, x[\text{give}(e) \land \text{AG}(e, j) \land \text{GOAL}(e, m) \land \text{TH}(e, x) \land \text{book}(x)]$

By reifying the propositional content of the action as a first-order individual in the model, Davidson was able to apply standard first-order logical inference procedures to handle entailments that had previously required higher-order functional behavior. For example, as with the optional arguments to the event in (8) above, both spatial and temporal prepositional phrases modify the event directly, shown in (13b), and not the entire predicate, as seen in (13c).

(13) a. Brutus stabbed Caesar in the Forum in the morning.

 b. $\exists e[\text{stab}(e) \wedge \text{AG}(e,b) \wedge \text{PAT}(e,c) \wedge \text{LOC}(e,f) \wedge \text{TIME}(e,m)]$

 c. $\text{TIME}(\text{LOC}(\text{stab}(b,c),f),m)$

The template described above, where an atomic event is introduced along with the participants playing specific semantic roles in this event, is also adopted in the representation used in VerbNet, where it provides a computational resource for English verbs, their valencies, and detailed syntactic–semantic descriptions of the constructions associated with each word sense (Kipper et al., 2008).

Now consider how the example in (12ba) is treated within the situation calculus. As mentioned previously, the focus within AI and the planning community was originally on registering and monitoring the state of the world and how properties (fluents) in the world change from one state to the next. Fluents are time-varying properties of individuals. There is no single individual event of "giving" in the situation calculus, because actions are not state descriptions but rather are functions that map states to states and hence act as *state transformers*. The action of giving, for example, has two fluents identifying possession of an object, each associated with a state; i.e., the beginning and end states of the event.

(14) a. $\exists s_1, t_1[\text{have}(j,x,s_1) \wedge book(x) \wedge \text{time}(s_1) = t_1]$

 b. $\exists s_2, t_2[\text{have}(m,x,s_2) \wedge \text{time}(s_2) = t_2]$

To model the event in (12b), the initial state, s_1, is changed by the application of a state-to-state transducer, **give**, which indicates the state that results from its application; i.e., s_2:

(15) $\lambda s_2 \exists x, y, z[\text{have}(z, y, \text{Result}(\textbf{give}(x, y, z), s_2))]$

Though this adequately captures the change in state within the world, where John had the book and now Mary has the book, there are two things missing in this analysis: (a) there is no quantified reference to the change of state itself in the model (i.e., the transition) and (b), there is no event variable associated with any linguistic expression in (12b) denoting this transition. That is, the verbal predicate *give* is not represented at all. This makes the situation calculus difficult to use for modeling natural language in a compositional manner, without some modifications or enrichments.

One such modification was made by McDermott (1982), who abandoned the classical situation calculus notion of events as state transformers. Rather, he defined an event as a *set of intervals* over which a proposition is minimally true (i.e., it happens once): this theory subsequently became an important model for

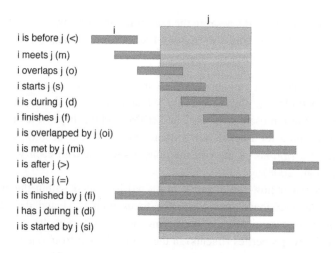

Figure 1.1 Allen's (1984) temporal interval relations.

problem solving and planning paradigms in AI. This is essentially the same
intuition that Allen (1984) adopted for his definition of event. A somewhat
different approach was taken by Kowalski and Sergot (1989), where events are
assumed as primitives in the model, acting as *updates* on the state of the world.
In this sense they are *additive* information operations. More specifically, they
are seen as actions that initiate or terminate the properties of individuals (the
fluents we encountered in the situation calculus).

One of the most influential argument reification methods to be developed
within the AI tradition is Allen's interval temporal logic (Allen, 1983). Allen
(1984) can be seen as an attempt to model events directly in the logic, while
also considering their temporal interval properties (as shown in Figure 1.1)
for planning purposes, within general AI concerns. In this system, temporal
intervals are considered primitives and constraints (on actions, etc.) are
expressed as relations between intervals. There are 13 basic (binary) interval
relations, where 6 are inverses of the other, excluding equality.

Allen (1984) made a basic distinction between *properties* (fluents) and
occurrences, which are similar to Davidson's events and Goldman's actions
(Davidson, 1967; Goldman, 1970). As in the situation calculus, a property, p,
holds, if and only if it is true during a specified temporal interval, t. This
predicate is defined in terms of a downward monotonic subinterval property
(Allen, 1984).

(16) **holds**$(p,t) \leftrightarrow \forall i[in(i,t) \rightarrow$ **holds**$(p,i)]$

Occurrences are a sort of generalized eventuality category that divide into two classes: *processes* and *events*. Processes are characterized as **occurring**, whereas events **occur**. This is essentially identical to Parsons' distinction between **Hold** and **Cul** (Parsons, 1990). As a result, Allen's theory is able to address one of the major issues fundamental to the linguistic approach to event representations, namely, semantic compositionality. By differentiating the satisfaction conditions between the different event types (property, process, and event), Allen's theory can be directly adapted as an interpretation consistent with linguistic treatments of event semantics at the sentence level.

The other major influence in AI promoting the role of events in formal reasoning comes from Hobbs and his colleagues (Hobbs et al., 1987). Hobbs introduced a parsimonious method of treating events as reified first-order individuals in the logic and the model, with an operator he called *nominalization* (Hobbs, 1985). For example, for any predicate, P, in the language, we can generate its nominalized form, $P^{\textbf{Nom}}$, as follows:

(17) $\forall x \forall P [P(x) \rightarrow \exists e [P^{\textbf{Nom}}(e,x) \wedge Exists(e)]]$

The *Exists* predicate can be seen as a domain updating operation in the model, ensuring that this individual has the proper extension. As with Allen's interval logic or Davidson's event logic, we can restrict our reasoning to first-order inferences and avoid complications arising from higher-order modifiers and operators. Unlike these approaches, however, Hobbs sees nominalization as a general operation for enriching the ontology, one that can apply to a broad range of conceptual domains, including scales, times, materials, and so on. This general strategy of how ontological types relate to surface realization is given linguistic grounding in Croft (1991), where it is evidenced in language data through a number of typologically broad constructions.

Interestingly, Hobbs' method of reification along with Allen's interval-based notion of events together form the interpretive core of TimeML (Pustejovsky et al., 2003), ISO-TimeML (Pustejovsky et al., 2010), the multilingual resources built on ISO-TimeML community (Im et al., 2009; Bittar et al., 2011; Caselli et al., 2011), as well as the shared tasks based on ISO-TimeML (Verhagen et al., 2007, 2010; UzZaman et al., 2013). ISO-TimeML treats an event as a cover term for any linguistic predicate, as mentioned in a text, that happens or occurs (as with Parsons' and Allen's distinction). A description of the major event categories identified in ISO-TimeML is given below.

(18) a. VERBAL EVENT PREDICATES:
         The missile **sank** the ship.
         The car **hit** the pedestrian.

  b. NOMINAL EVENTS:

  The **meal** was after the **speech**.

  An **alarm** went off during the **workshop**.

  c. NOMINALIZATIONS:

  The **explosion** occurred at noon.

  The **arrival** of the train was late.

  d. ADJECTIVAL EVENT PREDICATES:

  Mary closed the **open** door.

  They observed the **moving** truck.

  e. PREPOSITIONAL PHRASE PREDICATES:

  John is **on board**.

  Sophie is **in the house**.

As is evident from this list, events can be punctual, last for a period of time, have a logical culmination or no natural termination, or describe states or circumstances, as in the situation calculus. The representation of events as reified intervals with constraints can be mapped to formal calculi used in temporal reasoning, for example DAML-Time (Hobbs and Pustejovsky, 2003), as well as interval temporal logic (Pratt-Hartmann, 2007). This strategy also allows one to interpret the ordering of events in discourse and narratives as an interval constraint satisfaction problem, which has had a significant influence on recognizing narrative event chains and identifying event schemas (Chambers and Jurafsky, 2008, 2009), as well as more recent work on script learning and frame induction (Cheung et al., 2013; Pichotta and Mooney, 2014).

If we interpret Allen's theory directly in terms of a Davidsonian event variable, as with Parsons' treatment discussed above, we can maintain syntactic and semantic compositionality, but we will still lack any representation that reflects the change of state accompanying actions, as with the situation calculus. As it happens, most implementations of Allen's interval calculus are deployed for tracking state-change in planning scenarios or constraint solving problems in NLP involving temporal intervals, rather than for sentence-level linguistic analysis.

What this discussion reveals is that though the underlying formal mechanisms of the situation calculus and event semantics are quite similar, their surface realizations are extremely different. The former focuses on the language of change and state-based situational representations, whereas the latter is concerned with the individuation of events that are denoted by complete sentential expressions. In the next section, we see how these two representational approaches have been integrated into more expressive languages that can address the core issues in both planning and discourse as well as sentence-level compositionality. We discuss first how to *encode* object properties that change, as subevents in the meaning representations for sentences. We then show how to *track* these object changes over the subevent structures themselves.

1.3 Modeling the Substructure of Events

Consider the philosophical presuppositions associated with the two perspectives discussed above. From an ontological standpoint, the componential structure of *actions* has been taken for granted in AI approaches to modeling change: a CLOSE action brings about a change in state from OPEN(Y) to NOT(OPEN(Y)). Within linguistics, the componential structure of *words* (not actions or events) has been traditionally of considerable importance, in addition to their various subclasses. To bring these two views closer together, we need to see how words can be associated with the componential structure of actions. But in order to represent the internal structure of events, one must first understand how the meanings of event-denoting expressions are to be represented.

How does this play out? In a logical framework, there are two fundamental ways of representing meaning: (i) the meaning of an accomplishment verb, for example *close*, is the predicate CLOSE, such that a sentence of the form *X closes Y* is mapped to CLOSE(X,Y); or (ii) the meaning of *close* is decomposed into the meaning of primitive elements; e.g., CAUSE(X,BECOME(NOT(OPEN(Y)))).

As generative semanticists such as McCawley (1971) and Lakoff (1970) demonstrated, by decomposing the meaning of accomplishment verbs into a causative component along with a result component, we can explain a number of apparent scope ambiguities with adverbs and other modifiers. For example, in (19), *again* can take scope over the entire expression ((19b), the external reading) or the resulting state ((19c), the internal reading).

(19) a. The astronauts entered the atmosphere again.

     b. AGAIN(ACT(X, BECOME(IN(X,ATMOSPHERE))))

     c. ACT(X, BECOME(AGAIN(IN(X,ATMOSPHERE))))

Dowty (1979) developed this decompositional strategy into a fully compositional semantic theory, providing an elegant interpretation for a broad range of linguistic constructions. Interestingly, however, there are still no events in Dowty's theory, not even at the atomic level, because he adopted a classical model with propositional interpretation functions.

Jackendoff (1983), on the other hand, did introduce atomic events into his meaning representations, what he called "conceptual structures." In Jackendoff (1990) he also assumed that eventualities can be referenced as conceptual categories selected by predicates or functions in the language.

Pustejovsky (1991) can be seen as an attempt to merge the event semantics of Davidson with the structured decomposition of Dowty and Jackendoff, by introducing the notion of subevent structure. In this approach, rather than decomposing an atomic event into predicative primitives, the event itself is decomposed into subevents, each with predicative content (cf. Moens and Steedman, 1988; Pustejovsky, 1988).

(20) a. EVENT → STATE | PROCESS | TRANSITION
      b. STATE: → e
      c. PROCESS: → $e_1 \ldots e_n$
      d. TRANSITION$_{ach}$: → STATE STATE
      e. TRANSITION$_{acc}$: → PROCESS STATE

This is accompanied by meaning-forming rules for event composition, giving rise to the relationships expressed by decomposed meanings. For example, an accomplishment event such as *close* is made up of two aspectually salient parts, a preparatory process with the meaning "ACT(X,Y) ∧ ¬ CLOSED(Y)" and a result state with the meaning "CLOSED(Y)." Event structure, in fact, distinguishes the different Aktionsarten in terms of how subevents are structured (cf. (21)), which is a central component of the lexically driven compositionality in GL (Pustejovsky, 1995).

(21) a. STATE: a simple event, evaluated without referring to other events: *be sick, love, know*

$$S$$
$$|$$
$$e$$

      b. PROCESS: a sequence of events identifying the same semantic expression: *run, push, drag*

$$P$$

$$e_1 \ldots\ldots\ldots e_n$$

      c. TRANSITION: an event identifying a semantic expression evaluated with respect to its opposition: *give, open; build, destroy*
         Two-state transition (ACHIEVEMENT): where $\neg\phi \in S_1$, and $\phi \in S_2$

Extended transition (ACCOMPLISHMENT): where $\neg\phi \in P$, and $\phi \in S$

By making explicit reference to the subevents associated with the internal structure of events, this approach enables event representations and the inference systems they support to directly reference and quantify them. Hence, unlike the primitive predicates in Dowty's theory, subevents can be quantified in the logical form of the sentence, in the same way that arguments can be. Consider the inferences associated with the sentences in (22), for example.

(22) a. The destroyer is sinking the boat.
$\exists e_1, x, y[\text{sink\_act}(e_1, x, y) \wedge \text{destroyer}(x) \wedge \text{boat}(y)]$

   b. The destroyer sank the boat.
$\exists e_1, e_2, x, y[\text{sink\_act}(e_1, x, y) \wedge \text{destroyer}(x) \wedge \text{boat}(y) \wedge \text{sink\_result}$
$(e_2, y) \wedge e_1 < e_2]$

   c. The boat sank.
$\exists e_2, e_1, y, x[\text{sink\_result}(e_2, y) \wedge \text{boat}(y) \wedge \text{sink\_act}(e_1, x, y) \wedge e_1 < e_2]$

There are distinct advantages to *encoding* state change directly in event structure. Notice that the logical form of the causative (22b) differs from the inchoative (22c) only in the explicit identification of a specific causer. The introduction of an unspecified causer allows the event to be linked in a discourse, where an antecedent or subsequent event might identify the agent. Furthermore, such a representation is essential for recognizing any temporal sequencing that occurs within an event and any changes in state that might have occurred (Pustejovsky, 2005; Mani and Pustejovsky, 2012).

Explicit subevent representations have proved useful, if not crucial, for some types of textual inference, such as *recognizing textual entailment* (RTE; Dagan et al., 2013) and the more recent *natural language inference* (NLI) challenge (Bowman et al., 2015).[1] For example, in order to identify the appropriate discourse relations in a narrative or discourse, it is helpful to

---

[1] The importance of subevent representation and tracking is discussed in Chapter 3 and the relevance of larger narrative event structures to inference is detailed in Chapters 4 and 6.

know how the events relate to each other semantically and therefore causally. Consider the discourse below.

(23)   a. The vase broke.

$\exists e_2, e_1, x, y[\text{broken}(e_2, y) \wedge \text{vase}(y) \wedge \text{break\_act}(e_1, x, y) \wedge e_1 < e_2]$

     b. John pushed it off the shelf.

$\exists e_3, e_4, z[\text{push\_act}(e_3, j, z) \wedge \text{vase}(z) \wedge \text{push\_result}(e_4, z) \wedge e_3 < e_4]$

In (23), because of the state resulting from the pushing event, we can conclude that $e_2 = e_4$; further, because $e_1 = e_3$, we have an *explanation* relation between (23b) and (23a) (Hobbs, 1982; Asher and Lascarides, 2003; Im and Pustejovsky, 2010).

The discussion above has focused on the identification and encoding of subevent structure for predicative expressions in language. In subsequent work within GL (Pustejovsky and Moszkowicz, 2011; Mani and Pustejovsky, 2012), event structure is enriched to not only *encode* but dynamically *track* those object attributes modified in the course of the event (the location of the moving entity, the extent of a created or destroyed entity, etc.). The resulting event structure representation is called a *dynamic event structure* (Pustejovsky, 2013). Starting with the view that subevents of a complex event can be modeled as a sequence of states (containing formulae), a dynamic event structure explicitly labels the transitions that move an event from state to state (i.e., programs).[2]

A dynamic approach to modeling updates makes a distinction between formulae, ϕ, and programs, π. A formula is interpreted as a classical propositional expression, with assignment of a truth value in a specific state in the model (Harel et al., 2000). For our purposes, a state is a set of propositions with assignments to individual variables at a specific frame. We can think of atomic programs as input/output relations, that is relations from states to states, and hence interpreted over an input–output state–state pairing. The model encodes three kinds of representations: (i) predicative **content** of a frame; (ii) **programs** that move from frame to frame; and (iii) **tests** that must be satisfied for a program to apply. These include pretests, while-tests, and result-tests.

---

[2] Each event can be seen as a traced structure over a labeled transition system (van Benthem, 1995). The approach is similar in many respects to that developed in Fernando (2009, 2013) and Naumann (2001).

In this model, there are only two primitive event types: *states*, which are simply propositions describing a snapshot in time, and *transitions*, which are pairs of states connected by a function that moves from the first state to the second state (in some ways similar to the situation calculus representation). These two event types are illustrated in (24).[3]

(24)   a. State   b. Simple Transition

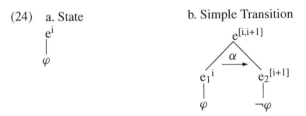

The structure in (24a) represents a **state** as a snapshot of the world in time, e^i, with the propositional content, φ. The event structure in (24b) illustrates how the program α takes the world from the state in e^i with content φ, to the adjacent state, e_2^{i+1}, where the propositional content has been negated, $\neg\varphi$. This structure corresponds directly to **achievements**. From these two types the other two Vendlerian classes can be generated, as we now demonstrate. **Processes** can be modeled as an iteration of simple transitions, where two conditions hold: the transition is a change in the value of an identifiable attribute of the object; every iterated transition shares the same attribute being changed. This is illustrated in (25a).

Finally, **accomplishments** are built up by taking an underlying process event, $e{:}\textsc{p}$, denoting some change in an object's attribute, and synchronizing it with an achievement (simple transition); that is, $e{:}\textsc{p}$ is unfolding while ψ is true, until one last step of the program α makes it the case that $\neg\psi$ is now true. This can be seen in the event structure in (25b).

(25)   a. Process   b. Accomplishment

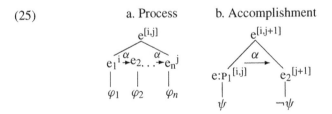

<hr>

[3] In Chapter 2, the classical event ontology is enriched substantially to accommodate concepts and relations required for robust processing and interpretation in NLP applications.

1.4 Enriching VerbNet with Event Dynamics

In order to operationalize an event semantics as a computational resource, the information needs to be encoded as frames in the meaning representations associated with the verbal predicates in the language. For modeling predicates with atomic event representations, VerbNet (Kipper et al., 2008) is an example of such an encoding. VerbNet is a lexicon of around 5,200 English verbs, organized primarily around Levin's (1993) verb classification. Classes in VerbNet are structured according to the verb's syntactic behavior, describing the diathesis alternations compatible with each verb (Bonial et al., 2011). Each VerbNet class contains semantic representations expressed as conjunctions of primitive predicates, such as **motion** or **cause** along with an atomic event variable **E**. Event participants that have syntactic relevance are identified with various stages of the event evoked by the syntactic frame. The manner in which a predicate (and its argument) is temporally positioned relative to another is accomplished through the higher-order relation **path_rel**, which requires reference to one of the second-order predicates, **Start**, **During**, or **End**. For example, the semantics for one intransitive frame in class **Run-51.3.2** is shown in (26).

(26) a. *Billy ran into a cafe.*

b. **motion**(during(E), Theme)
   path_rel(start(E), Theme, Initial_location, ch_of_loc, prep)
   path_rel(during(E), Theme, Trajectory, ch_of_loc, prep)
   path_rel(end(E), Theme, Destination, ch_of_loc, prep)

Hence, what classic VerbNet provides is a rich resource for *atomic* event representations associated with language predicates (i.e., English verbs).

Given our discussion from the previous section, however, there are several things to note about what is not expressed in the VerbNet semantics: (i) the representation is not inherently first-order; (ii) there are no reified subevents that can be referenced in discourse models or planning algorithms; (ii) and there is no mention of the actual change; i.e., the *opposition structure* that is implicated in a change-of-state event, such as *close* or *break*.

Because there is only a single event variable, any ordering or subsetting information needs to be performed as second-order operations. For example, temporal sequencing is indicated with the second-order predicates **start**, **during**, and **end**, which are included as arguments of the appropriate first-order predicates. Attempts to use VerbNet in human–computer interaction concluded that a first-order, enriched subevent representation would greatly facilitate the interaction between the language parsing and the planning components of the system (Narayan-Chen et al., 2017).

Interpreting (26a) in a first-order atomic representation, where we eliminate the **path_rel** relation and let participant roles act as relations, takes us part of the way, resulting in the event expression given in (27).

(27) $\exists e,x,l,p[\text{run}(e) \wedge \mathbf{Ag}(e,j) \wedge \mathbf{Init}(e,l) \wedge \mathbf{Dest}(e,x) \wedge \mathbf{Traj}(e,p) \wedge \text{cafe}(x)]$

As the expression in (27) makes clear, the VerbNet semantic representation includes reference to participants that *can* be realized syntactically but are not always present in a specific construction. A more conventional Davidsonian representation for (26a) would be that shown in (28).

(28) $\exists e,x[\text{run}(e) \wedge \mathbf{Ag}(e,j) \wedge \mathbf{Dest}(e,x) \wedge \text{cafe}(x)]$

This leaves the remaining issues unresolved, however. As Zaenen et al. (2008) pointed out, VerbNet is unable to support many temporal and spatial inferencing tasks, because the temporal ordering annotation is not complete or consistent throughout the database; e.g., for several motion classes, **End**(E) was given but not **Start**(E), and some classes involving change of location of participants (e.g., *gather, mix*) did not include a motion predicate at all. That is, from *The diplomat left Bhagdad* you cannot infer *The diplomat was in Bhagdad* (Brown et al., 2018). In addition, attempts to use VerbNet in robotics have resulted in the suggestion that the representation contain more specific causal and temporal relations. The current method of indicating causation, for example, simply had an **Agent** and the event variable E as arguments to a **Cause** predicate. This is somewhat misleading in that it could imply that the Agent causes all of E, including whatever state exists at **Start**(E).

A further step toward a proper subeventual meaning representation was proposed in Brown et al. (2018, 2019), where it was argued that, in order to adequately model change, the VerbNet representation must track the change in the assignment of values to attributes as the event unfolds. This includes making explicit any *predicative opposition* denoted by the verb. For example, simple transitions (achievements) encode either an intrinsic predicate opposition (*die* encodes going from $\neg dead(e_1,x)$ to $dead(e_2,x)$) or a specified relational opposition (*arrive* encodes going from $\neg loc\_at(e_1,x,y)$ to $loc\_at(e_2,x,y)$). Creation predicates and accomplishments generally also encode predicate oppositions. As we will describe briefly, GL's event structure and its temporal sequencing of subevents solves this problem transparently, while consistent with the idea that the sentence describes a single matrix event, E.

With the introduction of GL's event structure, the biggest change to VerbNet is the move from a tripartite division of the temporal span of any event to a model with explicitly quantified (and indexed) subevents, which can be increased or decreased to accommodate the complexity of the event and are ordered using Allen's relational calculus (Allen, 1983). This also eliminates the needs for second-order logic of **Start**(E), **During**(E), and **End**(E), allowing for more nuanced temporal relationships between subevents. The default assumption in this new schema is that e_1 precedes e_2, which precedes e_3, and so on. When appropriate, however, more specific predicates can be used to specify other relationships, such as **meets**(e_2, e_3), to show that the end of e_2 meets the beginning of e_3, or **while**(e_2, e_3) to show that e_2 and e_3 are cotemporal. The latter can be seen in Section 5.1 with the example of accompanied motion.

The second significant change is how causation is represented. Previously in VerbNet, the semantic form implied that the entire atomic event was caused by an Agent; i.e., **cause**(Agent, E). In the revised VerbNet-GL, adopting the GL event structure and assumptions consistent with our discussion above from AI and robotics, "events cause events." Thus, something an agent does (e.g., **do**$(e_2,$ Agent)) causes a state change or another event (e.g., **motion**$(e_3,$ Theme)), which would be indicated with **cause**(e_2, e_3). This is seen in (29).

(29) a. *The lion tamer jumped the lions through the hoop.*

   b. **motion**(during(E), Theme)
   path_rel(start(E), Theme, ?Initial_location, ch_of_loc, prep)
   path_rel(during(E), Theme, Trajectory, ch_of_loc, prep)
   path_rel(end(E), Theme, ?Destination, ch_of_loc, prep)
   cause(Agent, E)

To illustrate this change, consider the revised representation in (30) (Brown et al., 2018, 2019).

(30) *The lion tamer jumped the lion through the hoop.*
   has_location$(e_1,$Theme,?Initial_Location)
   do$(e_2,$Agent)
   motion$(e_3,$Theme,Trajectory)
   cause(e_2, e_3)
   has_location$(e_4,$Theme,?Destination)

Notice that the predicate **has_location** now has three arguments: an event, e_1; a **Theme** argument for the object in motion; and an **Initial_location** argument. The motion predicate is underspecified as to the manner of motion in order to be applicable to the 97 verbs in this VerbNet class. A final **has_location** predicate indicates the **Destination** of the **Theme** at the end of the event. Any uninstantiated roles in a frame are preceded by ?, such as **Initial location** and **Trajectory**.

Another way in which VerbNet has accommodated to incorporate an enriched event structure is the encoding of an event-based *opposition structure* to help track the change in object properties over time. This is best illustrated in the revised representation for the VerbNet class **change-of-state**. The representations for changes of state have two basic patterns, depending on whether the change is between absolute states or along a value continuum or scale. The first is illustrated in (31b), the representation for the **Die-42.4** class.

(31)   a. *John died.*

   b. **cause**(e_2, e_3)
      alive(e_1, Patient)
      ¬**alive**(e_3, Patient)

   c.

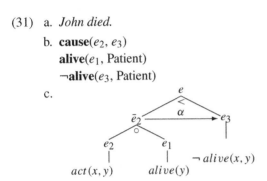

The same event template for relational opposition applies to transfer verbs; e.g., VerbNet class **give-13.1-1**. For example, sentence (32a) has the semantic representation in (32b) and event structure seen in (32c).

(32)   a. *Mary gave the book to John.*

   b. **transfer act**(e_2,x,y)
      have(e_1,x,y)
      ¬**have**(e_1,z,y)
      have(e_3,z,y)
      ¬**have**(e_3,x,y)

   c.

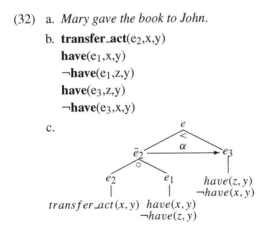

Other modifications to VerbNet semantic representations also include the reinterpretation of accomplishments such as *build* and *write* in terms of GL's dynamic event semantics (Brown et al., 2019).

1.5 Conclusions

In this chapter, I have discussed the distinct but related paths taken toward the interpretation of events by the AI and linguistics communities. An early focus on planning and goal satisfaction in many of the major areas of interest in AI led to a concern with *plan compositionality*, for which the situation calculus became a major representational vehicle for reasoning and inference. Plans were viewed as traversals from *state* to *state*; hence, the primitive units in the language were situations describing state behavior and content. From the philosophically inspired linguistic community, Davidson's notion of event was motivated by a concern to model propositional content of a sentence, rather than an abstract plan. Hence, the focus over the past 50 years in linguistics has been on *semantic compositionality*. I describe how recent work in event semantics has attempted to bridge this cultural and representational divide. The approach taken in dynamic event semantics incorporates the language of state-change from AI with the compositional constraints on linguistic behavior from linguistics.

Acknowledgments This work was funded in part by DTRA grant DTRA-16-1-0002; DARPA grant FA8750-18-2-0016; and DARPA grant W911NF-15-C-0238. I thank Olga Batiukova, Martha Palmer, and Nikhil Krishnaswamy for commenting on an earlier version of this chapter. All remaining errors are, of course, my own.

References

Allen, James. 1983. Maintaining Knowledge about Temporal Intervals. *Communications of the ACM*, **26**(11), 832–843.

Allen, James. 1984. Towards a General Theory of Action and Time. *Artificial Intelligence*, **23**, 123–154.

Asher, Nicholas, and Lascarides, Alex. 2003. *Logics of Conversation*. Cambridge University Press.

Bittar, André, Amsili, Pascal, Denis, Pascal, and Danlos, Laurence. 2011. French TimeBank: An ISO-TimeML Annotated Reference Corpus. Pages 130–134 of: *Proceedings of the 49th Annual Meeting of the Association for Computational*

Linguistics: Human Language Technologies: Short Papers – Volume 2. Association for Computational Linguistics.

Bonial, Claire, Corvey, William, Palmer, Martha, Petukhova, Volha V., and Bunt, Harry. 2011. A Hierarchical Unification of LIRICS and VerbNet Semantic Roles. Pages 483–489 of: *2011 IEEE Fifth International Conference on Semantic Computing*. IEEE.

Bowman, Samuel R., Angeli, Gabor, Potts, Christopher, and Manning, Christopher D. 2015. A Large Annotated Corpus for Learning Natural Language Inference. *arXiv preprint arXiv:1508.05326*.

Brown, Susan Windisch, Bonn, Julia, Gung, James, et al. 2019. VerbNet Representations: Subevent Semantics for Transfer Verbs. Pages 154–163 of: *Proceedings of the First International Workshop on Designing Meaning Representations*.

Brown, Susan Windisch, Pustejovsky, James, Zaenen, Annie, and Palmer, Martha. 2018. Integrating Generative Lexicon Event Structures into Verbnet. In: *Proceedings of the Eleventh International Conference on Language Resources and Evaluation (LREC 2018)*.

Caselli, Tommaso, Lenzi, Valentina Bartalesi, Sprugnoli, Rachele, Pianta, Emanuele, and Prodanof, Irina. 2011. Annotating Events, Temporal Expressions and Relations in Italian: The It-TimeML Experience for the Ita-TimeBank. Pages 143–151 of: *Proceedings of the 5th Linguistic Annotation Workshop*. Association for Computational Linguistics.

Chambers, Nathanael, and Jurafsky, Dan. 2008. Jointly Combining Implicit Constraints Improves Temporal Ordering. Pages 698–706 of: *Proceedings of the Conference on Empirical Methods in Natural Language Processing*. Association for Computational Linguistics.

Chambers, Nathanael, and Jurafsky, Dan. 2009. Unsupervised Learning of Narrative Schemas and Their Participants. Pages 602–610 of: *Proceedings of the Joint Conference of the 47th Annual Meeting of the ACL and the 4th International Joint Conference on Natural Language Processing of the AFNLP: Volume 2*. Association for Computational Linguistics.

Cheung, Jackie Chi Kit, Poon, Hoifung, and Vanderwende, Lucy. 2013. Probabilistic Frame Induction. *arXiv preprint arXiv:1302.4813*.

Croft, William. 1991. *Syntactic Categories and Grammatical Relations: The Cognitive Organization of Information*. Chicago: University of Chicago Press.

Dagan, Ido, Roth, Dan, Sammons, Mark, and Zanzotto, Fabio Massimo. 2013. Recognizing Textual Entailment: Models and Applications. *Synthesis Lectures on Human Language Technologies*, **6**(4), 1–220.

Davidson, Donald. 1967. The Logical Form of Action Sentences. *Essays on Actions and Events*, **5**, 105–148.

Dowty, David. 1979. *Word Meaning and Montague Grammar*. Dordrecht, The Netherlands: Kluwer.

Emerson, E. Allen, and Sistla, A. Prasad. 1984. Deciding Full Branching Time logic. *Information and Control*, **61**(3), 175–201.

Fernando, Tim. 2009. Situations in LTL as Strings. *Information and Computation*, **207**(10), 980–999.

Fernando, Tim. 2013. Segmenting Temporal Intervals for Tense and Aspect. Pages 30–40 of: *Proceedings of the 13th Meeting on the Mathematics of Language (MoL 13)*.

Finlayson, Mark A., Cremisini, Andreas, and Ocal, Mustafa. 2021. Extracting and Aligning Timelines. Pages 91–109 of: Caselli, Tommaso, Palmer, Martha, Hovy, Eduard, and Vossen, Piek (eds), *Computational Analysis of Storylines: Making Sense of Events*. Cambridge University Press.

Goldman, Alvin I. 1970. *Theory of Human Action*. Princeton, NJ: Princeton University Press.

Harel, David, Kozen, Dexter, and Tiuyn, Jerzy. 2000. *Dynamic Logic*. 1st ed. The MIT Press.

Hobbs, Jerry R. 1982. Towards an Understanding of Coherence in Discourse. Pages 223–243 of: Hobbs, Jerry R., and Lehnert, W. (eds.), *Strategies for Natural Language Processing*. Lawrence Erlbaum.

Hobbs, Jerry R. 1985. Ontological Promiscuity. Pages 60–69 of: *23rd Annual Meeting of the Association for Computational Linguistics*. Chicago: Association for Computational Linguistics.

Hobbs, Jerry R., Croft, William, Davies, Todd, Edwards, Douglas, and Laws, Kenneth. 1987. Commonsense Metaphysics and Lexical Semantics. *Computational Linguistics*, **13**(3–4), 241–250.

Hobbs, Jerry, and Pustejovsky, James. 2003. Annotating and Reasoning about Time and Events. In: *Proceedings of AAAI Spring Symposium on Logical Formalizations of Commonsense Reasoning (Stanford, CA, March 2003)*.

Im, Seohyun, and Pustejovsky, James. 2010. Annotating Lexically Entailed Subevents for Textual Inference Tasks. Pages 204–209 of: Murray, R. Charles, and Guesgen, Hans W. (eds.), *Proceedings of the 23rd International Florida Artificial Intelligence Research Society Conference (FLAIRS-23)*. Daytona Beach, FL.

Im, Seohyun, You, Hyunjo, Jang, Hayun, Nam, Seungho, and Shin, Hyopil. 2009. KTimeML: Specification of Temporal and Event Expressions in Korean Text. Pages 115–122 of: Riza, Hammam, and Sornlertlamvanich, Virach (eds.), *Proceedings of the 7th Workshop on Asian Language Resources*. Association for Computational Linguistics.

Jackendoff, Ray. 1983. *Semantics and Cognition*. Vol. 8. The MIT Press.

Jackendoff, Ray. 1990. *Semantic Structures*. Vol. 18. MIT Press.

Kamp, J. A. W. 1968. *Tense Logic and the Theory of Linear Order*. Ph.D. Thesis, University of California, Los Angeles.

Kipper, Karin, Korhonen, Anna, Ryant, Neville, and Palmer, Martha. 2008. A Large-Scale Classification of English Verbs. *Language Resources and Evaluation*, **42**(1), 21–40.

Kowalski, Robert, and Sergot, Marek. 1989. A Logic-Based Calculus of Events. Pages 23–55 of: Schmidt, J. W., and Thanos, C. (eds.), *Foundations of Knowledge Base Management*. Berlin: Springer.

Lakoff, George. 1970. *Irregularity in Syntax*. Holt, Rinehart, and Winston.

Levin, Beth. 1993. *English Verb Classes and Alternations: A Preliminary Investigation*. University of Chicago press.

Mani, Inderjeet, and Pustejovsky, James. 2012. *Interpreting Motion: Grounded Representations for Spatial Language*. Oxford University Press.

McCarthy, John. 1963. *Situations, Actions, and Causal Laws*. Tech. Rep., Stanford University, Department of Computer Science.

McCarthy, John, and Hayes, Patrick. 1969. *Some Philosophical Problems from the Standpoint of Artificial Intelligence*. Stanford University.

McCawley, James D. 1971. Prelexical Syntax. *Monograph Series on Languages and Linguistics*, **24**, 19–33.

McDermott, Drew. 1982. A Temporal Logic for Reasoning about Processes and Plans. *Cognitive Science*, **6**(2), 101–155.

Moens, Marc, and Steedman, Mark. 1988. Temporal Ontology and Temporal Reference. *Computational Linguistics*, **14**, 15–28.

Narayan-Chen, Anjali, Graber, Colin, Das, Mayukh, et al. 2017. Towards Problem Solving Agents That Communicate and Learn. Pages 95–103 of: Bansal, Mohit, Matuszek, Cynthia, Andreas, Jacob, Artzi, Yoav, and Bisk, Yonatan (eds.), *Proceedings of the First Workshop on Language Grounding for Robotics*.

Naumann, Ralf. 2001. Aspects of Changes: A Dynamic Event Semantics. *Journal of Semantics*, **18**(1), 27–81.

Parsons, Terence. 1989. The Progressive in English: Events, States and Processes. *Linguistics and Philosophy*, **12**(2), 213–241.

Parsons, Terence. 1990. *Events in the Semantics of English*. Vol. 5. Cambridge, MA: MIT Press.

Pichotta, Karl, and Mooney, Raymond. 2014. Statistical Script Learning with Multi-argument Events. Pages 220–229 of: Wintner, Shuly, Goldwater, Sharon, and Riezler, Stefan (eds.), *Proceedings of the 14th Conference of the European Chapter of the Association for Computational Linguistics*.

Pnueli, Amir. 1977. The Temporal Logic of Programs. Pages 46–57 of: *18th Annual Symposium on Foundations of Computer Science (SFCS 1977)*. IEEE.

Pratt-Hartmann, I. 2007. From TimeML to Interval Temporal Logic. Pages 166–180 of: Geertzen, J., Bunt, H. C., Thijsse, E., and Schiffrin (eds.), *Proceedings of the Seventh International Workshop on Computational Semantics (IWCS-7)*.

Prior, A. N. 1957. *Time and Modality*. Oxford: Clarendon Press.

Pustejovsky, James. 1988. The Geometry of Events. Tenny, C. (ed.), *Studies in Generative Approaches to Aspect*.

Pustejovsky, James. 1991. The Syntax of Event Structure. *Cognition*, **41**(1), 47–81.

Pustejovsky, James. 1995. *The Generative Lexicon*. Cambridge, MA: MIT Press.

Pustejovsky, James. 2005 (August). *Generative Lexicon and Type Theory*. ESSLLI Summer School, Edinburgh, Scotland.

Pustejovsky, James. 2013. Dynamic Event Structure and Habitat Theory. Pages 1–10 of: Pustejovsky, James (ed.), *Proceedings of the 6th International Conference on Generative Approaches to the Lexicon (GL2013)*. Association for Computational Linguistics.

Pustejovsky, James, Castao, José, Ingria, Robert, et al. 2003. TimeML: Robust Specification of Event and Temporal Expressions in Text. In: Bos, Johan, and Koller, Alexander (eds.), *Fifth International Workshop on Computational Semantics (IWCS-5)*.

Pustejovsky, James, Lee, Kiyong, Bunt, Harry, and Romary, Laurent. 2010. ISO-TimeML: An International Standard for Semantic Annotation. In: Calzolari, Nicoletta, Choukri, Khalid, Maegaard, Bente (eds.), *Proceedings of the Seventh*

International Conference on Language Resources and Evaluation (LREC'10). Valletta, Malta: European Language Resources Association.

Pustejovsky, James, and Moszkowicz, Jessica L. 2011. The Qualitative Spatial Dynamics of Motion in Language. *Spatial Cognition & Computation,* **11**(1), 15–44.

Reichenbach, Hans. 1947. *Elements of Symbolic Logic.* London: Collier-Macmillan.

Tenny, Carol, and Pustejovsky, James. 2000. *Events as Grammatical Objects: The Converging Perspectives of Lexical Semantics and Syntax.* CSLI Publications, Center for the Study of Language and Information.

UzZaman, Naushad, Llorens, Hector, Derczynski, Leon, et al. 2013. SemEval-2013 Task 1: TempEval-3: Evaluating Time Expressions, Events, and Temporal Relations. Pages 1–9 of: Manandhar, Suresh, and Yuret, Deniz (eds.), *Second Joint Conference on Lexical and Computational Semantics (*SEM): Volume 2. Proceedings of the Seventh International Workshop on Semantic Evaluation (SemEval 2013).* Atlanta: Association for Computational Linguistics.

van Benthem, Johannes Franciscus Abraham Karel. 1995. Logic and the Flow of Information. Pages 693–724 of: *Studies in Logic and the Foundations of Mathematics,* Vol. 134. Elsevier.

Verhagen, Marc, Gaizauskas, Robert, Schilder, Frank, et al. 2007. Semeval-2007 Task 15: Tempeval Temporal Relation Identification. Pages 75–80 of: Agirre, Eneko, Màrquez, Lluís, and Wicentowski, Richard (eds.), *Proceedings of the Fourth International Workshop on Semantic Evaluations (SemEval-2007).*

Verhagen, Marc, Sauri, Roser, Caselli, Tommaso, and Pustejovsky, James. 2010. SemEval-2010 Task 13: TempEval-2. Pages 57–62 of: Erk, Katrin, and Strapparava, Carlo (eds.), *Proceedings of the 5th International Workshop on Semantic Evaluation.* Association for Computational Linguistics.

Vossen, Piek, Caselli, Tommaso, and Segers, Roxane. 2021. A Narratology-based Framework for Storyline Extraction. Pages 130–147 of: Caselli, Tommaso, Palmer, Martha, Hovy, Eduard, and Vossen, Piek (eds), *Computational Analysis of Storylines: Making Sense of Events.* Cambridge University Press.

Zaenen, Annie, Bobrow, Daniel G., and Condoravdi, Cleo. 2008. The Encoding of Lexical Implications in VerbNet Predicates of Change of Locations. In: Calzolari, Nicoletta, Choukri, Khalid, Maegaard, Bente, et al. (eds.), *LREC.*

2

The Rich Event Ontology

Ontological Hub for Event Representations

Claire Bonial, Susan W. Brown, Martha Palmer,
and Ghazaleh Kazeminejad

Abstract. This chapter reviews the current landscape of ontological and lexical resources that motivated the development of the Rich Event Ontology (REO). Aimed at a whole that is greater than the sum of its parts, REO functions as a conceptual organization of event types that facilitates mapping between FrameNet, VerbNet, and the Entities, Relations, and Events corpus annotation from the Linguistic Data Consortium.

2.1 Introduction

Lexical resources are the foundation of many natural language processing (NLP) tasks, such as word sense disambiguation, semantic role labeling, and question answering. Manually crafted resources such as WordNet (Fellbaum, 1998), VerbNet (Kipper et al., 2008), and FrameNet (Baker et al., 1998) and their accompanying annotated corpora have required a great deal of time and resources to construct, reflecting their value to NLP but also making it intractable to meet the demand for such resources on a large scale in a variety of languages. Somewhat independently, there has been an explosion of efforts in the construction of ontologies as part of the Semantic Web (Berners-Lee et al., 2001). These ontologies facilitate machine reasoning over data that were previously only available for human consumption. Unfortunately, the progress to integrate computational lexical resources into the Semantic Web (e.g., Eckle-Kohler et al., 2015) has been somewhat slow and difficult, given that conversion of resources like FrameNet, with its complex ontological relations, into the minimalist Resource Descriptive Framework (RDF) schema used in the Semantic Web is not trivial (Scheffczyk et al., 2006). Despite the challenges, there is tremendous value to bringing ontological and lexical resources together—much as WordNet's incorporation of structuring relations into a lexical resource was a tremendous boon to NLP, further integration of these two fields can lead to major contributions.

In this chapter, we survey work that demonstrates the variety of ways and extents to which lexical resources and ontologies can be integrated beneficially, and we provide our own case study illustrating these benefits in the development of the Rich Event Ontology (REO). First, we focus on ontologies—related work marrying ontologies to lexical resources as well as a description of the basic structure and organizing principles of REO, which offers a novel hierarchy of event concepts capable of linking disparate semantic role labeling (SRL) resources and adds typical temporal and causal relations between events. We then turn our focus to SRL resources and describe both related work and the SRL resources leveraged in REO. We demonstrate how bringing together SRL resources into an ontological hub like REO can greatly expand the conceptual coverage of events beyond any single resource and facilitate deeper reasoning about events, such as script or storyline extraction.[1] We close with a discussion of future work in which we further leverage ontologies and linguistic resources together.

2.2 Ontologies

Ontology is traditionally a subfield of philosophy, defined as the science of what is—the various types and categories of objects and relations in existence. Aristotle was one of the most prominent early ontologists, whose ideas laid out in *Categories* and *Metaphysics* clearly influence the distinctions made in many of the ontologies described herein.[2] Within computational efforts, an ontology can be defined as a computer-readable vocabulary of a particular domain. Thus, there is some overlap with lexical resources such as dictionaries; however, ontologies are *structured* to demonstrate various relationships between words, including the common *is-a* subclass relations that indicate the type or category of an ontology entry (WordNet stands out as a lexical resource with ontological structuring). This structure facilitates a computer system's understanding of type relationships and, in combination with other relations, can enable more complex querying and reasoning over the ontological concepts.

Many of the ongoing efforts to create large, computer-readable ontologies, such as YAGO (Suchanek et al., 2007), FreeBase (Bollacker et al., 2008), and

---

[1] Events in REO are "perdurants" defined in Section 2.2.2.
[2] For a clear summary of Aristotle's ideas and how they have been adapted in a modern ontology, see Smith (2000).

DBpedia (Bizer et al., 2009), focus on things or objects, especially named entities, as opposed to events or qualities. Here, we focus on ontological resources that include or concentrate on events. These are numerous and growing, because ontologies often need to be tuned to a particular domain and end goal. Thus, we highlight the ontologies that were most relevant to the development of the type of ontology we sought to create with REO. For each resource, we attempt to briefly describe how it uniquely brings together lexical and ontological information, as well as the high-level category distinctions, principles behind category distinctions, and basic relations it encompasses.

2.2.1 Related Work: Ontologies

Manually Crafted

WordNet (Fellbaum, 1998) is a large electronic database of English words with ontological structure; it represents one of the first large-scale efforts to add such structure to a dictionary-like resource. WordNet is divided firstly into syntactic categories – nouns, verbs, adjectives, and adverbs – and secondly by semantic relations, including synonymy (given in the form of "synsets"), antonymy, hyponymy (e.g., *tree* is a hypernym of *maple*), and meronymy (part–whole relations). These relations make up a complex network of associations that is both useful for computational linguistics and NLP and also informative in situating a word's meaning with respect to others. The highest-level semantic distinction made is between concrete entities and abstract entities, with events falling under abstract entity.

The Suggested Upper Merged Ontology (SUMO; Pease et al., 2002) is a formal ontology that maps to the WordNet lexicon. SUMO serves as the upper-level ontology for a variety of domain ontologies, varying in focus from emotions to weapons of mass destruction. Like WordNet, SUMO also makes a primary distinction between physical entities and abstract entities. However, SUMO's next distinction for physical entities is between objects and processes, such that most events are represented as physical, as opposed to abstract, entities. SUMO's extensive documentation and relations, including logical axioms, were leveraged for efficient expansion of the coverage of nonevent concepts in REO (see Section 2.2.2), as well as semi-automatic extraction of qualia relations currently being integrated into REO (see Kazeminejad et al., 2018).

The Descriptive Ontology for Linguistic and Cognitive Engineering (**DOLCE**; Masolo et al., 2003; Gangemi et al., 2002) is the first module of the WonderWeb Foundational Ontologies effort, the goal of which is to provide a library of ontologies that facilitate mutual understanding. DOLCE aims to model the conceptual categories underlying natural language and common sense, but, because it is intended to be one module in a library of ontologies, it does not itself include lexical mappings. Within DOLCE, a primary distinction is made between ENDURANT and PERDURANT (also sometimes called "continuants" and "occurrents," respectively), which we have adopted for REO. When present, endurants are wholly present, whereas perdurants extend in time by accumulating different temporal parts, so they are only partially present.

The Basic Formal Ontology (BFO; Smith et al., 2014) is intended to be an upper-level ontology to support the creation of lower-level domain ontologies; therefore, it is designed to be neutral with regard to the domains to which it is applied. BFO and DOLCE share many goals and properties, including an initial split between CONTINUANT (entities that can be sliced to yield parts only along spatial dimensions; e.g., *table*) and OCCURRENT (entities that can be sliced along spatial and temporal dimensions to yield parts; e.g., events— *childhood, throwing*).

The Event and Implied Situation Ontology (ESO) focuses on pre- and postsituations with respect to some event type, making explicit how a participant's pre- and poststates change in an event (Segers et al., 2015). ESO was developed as part of the NewsReader project (Vossen et al., 2016), which exploits SRL technology to process millions of English news articles on the global automotive industry from 2003 to 2013. It is another excellent case study in bringing together lexical and ontological resources. The 59 event types included (in version 1) are those relevant to the automotive domain – CHANGE OF POSSESSION, MOTION, etc. Mappings between FrameNet frames and frame elements (see Section 2.3 for more details on FrameNet) and the ESO event types and roles are needed to translate role annotations provided by an SRL module to ontology vocabulary. ESO leverages SUMO to derive the hierarchical structure of events.

The Brandeis Semantic Ontology (BSO) was developed to provide a resource capturing the Generative Lexicon theory of linguistic semantics, a basic tenet of which is the distributed nature of compositionality in language— spreading the semantic load across all constituents as opposed to verb-based approaches (Pustejovsky et al., 2006). Qualia relations are at the heart of this theory and are a primary piece of lexical information represented for each entry in the ontology. The ontology structure makes a basic category distinction between ENTITY, EVENT, and PROPERTY. Each of these, in turn, is divided into the subtypes NATURAL, ARTIFACTUAL, and COMPLEX, which are characterized by the presence or absence of particular qualia relations. The value of qualia relations has been demonstrated for a variety of NLP applications, including furnishing world knowledge for artificial agents (e.g., McDonald and Pustejovsky, 2013; Pustejovsky et al., 2017; Narayana et al., 2018). This motivated us to integrate qualia relations into REO (see Section 2.2.3).

The Rochester Interactive Planning System (TRIPS) LF Ontology was developed to serve as a lexicon for deep syntactic and semantic parsing with the TRIPS parser—a dialogue assistant applied to a variety of different application domains (Dzikovska et al., 2004). This ontology was built by manually combining features from different lexical resources. FrameNet was leveraged for semantic predicates in the system and was the basis for generalized roles, VerbNet was used for the syntax–semantics mapping included in each frame/lexicon entry, and EuroWordNet (Vossen, 1997) was used to gather selectional restrictions on roles. The ontology top level consists of two artificial, empty top nodes that serve as parents for the contentful entries starting at the second level.

Automatically Induced

There are a growing number of automatically induced ontologies, which may rely to a greater or lesser extent on manual resources for seed structure and/or content. Although we focus on manually created resources, assuming they can be leveraged for mappings to automatically induced ontologies that incorporate them, we would like to note the Predicate Matrix (De Lacalle et al., 2014), BabelNet (Navigli and Ponzetto, 2012), ConceptNet (Speer and Havasi, 2013), and the Never-ending Language Learner (NELL) system (Betteridge et al., 2009) as automatically derived resources that also showcase the merits of leveraging lexical resources and ontologies together.

Ontologies for Annotation Schema Interoperability

Two existing efforts that deserve special attention are UBY (Gurevych et al., 2012) and the Ontologies for Linguistic Annotation (OLiA; Chiarcos and Sukhareva, 2015). Like our goal of facilitating mapping among different SRL resources, both UBY and OLiA share a primary goal of bringing together the disparate labeling schemas of lexical resources into one, interoperable ontological resource.

UBY is a lexical–semantic resource combining information from expert and collaboratively constructed resources for both English and German – for example, English WordNet and German Wiktionary. The structure of UBY reflects the intention to capture lexical–semantic information, as opposed to world knowledge. Thus, a LEXICON node has direct subclasses such as

LEXICALENTRY, SYNSET, SEMANTICPREDICATE, etc. UBY also provides sense alignments across the included resources by converting existing alignments and automatically inferring additional alignments both within resources of the same language and across languages.

OLiA was developed to provide a terminological backbone between several prominent repositories of annotation terminology. The architecture of OLiA consists of (i) a main reference model that specifies the common terminology that different annotation schemas can refer to in order to facilitate interoperability; (ii) multiple external reference models with their own annotation terminologies, such as GOLD; and (iii) multiple annotation models (32 models for about 70 different languages), which capture both the annotation tag and concrete individuals instantiating that tag. For each of the external reference and annotation models there is a linking model that specifies the relationship between that model and the reference model. The categories in the OLiA reference model and the annotation models included are largely morphological and syntactic in nature, with only a few semantic categories.

We find the architecture of OLiA to be uniquely valuable because, unlike many resources that provide a direct mapping between resources, providing the pivot of a reference model enables recovery of information about sources and the extent or types of mismatches between models. Furthermore, it introduces a clear distinction between the externally provided information and the ontology engineer's interpretation of that information. Given the value of this architecture, we adopt it for our own ontology structure, described in the next section.

2.2.2　The Rich Event Ontology

As we have seen, many existing ontological resources focus on representing world knowledge, in the philosophical tradition of ontology, and may or may not include lexical resources mapping to those concepts. In contrast, WordNet, UBY, and OLiA focus on representing lexical and morpho-syntactic information. The REO aims to represent lexical event semantic information; thus, we hope to capture both commonsense world knowledge about events and their participants, as well as lexical information on how these concepts are realized and tagged in various English annotation schemas.

REO unifies the existing SRL schemas FrameNet, VerbNet, Automatic Content Extraction (ACE; Doddington et al., 2004), and its spinoff, the Rich Entities, Relations and Events (ERE; Song et al., 2015). REO unifies the disparate schemas by providing an independent conceptual backbone through which they can be associated, and it augments the schemas with event-to-event causal and temporal relations. The ontology was developed, in part, in response to unsuccessful efforts to map directly between FrameNet and the small set of disparate event types in (ERE). The difficulty was mainly due to differences in the granularity of events described by the FrameNet frames and ERE event types and inconsistencies in how the resources divided the semantic space.

FrameNet (FN), ERE, and VerbNet (VN) have wide-coverage lexicons of events, and they contribute annotated corpora and additional semantic and syntactic information that can be crucial to identifying events and their participants. REO serves as a shared hub for the disparate annotation schemas and therefore enables the combination of SRL training data into a larger, more diverse corpus, as well as expanding the set of lexical items associated with each event type. By adding temporal and causal relational information, the ontology also facilitates reasoning on and across documents, revealing relationships between events that come together in temporal and causal chains to build more complex scenarios.

After considering the somewhat unique purposes and structures of each of the existing ontologies described in Subsection 2.2.1, we have selected a top-level concept, ENTITY, with an initial distinction between ENDURANT and PERDURANT entities (inspired by DOLCE and BFO). We define ENTITY as a unique thing or set of things in the world. We define ENDURANTS as those entities that can be observed/perceived as a complete concept, no matter which given snapshot of time; that is, were we to freeze time, we would still be able to perceive the entire endurant—for instance, a specific person, place, or organization—that typically functions as a participant. We define PERDURANTS as those entities for which only a part exists if we look at them at any given snapshot in time. Variously called events, processes, activities, and states, perdurants have temporal or spatial parts and participants. Beyond this primary distinction, our ontology makes secondary distinctions between PHYSICAL and NONPHYSICAL endurants, as well as EVENTIVE and STATIVE perdurants. Below this level, the semantic space was divided with an eye toward sub-event structures and event participants to facilitate the linking of event types to SRL resources.

The structure of REO, illustrated in Figure 2.1, consists of a main "reference" ontology of generic event types and individual OWL (Web Ontology Language) "resource" ontologies. The relationships between the generic event types in the reference ontology and the event designations made in a particular annotated data resource are spelled out in various "linking models" that import both the reference ontology and a resource ontology. In the example shown in Figure 2.1, REO DISCHARGE events map to the Releasing frame in FN and the

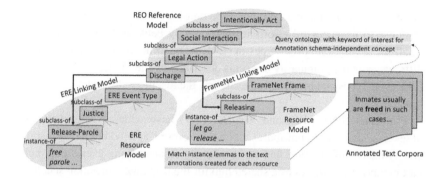

Figure 2.1 OWL resource models are linked to REO reference model in linking models (ACE and VN linking models not shown).

Release-Parole event type in ERE.[3] Additional indirect mappings are detailed in Brown et al. (2017). Individual words within the resource classes can be detected in text to find a wide variety of mentions of each event type, or one can query the ontology for words associated with an event of interest to view its participants and its relations to other events that are independent of the various lexical resource schemas.

As an ontology meant to provide a shared vocabulary of SRL annotation resources, the development of REO has focused on how to structure onto-logical relations between the events and states included in these resources (ACE, ERE, VN, FN). Although our intention has never been to create a detailed ontology of the endurant entities that serve as the participants in these events/states, such information is needed to generalize and map it across resources, as well as provide some insights into selectional restrictions generally and qualia relations specifically (see Section 2.2.3). Thus, we opted to integrate REO with an existing ontology containing the type of information on participants that we were interested in. Given the detailed information on objects and accompanying information such as HASPURPOSE in SUMO, we decided that it was best suited to our needs and elected to leverage SUMO to extend our coverage of endurant entities and facilitate the addition of qualia relations between endurant and perdurant entities.

PERDURANTS largely map to what SUMO deems PROCESSES, and, although many ENDURANTS map to what SUMO deems OBJECTS, there were also

---

[3] Other mappings between ERE and FN are necessarily more indirect; for example, with respect to the COMMUNICATION node in REO, ERE, and ACE (as related projects, ERE and ACE share similar event classes) only map to Instrument communication and Statement, whereas FN has mappings to nearly all daughters, as does VN, and VN maps to the mother Communication node as well.

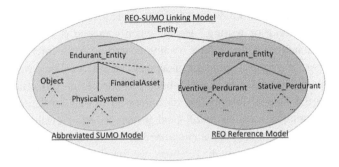

Figure 2.2 REO-SUMO linking model: REO specifies the PERDURANTS of the model, and SUMO specifies the ENDURANTS.

a variety of useful concepts in SUMO that seemed to fit the definition of an ENDURANT, including FINANCIALASSET, GRAPH, and PHYSICALSYSTEM, among others. To flesh out the ENDURANT portion of REO, we opted to integrate from SUMO all daughters of OBJECT and the classes just mentioned as daughters of our ENDURANT class. Specifically, this was done in a linking model like those described earlier. The linking model imports an abbreviated OWL version of SUMO (containing only the ENDURANT-compatible classes, their documentation that provides a description of what they are, and their associated WordNet sense keys) and the REO OWL reference model. The resulting model has all of the REO event ontology nested under PERDURANT and the extracted SUMO content nested under ENDURANT (see Figure 2.2). In Section 2.2.3 we describe how qualia relations are integrated to relate the objects and events, or endurants and perdurants, in the ontology.

REO remains under development; currently the suite of ontologies together encompass over 7,000 classes with over 27,000 unique individuals, which are the resource class members, such as verb types from VerbNet. Presently, there are 18 different annotation properties in the ontology, including REO definitions and WN sense key mappings. There are 60 object properties, which include the HAS_REFERENCE_GROUP relation that maps classes in the reference ontology to classes in the resource models, as well as the temporal and causal relations, such as TYPICALLY_PRECEDES and HAS_SUBEVENT.

2.2.3 Qualia in REO

Generative Lexicon qualia relations include an entity's function, origin, parts, and type (Pustejovsky, 1995). As part of our world knowledge, qualia relations represent our familiarity with the essence of entities and relations between them. For instance, we know that the prototypical function of a desk is "to sit at while reading or writing." Hence, when someone is sitting at a desk, we naturally infer that she or he is reading or writing. Such inferences are an essential part of a natural language understanding system. Thus, we sought to incorporate qualia relations in REO, but we wanted to do this efficiently by leveraging the kind of information encompassed in qualia relations already implicitly captured in other ontological resources. After evaluating several machine-readable ontologies (as mentioned in Section 2.2.1) as a resource to semiautomatically extract qualia relations, we found SUMO (Niles and Pease, 2001) to have the highest potential for achieving our purpose. In SUMO, we used two types of data for extracting qualia relations, including logical and textual data. First, we used the higher-order logical axioms embedded in SUMO. Each axiom is a conjunction of smaller logical relations that are connected via other relations or logical operators and represents the semantics of each entity. We used a number of SUMO relations to extract qualia relations from these axioms (Kazeminejad et al., 2018). Second, we performed regular expression searches in each entity's documentation, employing textual clues such as "purpose is," "intended to," or "designed for," which could indicate the telic quale.

Before implementing the extracted qualia relations in REO, we did a sanity check on the results using human judges. An online annotation system was developed and linguists annotated each extracted relation with their judgment (Kazeminejad et al., 2018). After validation, the extracted qualia relations were integrated into REO, enabling their use in knowledge representation and reasoning.

2.3 Semantic Role Labeling

Semantic roles, also called "thematic roles," refers to general classes of participants in a sentence and attempt to define the relation of the participant to the event. In the sentence *Fred gave Maria a book*, we must know which thing in the world *Fred* refers to and also that he is the agent of the action. We must know that the book is the gift and Maria the recipient instead of the other way around. Participants in an eventuality have a particular semantic role regardless of the syntactic format of the sentence. For example, in *Fred gave a book to Maria, Maria* is still the recipient, even though *Maria* is syntactically now an object of a preposition instead of a direct object.

Identifying the semantic roles of the participants is part of the more general task of understanding the semantics of the event, which has certain semantic components regardless of the specific verb used. Whether a speaker talks of *giving*, *handing*, or *passing*, there is always a transfer of an entity from the giver to a recipient. Grouping verbs with similar semantics allows us to refer to their shared semantic components and participant types.

In addition to furthering our understanding of how language communicates meaning, these theories of semantic roles and classes of semantically related verbs have improved several important NLP tasks. By labeling the semantic roles of participants in large amounts of text, machine learning models have improved information extraction (Bastianelli et al., 2013), question-answering systems (Yih et al., 2016), and machine translation (Xiong et al., 2012), among others.

2.3.1 Theories of Semantic Roles

Although the idea of semantic roles has fairly widespread acceptance in linguistics, an exact definition and a canonical list of the roles have never been agreed upon. Fillmore (1968) introduced the notion of "deep" cases as verb arguments with semantic types, such as agentive, instrumental, and locative, and set off a debate as to what the categories are and how to identify an entity's type. In largely contemporaneous work, Jackendoff (1987) explored thematic roles as an important aspect of the interface between semantics and syntax.

As linguists put these theories into practice, a loose set of 10 to 20 roles emerged, with Agent, Patient, Instrument, Theme, and a few others as the most widely accepted roles. However, using a strict set to label participants in actual text proved difficult to do consistently. Often, a participant did not "fit" the criteria for a certain role or it would have characteristics that partially fit multiple roles.

Over the next couple of decades, Baker et al. (1998) developed the influential theory of Frame Semantics, which describes the conceptual structure of events in terms of frames or schemas, with specific roles, or "frame elements," defined for each frame. Rather than focusing on generalizations about roles across event types, he moved away from a small set of roles to develop a large, unbounded set of richly described, specific relations between participants in event types. Fillmore's theory served as the basis for the lexical resource FrameNet (see Section 2.3.2).

Dowty (1991) took the opposite approach, instead defining the characteristics of a prototypical Agent and a prototypical Patient. This influential theory informed the argument labels in the widely used SRL resource, PropBank (Palmer et al., 2005), which we are integrating into REO currently.

Levin (1993) circumvented strict categories of roles by instead focusing on the syntactic alternations that characterized classes of verbs with similar semantics. She pointed out that meaning is largely preserved across syntactic alternations. For example, *Fred gave Maria the book* means much the same thing as *Fred gave the book to Maria*. Levin does not call out *Maria* as a Recipient, but the implication is that she has the same relation to the event in both sentences, regardless of labeling. In this work, Levin categorized thousands of English verbs into classes based on their participation in syntactic alternations. These classes all demonstrate some amount of semantic similarity, from very general (e.g., verbs of changes of state) to very specific (e.g., verbs of cutting). These classes form the core of the lexical resource VerbNet (see Section 2.3.2).

2.3.2 Semantic Role Labeling Resources in REO

These linguistic resources attempt to apply these theories of semantic roles and verb classes to large numbers of English predicates. The resources described here differ in the semantic granularity of their semantic role types. They also differ in the focus of their groupings: FrameNet groups verbs purely on semantics, VerbNet on the semantics as reflected in syntactic variation, and ERE/ACE on predetermined domains of interest. The resources have been widely used for the NLP task of SRL, which requires large amounts of annotated data. These particular SRL resources were selected for inclusion in REO because of the extant large-scale corpora manually annotated with each SRL schema. The desire to increase the data available without expensive and time-consuming annotation has led to efforts to map from the classes and roles of one resource to another. As described in Section 2.2, the difficulty of one-to-one mappings between resources such as ERE and FrameNet motivated linking them via an ontology in REO (see Figure 2.3). REO offers conceptual levels that abstract away from low-level, resource-specific differences. In this section, we describe and compare the resources included in REO.

FrameNet, based on Fillmore's frame semantics (Baker et al., 1998), groups verbs, nouns, and adjectives into "frames" based on "frame elements" that evoke the same semantic frame: a description of a type of event, relation, or entity and the participants in it. For example, the APPLY_HEAT frame includes the frame elements COOK, FOOD, HEATING_INSTRUMENT, TEMPERA-TURE_SETTING, etc. The resource currently has over 1,224 frames that connect over 13,000 lexical units (i.e., word senses). These frame elements have been used as semantic role labels in NLP. The "net" of frames makes up a rather

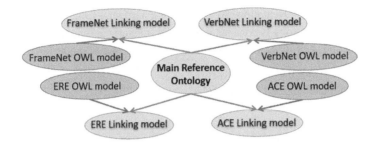

Figure 2.3 Modular architecture of REO showing the lexical resource models.

complex network, including simple *is-a* inheritance relations as well as more complex relations such as *Precedes* and *PerspectiveOn*.

These relations highlight important aspects of many frames; for example, the APPLY_HEAT frame is *UsedBy* the COOKING_CREATION frame. Often, however, the frames involved are not anchored to the main *is-a* hierarchy. In addition, the automatic reasoning capabilities of ontologies implemented in OWL are restricted to strictly logical relationships between classes. The complexity of FN precludes complete representation in OWL, as others have found (e.g., Scheffczyk et al., 2006).

VerbNet, based on Levin (1993), groups verbs into "classes" using their compatibility with certain syntactic alternations (e.g., "the causative–inchoative alternation"—*She rolled the ball down the hill* vs. *The ball rolled down the hill*). Although the groupings are primarily syntactic, the classes do share semantic features as well, because, as Levin posited, the syntactic behavior of a verb is largely determined by its meaning. Each VN class specifies its member verbs and their typical participants (i.e., semantic roles), lists the syntactic patterns, or subcategorization frames, they are all compatible with, and connects those patterns to semantic representations (Kipper et al., 2008).

By linking to VN, the ontology gains valuable syntactic information about how events are expressed in English. Generally, a VN class is linked in a one-to-one relation to one of the main reference ontology classes. A class's syntactic alternations, however, sometimes cut across semantic distinctions made by the main ontology. For example, events expressible with causative–inchoative alternations are grouped in the same VN class but are divided in the main ontology (because the main ontology makes distinctions based on the number and types of event participants). For these VN classes, we link an ontology class to specific subcategorization frames in a class, using VN thematic roles to distinguish the appropriate frames. These cases coincide with places where

VN's semantic representation also differs for a particular frame, indicating that the reference ontology is consistent with VN semantic distinctions.

In (1) and (2) we compare VN and FN semantic role schemas.

(1) a. *Fred gave Maria a book.*
     b. Agent Recipient Theme (VN)
     c. Donor Recipient Theme (FN)

(2) a. *Fred told Maria about a book.*
     b. Agent Recipient Topic (VN)
     c. Speaker Addressee Message (FN)

Using broad VN roles, the arguments in each sentence have largely the same roles, whereas the FN labels place the arguments in different and much more specific categories. Both approaches have their advantages: broad labels allow generalization, whereas more specific labels can be associated with fine-grained inferences. They also each have their disadvantages. Because not all arguments fall neatly into a small set of roles, the VN set can lead to inconsistencies when it is used to annotate text. Very specific roles are easier to apply consistently, but the large number of specific FN roles leads to few labeled instances of each role, a major detriment to machine learning techniques. REO facilitates leveraging the strengths of both sets of roles together and can potentially allow for "backoff" from a finer-grained role label to a coarser-grained label to overcome data sparsity issues.

ERE is a slight expansion of the **ACE** project's semantic role annotation schema. The goal of the ERE and ACE projects is to provide a shallow representation of the meaning of the text by marking up events, the entities involved in them, and any coreference between these. Annotated events are limited to certain types of interest to the defense community, with top-level types of Life, Movement, Transaction, Business, Conflict, Manufacture, Contact, Personnel, and Justice events.

Within REO, both the FN and VN resource ontologies model lexical units and class members, respectively, as individuals that represent lemmas, which may be used as references for particular event concepts. Because ERE and ACE are resources developed specifically for annotating training data, they do not predefine the lexical "triggers" of event types. Instead, these are always discovered in context. Thus, ACE and ERE provide a data-driven, bottom-up perspective on event semantics that is distinct from the other resources. Their models in REO include as individuals English lemmas that have been annotated either in the freely available ACE 2005 Multilingual Training Corpus (Walker et al., 2006) or the as-of-yet-unreleased ERE corpus, respectively.

2.3.3 Evaluation: Expanding Event Detection

As a preliminary evaluation of how linking these lexical resources via an ontology can improve NLP tasks, we looked at leveraging REO to support event detection in information extraction (IE) systems (Brown et al., 2017). For various reasons, many existing IE systems are limited to the detection of events marked up in the ACE data. To avoid the need for additional manually annotated data, REO and its associated lexical resources can be used in backoff techniques to augment the trigger words associated with certain event types, thus expanding the domain of application. We tested this idea by examining the reference groups associated with the LEGAL ACTION portion of the ontology. LEGAL ACTION is the parent class of several subclasses, including ARREST, SUE, and DECLARE BANKRUPTCY. We first established a baseline of what a typical system, trained on ACE, might recognize as triggers associated with LEGAL ACTION event concepts. We followed all ACE types and subtypes linked to the subclasses of LEGAL ACTION via the HASREFERENCEGROUP relation and extracted the individuals that had been tagged as triggers for them, finding 102 lexemes in total. Presumably, systems trained on ACE data have the potential to recognize these lexemes as triggers of the LEGAL ACTION events.

To determine how the ontology may help to move beyond this baseline, we accessed the lexemes in the reference groups associated with LEGAL ACTION in ERE, FN, and VN, which added groups of 204, 69, and 14 lexemes, respectively. Thus, we were able to expand the LEGAL ACTION vocabulary from 102 words to 389. In addition, the resources seem to be making unique contributions: only 17 of the 389 lexemes are duplicated from one resource to another. This expansion highlights the potential for the ontology to overcome data sparsity by combining resources. Although word embeddings have the potential to expand IE vocabulary as well, they lack the frame relations we get from FN or the syntactic alternations from VN.

2.4 Conclusions, Gaps, and Future Work

This chapter describes existing ontologies and lexical resources that play prominent roles in NLP. It presents REO as a rich event ontology specifically designed to provide a conceptual bridge between informative semantic role labeling resources, such as FrameNet, VerbNet, and the Linguistic Data Consortium's Entities, Relations, and Events. Thus, REO supports mapping between specific event types of different resources and enables the merging of associated annotated corpora and expanding sets of related event triggers.

There are clear benefits to this marriage of ontological and lexical resources. However, by itself, this is still insufficient. To truly leverage the information in these resources and harness it to modern NLP, the next step is a much closer interweaving of these types of symbolic resources with the current plethora of large-scale continuous vector representations that are transforming the field, such as Devlin et al. (2019). Exciting results are already being demonstrated by effective integration of neural net techniques and resources such as WordNet (Kumar et al., 2019), to name just one. Our goal of natural language understanding is elusive enough that we cannot ignore any tools at our disposal but instead must marshal a diverse and coordinated effort.

Acknowledgments We gratefully acknowledge the support of DTRA1-16-1-0002/Project 1553695, eTASC – Empirical Evidence for a Theoretical Approach to Semantic Components and DARPA 15-18-CwC-FP-032 Communicating with Computers, C3 Cognitively Coherent Human–Computer Communication (sub from UIUC) and Elementary Composable Ideas (ECI) Repository (sub from SIFT). Any opinions, findings, and conclusions or recommendations expressed in this material are those of the authors and do not necessarily reflect the views of DTRA, DARPA, or the U.S. government. In addition, we thank our anonymous reviewers for their constructive feedback.

References

Baker, Collin F., Fillmore, Charles J., and Lowe, John B. 1998. The Berkeley FrameNet Project. Pages 86–90 of: *Proceedings of the 17th International Conference on Computational Linguistics. Volume 1.* Association for Computational Linguistics.

Bastianelli, Emanuele, Castellucci, Giuseppe, Croce, Danilo, and Basili, Roberto. 2013. Textual Inference and Meaning Representation in Human Robot Interaction. Pages 65–69 of: Popescu, Octavian, and Lavelli, Alberto (eds.), *Proceedings of the Joint Symposium on Semantic Processing. Textual Inference and Structures in Corpora.*

Berners-Lee, Tim, Hendler, James, Lassila, Ora, et al. 2001. The Semantic Web. *Scientific American,* **284**(5), 28–37.

Betteridge, Justin, Carlson, Andrew, Hong, Sue Ann, et al. 2009. Toward Never Ending Language Learning. Pages 1–2 of: *AAAI Spring Symposium: Learning by Reading and Learning to Read.*

Bizer, Christian, Lehmann, Jens, Kobilarov, Georgi, et al. 2009. DBpedia-A Crystallization Point for the Web of Data. *Web Semantics: Science, Services and Agents on the World Wide Web,* **7**(3), 154–165.

Bollacker, Kurt, Evans, Colin, Paritosh, Praveen, Sturge, Tim, and Taylor, Jamie. 2008. Freebase: A Collaboratively Created Graph Database for Structuring Human

Knowledge. Pages 1247–1250 of: *Proceedings of the 2008 ACM SIGMOD International Conference on Management of Data*. ACM.

Brown, Susan, Bonial, Claire, Obrst, Leo, and Palmer, Martha. 2017. The Rich Event Ontology. Pages 87–97 of: Caselli, Tommaso, Miller, Ben, van Erp, et al. (eds.), *Proceedings of the Events and Stories in the News Workshop*.

Chiarcos, Christian, and Sukhareva, Maria. 2015. OLiA – Ontologies of Linguistic Annotation. *Semantic Web*, **6**(4), 379–386.

De Lacalle, Maddalen Lopez, Laparra, Egoitz, and Rigau, German. 2014. Predicate Matrix: Extending SemLink through WordNet Mappings. Pages 903–909 of: Calzolari, Nicoletta, Choukri, Khalid, Declerck, Thierry, et al. (eds.), *Proceedings of the Ninth International Conference on Language Resources and Evaluation (LREC'14)*. Reykjavik, Iceland: European Language Resources Association (ELRA).

Devlin, Jacob, Chang, Ming-Wei, Lee, Kenton, and Toutanova, Kristina. 2019. BERT: Pre-training of Deep Bidirectional Transformers for Language Understanding. Pages 4171–4186 of: Burstein, Jill, Doran, Christy, and Solorio, Thamar (eds.), *Proceedings of the 2019 Conference of the North American Chapter of the Association for Computational Linguistics: Human Language Technologies, Volume 1 (Long and Short Papers)*. Minneapolis, MN: Association for Computational Linguistics.

Doddington, George, Mitchell, Alexis, Przybocki, Mark, et al. 2004. The Automatic Content Extraction (ACE) Program – Tasks, Data, and Evaluation. In: Lino, Maria Teresa, Xavier, Maria Francisca, Ferreira, Fátima, Costa, Rute, and Silva, Raquel (eds.), *Proceedings of the Fourth International Conference on Language Resources and Evaluation (LREC'04)*. Lisbon: European Language Resources Association.

Dowty, David. 1991. Thematic Proto-Roles and Argument Selection. *Language*, **67**, 547–619.

Dzikovska, Myroslava O., Swift, Mary D., and Allen, James F. 2004. Building a Computational Lexicon and Ontology with FrameNet. Pages 53–60 of: Fillmore, Charles J., Pinkal, Manfred, Baker, Colllin F., and Erk, Katrin (eds.), *LREC Workshop on Building Lexical Resources from Semantically Annotated Corpora*.

Eckle-Kohler, Judith, McCrae, John Philip, and Chiarcos, Christian. 2015. lemonUby – A large, Interlinked, Syntactically-Rich Lexical Resource for Ontologies. *Semantic Web*, **6**(4), 371–378.

Fellbaum, Christiane (ed.). 1998. *WordNet: An Electronic Lexical Database*. Cambridge, MA: MIT Press.

Fillmore, Charles J. 1968. The Case for Case. Pages 1–25 of: Bach, E., and Harms, R. T. (eds.), *Universals in Linguistic Theory*. London: Holt, Rinehart and Winston.

Gangemi, Aldo, Guarino, Nicola, Masolo, Claudio, Oltramari, Alessandro, and Schneider, Luc. 2002. Sweetening Ontologies with DOLCE. Pages 166–181 of: Gómez-Pérez, Asunción, and Benjamins, V. Richard (eds.), *International Conference on Knowledge Engineering and Knowledge Management*. Springer.

Gurevych, Iryna, Eckle-Kohler, Judith, Hartmann, Silvana, et al. 2012. Uby: A Large-Scale Unified Lexical-Semantic Resource Based on LMF. Pages 580–590 of: Daelemans, Walter (ed.), *Proceedings of the 13th Conference of the European Chapter of the Association for Computational Linguistics.* Association for Computational Linguistics.

Jackendoff, Ray. 1987. The Status of Thematic Relations in Linguistic Theory. *Linguistic Inquiry*, **18**(3), 369–411.

Kazeminejad, Ghazaleh, Bonial, Claire, Brown, Susan Windisch, and Palmer, Martha. 2018. Automatically Extracting Qualia Relations for the Rich Event Ontology. Pages 2644–2652 of: Bender, Emily M., Derczynski, Leon, and Isabelle, Pierre (eds.), *Proceedings of the 27th International Conference on Computational Linguistics.* Santa Fe, NM: Association for Computational Linguistics.

Kipper, Karin, Korhonen, Anna, Ryant, Neville, and Palmer, Martha. 2008. A Large-Scale Classification of English Verbs. *Language Resources and Evaluation*, **42**(1), 21–40.

Kumar, Sawan, Jat, Sharmistha, Saxena, Karan, and Talukdar, Partha. 2019. Zero-Shot Word Sense Disambiguation Using Sense Definition Embeddings. Pages 5670–5681 of: Nakov, Preslav, and Palmer, Alexis (eds.), *Proceedings of the 57th Annual Meeting of the Association for Computational Linguistics.* Florence, Italy: Association for Computational Linguistics.

Levin, Beth. 1993. *English Verb Classes and Alternations: A Preliminary Investigation.* Chicago, IL: University of Chicago Press.

Masolo, Claudio, Borgo, Stefano, Gangemi, Aldo, Guarino, Nicola, and Oltramari, Alessandro. 2003. Wonderweb Deliverable d18, Ontology Library (Final). *ICT Project*, **33052**.

McDonald, David, and Pustejovsky, James. 2013. On the Representation of Inferences and Their Lexicalization. Page 152–169 of: Langley, Pat (ed.), *Proceedings of the Second Annual Conference on Advances in Cognitive Systems ACS*, Vol. 135. Cognitive Systems Foundation.

Narayana, Pradyumna, Krishnaswamy, Nikhil, Wang, Isaac, et al. 2018. Cooperating with Avatars through Gesture, Language and Action. Pages 272–293 of: Arai, Kohei, Kapoor, Supriya, and Bhatia, Rahul (eds.), *Proceedings of SAI Intelligent Systems Conference.* London: IEEE.

Navigli, Roberto, and Ponzetto, Simone Paolo. 2012. BabelNet: The Automatic Construction, Evaluation and Application of a Wide-Coverage Multilingual Semantic Network. *Artificial Intelligence*, **193**(Dec.), 217–250.

Niles, Ian, and Pease, Adam. 2001. Towards a Standard Upper Ontology. Pages 2-9 of: Guarino, Nicola, Smith, Barry, and Welty, Christopher (eds.), *Proceedings of the International Conference on Formal Ontology in Information Systems. Volume 2001.* FOIS '01. New York: Association for Computing Machinery.

Palmer, Martha, Gildea, Daniel, and Kingsbury, Paul. 2005. The Proposition Bank: An Annotated Corpus of Semantic Roles. *Computational Linguistics*, **31**(1), 71–106.

Pease, Adam, Niles, Ian, and Li, John. 2002. The Suggested Upper Merged Ontology: A Large Ontology for the Semantic Web and Its Applications. Pages 7–10 of: Pease, Adam (ed.), *Working Notes of the AAAI-2002 Workshop on Ontologies and the Semantic Web*, Vol. 28.

Pustejovsky, James. 1995. *The Generative Lexicon*. Cambridge, MA: MIT Press.

Pustejovsky, James, Havasi, Catherine, Littman, Jessica, Rumshisky, Anna, and Verhagen, Marc. 2006. Towards a Generative Lexical Resource: The Brandeis Semantic Ontology. In: Calzolari, Nicoletta, Choukri, Khalid, Gangemi, Aldo, et al. (eds.), *Proceedings of the Fifth International Conference on Language Resources and Evaluation (LREC'06)*. Genoa, Italy: European Language Resources Association.

Pustejovsky, James, Krishnaswamy, Nikhil, and Do, Tuan. 2017. Object Embodiment in a Multimodal Simulation. Pages 1–5 of: Chu, Vivian, Sinapov, Jivko, Bohg, Jeannette, Chernova, Sonia, and Thomaz, Andrea L. (eds.), *AAAI Spring Symposium: Interactive Multisensory Object Perception for Embodied Agents*.

Scheffczyk, Jan, Baker, Collin F., and Narayanan, Srini. 2006. Ontology-Based Reasoning about Lexical Resources. Pages 1–8 of: Oltramari, Alessandro, Huang, Chu-Ren, Lenci, Alessandro, Buitelaar, Paul, and Fellbaum, Christaine (eds.), *Proceedings of Workshop on Interfacing Ontologies and Lexical Resources for Semantic Web Technologies (OntoLex 2006)*.

Segers, Roxane, Vossen, Piek, Rospocher, Marco, et al. 2015. ESO: A Frame Based Ontology for Events and Implied Situations. *Proceedings of Maplex 2015*, February 9–10, Yamagata, Japan.

Smith, Barry. 2000. Objects and Their Environments: From Aristotle to Ecological Ontology. Pages 84–102 of: Frank, Andrew, Raper, Jonathan, and Cheylan, Jean-Paul (eds.), *Life and Motion of Socio-economic Units*. New York: Taylor & Francis.

Smith, Barry, Almeida, Mauricio, Bona, Jonathan, et al. 2014. *Basic Formal Ontology 2.0 Draft Specification and User's Guide*.

Song, Zhiyi, Bies, Ann, Strassel, Stephanie, et al. 2015. From Light to Rich ERE: Annotation of Entities, Relations, and Events. Pages 89–98 of: Hovy, Eduard, Mitamura, Teruko, and Palmer, Martha (eds.), *Proceedings of the 3rd Workshop on EVENTS at the NAACL-HLT*.

Speer, Robert, and Havasi, Catherine. 2013. ConceptNet 5: A Large Semantic Network for Relational Knowledge. Pages 161–176 of: Gurevych, Iryna, and Kim, Jungi (eds.), *The People's Web Meets NLP*. New York: Springer.

Suchanek, Fabian M., Kasneci, Gjergji, and Weikum, Gerhard. 2007. Yago: A Core of Semantic Knowledge. Pages 697–706 of: Williamson, Carey, and Zurko, Mary Ellen (eds.), *Proceedings of the 16th International Conference on World Wide Web*. Association for Computing Machinery.

Vossen, Piek. 1997. EuroWordNet: A Multilingual Database for Information Retrieval. Proceedings of the DELOS Workshop on Cross-Language Information Retrieval, March 5–7, Zurich.

Vossen, Piek, Agerri, Rodrigo, Aldabe, Itziar, et al. 2016. NewsReader: Using Knowledge Resources in a Cross-Lingual Reading Machine to Generate More Knowledge from Massive Streams of News. *Knowledge-Based Systems*, **110**, 60–85.

Walker, Christopher, Strassel, Stephanie, Medero, Julie, and Maeda, Kazuaki. 2006. *ACE 2005 Multilingual Training Corpus*. Philadelphia: Linguistic Data Consortium.

Xiong, Deyi, Zhang, Min, and Li, Haizhou. 2012. Modeling the Translation of Predicate-Argument Structure for SMT. Pages 902–911 of: Li, Haizhou, Lin,

Chin-Yew, Osborne, Miles, Lee, Gary Geunbae, and Park, Jong C. (eds.), *Proceedings of the 50th Annual Meeting of the Association for Computational Linguistics: Long Papers – Volume 1*. Association for Computational Linguistics.

Yih, Wen-tau, Richardson, Matthew, Meek, Chris, Chang, Ming-Wei, and Suh, Jina. 2016. The Value of Semantic Parse Labeling for Knowledge Base Question Answering. Pages 201–206 of: Erk, Katrin, and Smith, Noah A. (eds.), *Proceedings of the 54th Annual Meeting of the Association for Computational Linguistics: Volume 2. Short Papers*.

3

Decomposing Events and Storylines

William Croft, Pavlína Kalm, and Michael Regan

Abstract. Stories are typically represented as a set of events and temporal or causal relations among events. In the metro map model of storylines, participants are represented as histories and events as interactions between participant histories. The metro map model calls for a decomposition of events into what each participant does (or what happens to each participant), as well as the interactions among participants. Such a decompositional model of events has been developed in linguistic semantics. Here, we describe this decompositional model of events and how it can be combined with a metro map model of storylines.

3.1 Introduction: Events within Stories and Events within Events

Stories are typically represented as a set of events and temporal or causal relations among events (see Chapter 6). Linguistically, this is manifested by implicit or explicit relations between clauses. Explicitly, there are coordinating and subordinating conjunctions expressing temporal, causal or other relations between events and time expressions that can be used to determine temporal relations. Implicitly, the order of sentences in a document often reflects temporal and sometimes causal relations.

The storyline approach to discourse structure we present here is similar to metro map models of storyline analysis (Shahaf et al., 2012; van Erp et al., 2014). A storyline is a time-sequenced series of intersecting paths in a graph-like structure that represents the interactions of entities and events. Like van Erp et al. (2014), our storylines are "entity-centered," in the sense that the representation is centered around participant histories over time (edges in the graph), which contain the events that the participant is engaged in. Participants are related to each other via the events that they interact in (at the graph nodes). We envision that storylines will be useful for data analytics as a tool to visualize participant histories and for causal inference.

We argue that an entity-centered approach is a better model of storyline analysis than the more "event-centered" models. In this context, event-centered means the representation is centered around events and their temporal and causal relations. In the task of summarizing events and entities and their relations, an analyst requires a logical means to cluster information. With a storyline, information is organized by the participants involved, which may serve as an interpretative model for the connections among events (Caselli and Vossen, 2016). In addition, the salience of events may be determined by a metric based on interactions of interest. A rich model will also include event–event causal relations, which we believe will be inferable in part based on participant interactions.

One needs a model of event structure to go with a storyline approach, specifically a model that clearly indicates what each participant does or what happens to each participant in a particular event. Thus, the participant's history – the central representation in an entity-centered storyline – will consist of a joint representation for what each participant does or what happens to each participant over the time course of the story.

Most analyses of event structure in text assume that a single clause headed by a verb denotes a single event. However, participants in a mono-clausal event interact causally as well, and monoclausal events unfold in temporal phases. These observations underlie the decompositional analyses of verb meaning found widely in theoretical linguistics, as surveyed in Levin and Rappaport Hovav (2005) and also in computational linguistics (e.g., Narayanan, 1997). Many of the event decompositions in linguistics do not explicitly represent the temporal dimension and distribute participants across different event components. Such representations do not lend themselves well to integration with storyline analysis.

The model of event decomposition in Croft (2012) synthesizes discoveries in verbal semantics and accounts for crosslinguistic generalizations about the grammar of verbs. It is relevant to the analysis of events within stories in that the monoclausal event is decomposed in terms of time, causation, and qualitative state or change.

Croft's analysis of events explicitly represents time as a geometric dimension, as part of the representation of aspect – the structure of events as they unfold in successive phases over time. In addition to explicit representation of the temporal dimension, Croft introduces a second dimension, qualitative states, to model change over the course of the event. These two dimensions allow one to represent directly the prestate and poststate of events (Im and Pustejovsky, 2010; Segers et al., 2016) as different states on the qualitative dimension and as different points of time on the temporal dimension.

Croft's analysis also decomposes events into distinct subevents for each participant. The subevents directly represent the interactions of participants, instead of representing them indirectly and incompletely by semantic role labels. Having distinct subevents for each participant allows for a model of stories where stories are made up of participant histories; that is, the participant's existence through time. A participant history is in turn made up of subevents, namely, the states and processes that the participant has or undergoes during each interval of time. The participant histories are related to each other through participant interactions; that is, subevent relations within events at certain times. This model of subevents is similar to the model of stories in van Erp et al. (2014), who used a modified metro map visualization (Shahaf et al., 2012), with participants as "lines" and events as "stations."

For our storyline analysis, event meaning is decompositional: a node in a storyline graph represents a multiparticipant event composed of a set of subevents, one for each participant, with participant interaction defined in terms of causal and noncausal relations. Characteristics of each participant's subevent are defined along three dimensions: time (how the subevent unfolds over time), qualitative state (the role of the participant as an external agent or the resulting change it undergoes), and force-dynamic relations that describe the interactions between the participants in the event.

This chapter describes how we bring current theories of event structure decomposition from linguistics into computational linguistics and the potential application of these theories to the representation of the roles of participants in stories.

3.2 Constructions as Well as Verbs Determine the Internal Structure of Events

The first linguistic issue that must be addressed is where in the sentence the decompositional structure of events is encoded. It is generally assumed that events are expressed by verbs. But a major issue in annotation of verb meaning is that a verb can be construed in multiple ways, largely though not entirely depending on the clausal constructions in which it occurs.

For example, one and the same verb can describe events of different aspectual types (Moens and Steedman, 1988; Croft, 2012; examples from

Corpus of Contemporary American English [COCA; Davies, 2008, 1a–e] and
Google Books):

(1) a. He **touched** the tip of his hat, then left a few bills on the bar and slid
        off his stool.
     b. But **touching** the wound again and again, and remaining concentrated
        on the wound is not going to heal it.
     c. We can say the chair is **touching** the wall it is leaning against, but there
        really is not an encounter between them, but only a spatial relation of
        contiguity.
     d. Her fingers **touched** the ball, and she gripped.
     e. The desert **touches** the boundaries of rural and urban settlements alike.

Example (1a) describes an instant of contact (usually called semelfactive);
example (1b) an activity of repeated contact; example (1c) a transitory state
of maintained contact; example (1d) an achievement (instantaneous change)
from non-contact to contact; and example (1e) a stable physical relationship
between two landscape entities. The different aspectual interpretations are
constrained partly by the tense–aspect construction (simple past, simple
present, progressive) but also partly by contextual factors – for example, (1a)
and (1d) are both simple past but have different aspectual interpretations.

The same ambiguity is found in the force-dynamic structure of events
denoted by a single verb. Examples (2a–2e) illustrates the ambiguities, with
the standard labels for the force-dynamic type given in brackets (examples
from COCA and Google Books):

(2) a. She flailed with her feet to get her balance and managed to **kick** the
        chair. [contact]
     b. So he's going to shoot if I have to **kick** him black and blue. [change of
        state]
     c. **Kick** the ball into Lake Michigan … [ballistic motion]
     d. Go on, **kick** him the ball and let's see what he'll do with it. [transfer]
     e. You **kick** wildly at the plastic bottle, finally knocking it loose. [cona-
        tive – action aimed toward a target entity]

Thus, a semantic annotation of the event expressed by a clause cannot rely
simply on a verb's lexical semantics taken out of grammatical context.

There is a strong correlation between a construction's form and the
semantics of the event. That is, particular argument structure constructions
have meaning, as construction grammarians have argued (Fillmore et al.,
1988; Goldberg, 1995, 2006). The correlation is not perfect: there is some

lexical idiosyncrasy in the choice of prepositions for some argument structure constructions, for example. Nevertheless, the need for semantic annotation of event structure partly independent of a verb's lexical semantics is evident from the many-to-many mappings between verbs and argument structure constructions.

The goal of an annotation scheme is to allow annotators to identify semantic types and properties in a text with a degree of reliability to make the manually annotated corpus useful for training and also to allow automated integration with formal reasoning (Mani and Pustejovsky, 2012). We therefore propose an annotation scheme with holistic labels for aspectual and causal event types. Force-dynamic and aspectual structure are annotated separately from verb meaning and from each other, because verb meaning does not wholly determine aspectual or force-dynamic interpretation. The aspectual and causal event types for a clause are the product of the combination of the verb meaning and the tense–aspect and argument structure constructions of the clause. The holistic annotation relieves the annotator of identifying the contribution of the construction vs. the predicate to the event's semantic structure. The aspectual and force dynamic annotations can be translated into the decompositional analyses described in this chapter, which can in turn form the basis of formal reasoning about the events in a text.

3.3 Time and Qualitative State (Change)

3.3.1 The Semantics of Aspect

The semantic analysis of aspect is considerably more fine-grained than that used in previous annotations in computational linguistics (Siegel and McKeown, 2001; Zarcone and Lenci, 2008; Mathew and Katz, 2009; Friedrich and Palmer, 2014; Xue and Zhang, 2014). It has long been known that the four-way aspectual classification of events by Vendler (1957) into states (static), activities (dynamic, durative, unbounded), achievements (dynamic, punctual, bounded) and accomplishments (dynamic, durative, bounded) does not appear to include a number of other aspectual types that have been described in the linguistics literature. The decomposition of aspect into time and qualitative state allows us to represent all of the observed aspectual types of simple verbs.

Semanticists have identified a number of different aspectual types of events, most of which can be analyzed as special cases of Vendler's categories of states, achievements, activities and accomplishments (Vendler, 1957;

Croft et al., 2016). States lack change on the qualitative dimension. Some states are inherent properties of an individual (*She is French*), others are reversible (*The window is open*) or irreversible (*The window is broken*), and still others exist only in a point of time (*The sun is at its zenith*; Carlson, 1979; Talmy, 1985; Mittwoch, 1988).

Achievements represent a transition, construed as instantaneous, from one qualitative state to another. Directed achievements transition to a result state (*The window broke*; Talmy, 1985). Accomplishments represent a gradual change on a qualitative dimension over time, attaining a natural endpoint. Incremental accomplishments represent a measurable, monotonic change (*She ran into the gym*), whereas nonincremental accomplishments describe an activity that is not monotonic before achieving the result state (*He repaired the computer*; Croft, 1998; Rothstein, 2004). Activities represent change that does not have a natural endpoint. Directed activities represent a monotonic change (*The balloon rose*; Dowty, 1979; Talmy, 1985; Bertinetto and Squartini, 1995), whereas the change described by undirected activities is nonmonotonic (*The fans were dancing*).

There is another Vendler-like category: processes that terminate, returning to the base state. These events, which we call *endeavors*, are temporally bounded but not by reaching a natural endpoint. They may be directed or undirected. Semelfactives, which transition to the result state and back to the initial state (*The light flashed*; Talmy, 1985; Jackendoff, 1991; Smith, 1991) are punctual endeavors. Endeavors are not lexicalized as such in English, but certain subevents in complex events are endeavors. In Russian, there are lexicalized endeavors (Forsyth, 1970). Undirected endeavors are derived from undirected activities with the prefix *po-*, as in *On po-spal posle obeda* "He had a sleep after dinner." Directed endeavors are derived from directed activities with the prefixes *pri-*, *pod-*, and *nad-*, as in *On pri-otkryl dver'* "He opened the door a little."

Croft's graphic representations of two aspectual types are given in Figure 3.1.

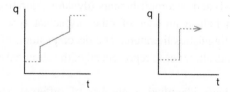

Figure 3.1 Aspectual representation of an incremental accomplishment and an irreversible directed achievement.

The incremental accomplishment includes five phases: the rest state, the inception transition, the directed change, the completion transition and the (transitory) result state. The directed change and the transitions that bound it (solid line) are profiled (Langacker, 1987); that is, they are the phases encoded by the sentence. The directed achievement consists only of the rest state, the transition and the permanent result state; only the transition is profiled.

3.3.2 Formalization of Aspectual Structure

Our formalization uses the interval calculus for both the temporal and qualitative dimensions (Allen, 1984; Mani and Pustejovsky, 2012) and the commonsense knowledge axioms of Gordon and Hobbs (2017). We model the qualitative structure of a subevent by the qualitative dimension q orthogonal to the time dimension t. Different verbs or predicates define different relevant qualitative states for each participant subevent. Hence, each subevent has a distinct set of qualitative states. One can consider each predicate's set of qualitative states as an interval on the q dimension. Alternatively, each predicate can be thought of as representing a distinct qualitative dimension (see Section 3.6).

Following Allen (1984), we represent "points" in time as very small intervals. One reason for treating points as the smallest intervals is that an event that is construed as occurring in an "instant" (*The bridge collapsed*) may also be construed as occurring over an interval (*The bridge is collapsing*). We would represent these two construals as both occurring over intervals with different granularities (Hobbs, 1985) such that there are no smaller intervals than the event interval for the coarser-grained temporal metric, though this is the case for a finer-grained temporal one.

We analyze the structure of the qualitative dimension q for each subevent also using the interval calculus, which is not specific to time (Hobbs and Pan, 2004; Mani and Pustejovsky, 2012). Verbs and other predicates impose more specific structure on q.

All event types except inherent states have a rest state or base state, a point on the quality dimension that we designate b. Telic events also have a result state, which we designate r. The point r is also the quality expressed by a state predicate. Achievements have only b and r defined on the q dimension. Durative processes – that is, any event involving change over an extended interval – define qualities on a central extended interval between b and r that we designate c.

A phase is defined as a function from an interval i on t to an interval j on q. Phases can be distinguished by properties of the domain and/or range. A state is a phase whose range is a point on q. A process is a phase whose domain and range are extended on t and q, respectively. Processes may be monotonic $(\text{Mon}(p))$ or nonmonotonic.

A subevent has an aspectual type. Aspectual types are composite entities composed of one or more phases. Aspectual types are what is annotated; they correspond to the subtypes of the Vendler types described above, such as incremental accomplishments or semelfactives.

3.4 Causation

3.4.1 The Force Dynamics of Physical Events

Participant subevents cause other participant subevents; this is the domain of force dynamics (Talmy, 1976, 1988). Croft (2012) extended Talmy's notion of force dynamics to cover a wide range of asymmetric relations between participants.

Croft et al. (2016) proposed an analysis of the semantic types of argument structure constructions in terms of force-dynamic relations between participants, causal and noncausal, and the type of change that the theme participant undergoes. Among the most common types of force-dynamic relations are Force, the prototypical physical transmission of force relation, and Path, the spatial figure–ground relation.

Croft et al. (2016) defined four types of physical changes, based in part on different types of incremental theme (Dowty, 1991; Hay et al., 1999). The simplest change subevent of the affected entity in a causal interaction is a change of state of the entity; that is, a change in a scalar property of the entity as a whole (Hay et al., 1999).

Events involving change in a spatial figure–ground relation proceed in two different ways. Motion events of various kinds, such as *The boy ran across the road*, define a spatial path on the qualitative dimension that the figure traverses as a whole; for this reason, Dowty (1991) calls the figure a "holistic theme."

Application, removal, combining and separating events, such as *The man picked pears from the tree*, define a mereological change in the location of the figure on the qualitative dimension; this is Dowty's incremental theme proper. Covering and uncovering events, such as *I buttered the toast with hazelnut butter* and *They stripped the trees of bark*, differ from application and removal events in that the incremental change is conceptualized as happening to the ground object (toast, trees) rather than the figure.

Croft et al. (2016) defined another type of theme change, called a Design theme, for creation of an object with a certain identity, for events of creation (*They built a shelter*) and formation (*She carved a toy out of a stick*).

Another type of physical change not described by Croft et al. (2016) is the internal change of a single participant, such as *The flag fluttered*. Internal events often also express a locative relation: *The flag fluttered (over the fort)*. Finally, simple static location is included as an internal event type, albeit stative: *The flag is over the fort*.

The relations between subevents and properties of subevents summarized above cover most if not all of the inventory of physical processes expressed by simple verbs in English.

3.4.2 Mental Events

Mental events generally, though not always, occur oriented to some external situation: an entity, a static state of affairs or the occurrence of a dynamic event. Mental events have two primary participants: the person whose mental state/process is being described, usually called the *experiencer*, and the external situation (entity, etc.), called the *stimulus*; the stimulus of emotion predicates is also called the target/subject matter of emotion (T/SM) following Pesetsky (1995).

Mental events differ from physical events in two major ways. First, there is no physical transmission of force between the external situation and the person's mental state. Second, what is happening in the mind is not outwardly apparent to the observer. Hence, the speaker construes whether the mental event is a state or process and what the "direction" of causation is in mental events.

The semantics literature has described three common construals of the mental force dynamic relation between the experiencer and the stimulus. The Attend construal highlights the experiencer directing her or his attention to the stimulus (Viberg, 1983; Croft, 1993) and consistently expresses the experiencer as subject (Croft, 1993). The Attend construal corresponds to Levin's *Marvel* verb class (Levin, 1993; emotion verbs) and *Peer* verb class (perception verbs; Levin does not include cognition verbs, which usually take sentential complements).

The Affect construal highlights the stimulus causing a change in mental state of the experiencer (Croft, 1993; Zaenen, 1993; Pesetsky, 1995; Levin and Grafmiller, 2013; Doron, 2020) and consistently expresses the stimulus as subject (Croft, 1993). The Affect construal corresponds to Levin's *Amuse* verb class (emotion verbs); there are no basic perception verbs with this construal. Affect also describes the relation between an event and its beneficiary (or maleficiary).

The Experience construal construes the mental event as a stative relation holding between the experiencer and the stimulus. The Experience construal corresponds to Levin's *Admire* verb class (emotion verbs) and *See* and *Sight* verb classes (perception verbs). This construal allows either the experiencer as subject or the stimulus as subject; we distinguish the latter encoding as Experience*.

Two other force-dynamic mental construals were identified in the survey of mental events by Croft et al. (2018). Judge describes an active mental process mostly under the control of the experiencer, like Attend: it describes mental processes such as comparing, categorizing, inferring and measuring something, as in *more respondents judged it a threat*. Unlike Attend, however, Judge describes the result of the mental process; that is, the conclusion, classification or measurement arrived at.

Finally, Intend describes the relationship between a volitional agent and the agent's as-yet-unrealized, and possibly never realized, action with respect to the other participant, as in *This is the way to cook a chicken for any kind of cold chicken salad, Asian or Western*. Hence, the Intend relation can be used for purpose arguments for all types of events, not unlike Affect with respect to the beneficiary of an event.

3.4.3 Social Events and Event Nominals

Social events are little discussed in the theoretical linguistics literature. Social events are fairly extensively covered in VerbNet (Kipper et al., 2008) and more extensively in FrameNet (Fillmore et al., 2003). Nevertheless, this is a vast and relatively little explored domain. Our preliminary research indicates that the majority of verbs describing social events in VerbNet and FrameNet fall into three domains: transfer of possession, communication (transfer of information) and social role or status, either formal (marry, elect, hire) or informal (befriend, shun). Possession requires positing a social relation between persons and things (control). Communication invokes a mental relation (cognition), plus its transfer via language or other symbolic means. Social role or state requires positing a relation between a person/their role and a social structure.

There are four other force-dynamic novelties found (mostly) in social events. First, the force-dynamic image schemas for social events are predominantly metaphorical extensions of force-dynamic image schemas for physical events. For example, *I gave the book to him* uses the positive mereological figure Place image schema for transfer of possession.

Second, there is interpersonal force-dynamics. In addition to the asymmetric interpersonal interaction termed Inducive (Talmy, 1976; Croft, 1991), there is also a more symmetric and reciprocal type of interpersonal interaction, which we term Mutual.

Third, clauses describing social (and mental) events often have event nominals or sentential complements as arguments. It can be argued that event nominals and complements express participant subevents (Croft and Vigus, 2017, 2020). However, one also finds sentences in which that participant and its subevent are expressed as separate syntactic argument phrases, as in *Rebuilding a life in Black Forest won't completely free [her] [of the emotional turmoil that has marked the past year], she said.* As a result, we posit the additional annotations Engage and its negative, Refrain, to capture the relation between a participant argument phrase and its subevent event nominal.

Fourth, the social force dynamic interactions are not simply causal chains: they include at least cyclic interactions, as when a buyer gives money to a seller and the seller gives the goods to the buyer. In fact, there is some cyclicity in certain physical events as well. For example, in ingestion events, an Eater uses a Utensil, which moves the Food to the Eater's mouth, and the Eater consumes the Food, as in *Jill ate the chicken with chopsticks.* In vehicular motion events, a Rider enters a Vehicle, which then transports the Rider to a Destination, as in *Brenda went to Berlin by train.* These more complex interactions between participants have led us to distinguish the causal chain expressed by an argument structure construction from the more complex causal network that is evoked by the verb (Kalm et al., 2019).

3.4.4 Formalization of Force-Dynamic Structure

Events expressed by single clauses are analyzed as interactions between participants for multiparticipant events. For example, in *The rock broke the window*, the rock acted on the window. We analyze these force-dynamic relations as relations between subevents that are components of the participant's history. In our example, the rock's contact subevent caused the window's change of state subevent (the specific qualitative state being contributed by the semantics of the verb *break*). The rock's contact subevent is a component of the rock's history, and likewise the window's change of state event is a component of the window's history.

The unity of an event expressed by a single clause (verb and argument structure construction) is defined by the fact that all subevents of an event are simultaneous, what Croft (2012) called the temporal unity of events, and by the presence of force dynamic relations between the subevents.

We model the type of incremental change that a participant undergoes, described in Section 3.4.1, as a property of that participant's subevent or, more precisely, the qualitative dimension of that subevent. The types of change described in Section 3.4.1 are Property change (Prop), Motion (Mot), Mereological change (Mer), Design change (Des) and Internal change (Int).

We also provide an analysis of the qualities of subevents of the agent and instrument not discussed by Croft et al. (2016). Agents interact in physical processes using their body. Most of the time what the agent does is volitional; that is, a process involving mental as well as physical aspects of a person. For now, we model volitionality as the type of action that an agent engages in; that is, the agent's subevent has the property Vol. Instruments in physical events interact solely physically, of course, ultimately through some sort of contact. We model the interaction of instruments by attributing the property Contact to the instrument's subevent.

3.5 Annotation Scheme

The theoretical model described above has been implemented in an annotation scheme. We have tested the annotation scheme on texts in different genres, including newswire texts from the Richer Event Description (RED) corpus (O'Gorman et al., 2016; Croft et al., 2016, 2018) and *The Pear Stories*, a set of oral narratives compiled by Chafe (1980; Croft et al., 2017). We have also annotated several hundred VerbNet example sentences with this annotation scheme. The VerbNet annotations can be accessed online through the Unified Verb Index website.[1]

Our annotation scheme currently requires separate manual annotation of the aspectual and force-dynamic event structures for each argument structure construction.

The aspectual annotation uses a four-way categorization into State (stative, all types), Activity (unbounded processes), Performance (completed processes) and Endeavors (terminated processes). This is a coarse-grained version of an annotation scheme with a fine-grained set of aspectual types (Croft et al., 2016). In practice, however, we found that certain aspectual semantic distinctions are difficult to consistently annotate in texts: stable vs. transitory states, punctual vs. durative events and incremental vs. nonincremental change. These distinctions are neutralized in the four-category annotation scheme

[1] https://uvi.colorado.edu.

described in the text. Examples such as *He is driving* and *He is driving down the hill* are both annotated as Activity. However, an example such as *He drove the package to New York* is annotated as Performance because it describes a completed process.

The annotation of force-dynamic structure involves the annotation of up to three subevents, each with a single label. One is the "core" subevent, which is the most salient change that is asserted by the predicate. The "core" event has a Theme participant and possibly a second participant, such as the Ground object in a spatial relation. The "core" event is defined by the type of change that it involves:

- Property: COS (Change of State, one participant), Relation (two participants)
- Path: Motion
- Mereology: Place, Remove (figure is mereological theme); Provide/Cover, Deprive/Uncover (ground is mereological theme)
- Design: Create ("de novo"), Form (includes inputs to creation)
- Existence: Internal (figure without reference to ground), Location (internal change applies to figure), Dynamic Texture (internal change construed as applying to ground)
- Mental: Attend, Affect, Experience, Experience*, Judge, Intend

We also annotate the external cause of the "core" event, if any. The annotation categories for the external cause are as follows:

- Autonomous: no external cause
- Self-Volitional: no external cause; theme argument brings about action volitionally
- Physical: external physical cause
- Volitional: external volitional cause; no distinct instrument
- Instrumental: external volitional cause with distinct instrument

To demonstrate the annotation procedure, we briefly discuss our annotation of two motion examples in (3) from the VerbNet roll-51.3.1 class.

(3)   a. Bill rolled the ball down the hill. [Volitional Motion]
       b. The ball rolled down the hill. [Autonomous Motion]

The annotation label for the "core" event in both of the examples in (3) is the same: Motion. The examples describe a spatial figure-ground relation in which the entity *ball* moves holistically with respect to the Ground *hill*. The semantic difference between the two examples is reflected in the assignment of distinct annotation labels for the type of external cause. In the first example (3a), the core motion event is initiated by an external entity, a volitional agent, who applies physical force to the theme. The annotation label for the external cause in (3a) is Volitional. In the second example (3b), there is no external cause that brings about the motion event; it is annotated Autonomous because the motion theme *ball* denotes a nonvolitional entity.

We applied the annotation scheme for mental events to a set of sentences in a news corpus annotated in RED (Croft et al., 2018). Croft et al. (2018) reported 81% agreement for the causal structure annotation of 92 argument structure constructions that describe real-world events. A respectable level of interannotator agreement points to a working annotation scheme. We continue to refine the annotation scheme, and it will be expanded to apply to social events.

3.6 Visualization

We are also developing a visualization to capture the evolving interactions of participants over time. The basic idea is a modified metro map (Shahaf et al., 2012), in which the lines represent participant histories and the nodes represent interactions among participants; that is, clausal events. Figure 3.2 presents a visualization of the events, participants and interactions in the following passage:

124 he comes down, ... from the ladder,

125 and he's wearing an apron,

126 And he dumps them into some baskets ...

Clausal events are related to other clausal events through temporal relations and relations of shared participants, as in van Erp et al. (2014). As with other storyline visualizations, temporally sequenced events – Before, After and Meets in the interval logic – can be arranged horizontally, with sequenced events sharing participants aligned horizontally. Temporally overlapping events – Equal, Overlap, During and Contain – can be arranged vertically. Events whose temporal location is constrained but not totally specified would be situated relative to those events to which they hold temporal relations.

Of course, such metro maps get very tangled very quickly, because coherent narratives normally express many interwoven events with many different combinations of many different participants. Algorithms such as that of Liu

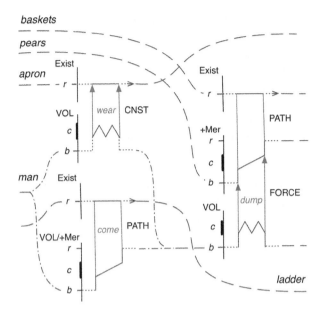

Figure 3.2 Event decomposition and interactions of participants.

et al. (2013) will, we hope, generate visually presentable metro maps of more complex participant interactions over time.

The primary innovation in the visualization is that the interactions between participants in a single clausal event are made explicit, as in Croft (2012) and Croft et al. (2016). That is, the nodes in the metro map visualization are elaborated as interactions between the participants. The roles of participants within a clausal event are kept separate because each participant has its own subevent. The qualitative states and changes of each participant are also explicitly represented. The visualization therefore describes not only the interactions that each participant engages in over the time of the story but also exactly what they do or what happens to them.

Precise representation of participants and their states in events requires addressing certain issues. A group of participants may act as a unit in some events but separately in other events:

41 they gather all the pears
42 and put them in the basket,
43 and one of the guys, helps him
44 brush off the dust,
45 and another guy picks up the rock,

In this case, we must allow the history for the group of three boys to split in order to represent the interaction of individual boys from the group with other entities (the cyclist and the rock).

In other cases, the same participant is playing different roles in two different events at the same time:

140 then he ... takes a pear,
141 after carefully watching the man in the tree.
142 Who's still picking.

The man in the tree is functioning as the target of the watching event in 141 at the same time that he is the agent of the picking event in 142.

In order to represent the distinct qualitative states of the man in the overlapping events, we allow a "virtual split" of the line representing the man's history, representing the different qualitative states of being watched and picking. Such virtual splits will be visualized in a distinct way from actual splits as found in passages 41–45 above. In Figure 3.2, we represent the virtual split of the man by dot-dashed lines.

3.7 Conclusion

The event decomposition developed in our research allows us to implement current models of event structure in theoretical linguistics. The event decomposition is also expandable to domains such as social events that are less well explored theoretically, because it is based on basic ontological dimensions of time, qualitative state and causation. Finally, the event decomposition can be integrated into a metro map representation of story structure that links participant histories to what happens to them, and between them, in the course of a narrative.

Acknowledgments The research was supported in part by grant HDTRA1-15-1-0063 by the Defense Threat Reduction Agency to William Croft.

References

Allen, James. 1984. Towards a General Theory of Action and Time. *Artificial Intelligence*, **23**, 123–154.
Bertinetto, Pier Marco, and Squartini, Mario. 1995. An Attempt at Defining the Class of 'Gradual Completion Verbs'. Pages 11–26 of: Bertinetto, Pier Marco, Bianchi,

Valentina, Higginbotham, James, and Squartini, Mario (eds.), *Temporal Reference, Aspect and Actionality*, Vol. 1. Torino, Italy: Rosenberg and Sellier.

Carlson, Gregory N. 1979. Generics and Atemporal When. *Linguistics and Philosophy*, **3**, 49–98.

Caselli, Tommaso, and Vossen, Piek. 2016. The Storyline Annotation and Representation Scheme (StaR): A Proposal. Pages 67–72 of: Caselli, Tommaso, Miller, Ben, van Erp, Marieke, Vossen, Piek, and Caswell, David (eds.), *Proceedings of the 2nd Workshop on Computing News Storylines (CNS 2016)*. Austin, TX: Association for Computational Linguistics.

Chafe, Wallace (ed.). 1980. *The Pear Stories*. New York: Ablex.

Croft, William. 1991. *Syntactic Categories and Grammatical Relations: The Cognitive Organization of Information*. Chicago: University of Chicago Press.

Croft, William. 1993. Case Marking and the Semantics of Mental Verbs. Pages 55–72 of: Pustejovsky, James (ed.), *Semantics and the Lexicon*. Dordrecht, The Netherlands: Kluwer Academic.

Croft, William. 1998. Event Structure in Argument Linking. Pages 21–63 of: Butt, Miriam, and Geuder, Wilhelm (eds.), *The Projection of Arguments: Lexical and Compositional Factors*. Stanford, CA: Center for the Study of Language and Information.

Croft, William. 2012. *Verbs: Aspect and Causal Structure*. Oxford University Press.

Croft, William, Pešková, Pavlína, and Regan, Michael. 2016. Annotation of Causal and Aspectual Structure of Events in RED: A Preliminary Report. Pages 8–17 of: Palmer, Martha, Hovy, Eduard, Mitamura, Teruko, and O'Gorman, Tim (eds.), *Proceedings of the Fourth Workshop on Events*. Austin, TX, USA: Association for Computational Linguistics.

Croft, William, Pešková, Pavlína, and Regan, Michael. 2017. Integrating Decompositional Event Structure into Storylines. Pages 98–109 of: Caselli, Tommaso, Miller, Ben, van Erp, Marieke, et al. (eds.), *Proceedings of the Workshop on Events and Stories in the News*. Vancouver: Association for Computational Linguistics.

Croft, William, Pešková, Pavlína, Regan, Michael, and Lee, Sook-kyung. 2018. A Rich Annotation Scheme for Mental Events. Pages 7–17 of: Caselli, Tommaso, Miller, Ben, van Erp, Marieke, et al. (eds.), *Proceedings of the Workshop on Events and Stories in the News*. Santa Fe, NM: Association for Computational Linguistics.

Croft, William, and Vigus, Meagan. 2017. Constructions, Frames and Event Structure. Pages 147–153 of: *The AAAI 2017 Spring Symposium on Computational Construction Grammar and Natural Language Understanding*. AAAI Tech. Rep. SS-17-02, AAAI Press. www.aaai.org/Library/Symposia/Spring/ss17-02.php

Croft, William, and Vigus, Meagan. 2020. Event Nominals and Force Dynamics in Argument Structure Constructions. Pages 151–183 of: Siegal, Elitzur Bar-Asher, and Boneh, Nora (eds.), *Perspectives on Causation*. Basel, Switzerland: Springer Nature.

Davies, Mark. 2008. *The Corpus of Contemporary American English (COCA)*. Available online at www.english-corpora.org/coca/.

Doron, Edith. 2020. The Causative Component of Locative and Psychological Verbs. Pages 395–416 of: Siegal, Elitzur Bar-Asher, and Boneh, Nora (eds.), *Perspectives on Causation*. Basel, Switzerland: Springer Nature.

Dowty, David. 1979. *Word Meaning and Montague Grammar*. Dordrecht, The Netherlands: Kluwer.

Dowty, David. 1991. Thematic Proto-Roles and Argument Selection. *Language*, **67**, 547–619.

Fillmore, Charles J., Johnson, Christopher R., and Petruck, Miriam R. 2003. Background to FrameNet. *International Journal of Lexicography*, **16**, 235–250.

Fillmore, Charles J., Kay, Paul, and O'Conner, Mary Catherine. 1988. Regularity and Idiomaticity in Grammatical Constructions: The Case of Let Alone. *Language*, **64**, 501–538.

Forsyth, James. 1970. *A Grammar of Aspect: Usage and Meaning in the Russian Verb*. Cambridge, UK: Cambridge University Press.

Friedrich, Annemarie, and Palmer, Alexis. 2014. Automatic Prediction of Aspectual Class of Verbs in Context. Pages 517–523 of: Toutanova, Kristina, and Wu, Hua (eds.), *Proceedings of the 52nd Annual Meeting of the Association for Computational Linguistics (Short Papers)*, Vol. 2. Association for Computational Linguistics.

Goldberg, Adele E. 1995. *Constructions: A Construction Grammar Approach to Argument Structure*. Chicago: University of Chicago Press.

Goldberg, Adele E. 2006. *Constructions at Work: The Nature of Generalization in Language*. Oxford NY: Oxford University Press.

Gordon, Andrew S., and Hobbs, Jerry R. 2017. *A Formal Theory of Commonsense Psychology: How People Think People Think*. Cambridge University Press.

Hay, Jennifer, Kennedy, Christopher, and Levin, Beth. 1999. Scalar Structure Underlies Telicity in 'Degree Achievements'. Pages 127–144 of: Matthews, Tanya, and Strolovitch, Devon (eds.), *Proceedings of SALT*, Vol. 9. Ithaca, NY: Cornell University Press.

Hobbs, Jerry R. 1985. Granularity. Pages 432–435 of: Joshi, Aravind Krishna (ed.), *Proceedings of the Ninth International Joint Conference on Artificial Intelligence, Volume 1*. San Francisco, CA: Morgan Kaufmann.

Hobbs, Jerry R., and Pan, Feng. 2004. An Ontology of Time for the Semantic Web. *ACM Transactions on Asian Language Information Processing*, **3**(1), 66–85.

Im, Seohyun, and Pustejovsky, James. 2010. Annotating Lexically Entailed Subevents for Textual Inference Tasks. Pages 204–209 of: Barták, Roman, and Bell, Eric (eds.), *Proceedings of the 23rd International Florida Artificial Intelligence Research Society Conference (FLAIRS-23)*. Daytona Beach, FL.

Jackendoff, Ray. 1991. Parts and Boundaries. *Cognition*, **41**, 9–45.

Kalm, Pavlína, Regan, Michael, and Croft, William. 2019. Event Structure Representation: Between Verbs and Argument Structure Constructions. Pages 100–109 of: Xue, Nianwen, Croft, William, Hajic, Jan, et al. (eds.), *Proceedings of the First International Workshop on Designing Meaning Representations (DMR 2019)*. Firenze, Italy: Association for Computational Linguistics.

Kipper, Karin, Korhonen, Anna, Ryant, Neville, and Palmer, Martha. 2008. A Large-Scale Classification of English Verbs. *Language Resources and Evaluation*, **42**(1), 21–40.

Langacker, Ronald W. 1987. *Foundations of Cognitive Grammar: Vol. I. Theoretical Prerequisites*. Stanford, CA: Stanford University Press.

Levin, Beth. 1993. *English Verb Classes and Alternations: A Preliminary Investigation.* University of Chicago Press.

Levin, Beth, and Grafmiller, Jason. 2013. Do You Always Fear What Frightens You? Pages 21–32 of: King, Tracy Holloway, and de Paiva, Valeria (eds.), *From Quirky Case to Representing Space.* CSLI Publications.

Levin, Beth, and Rappaport Hovav, Malka. 2005. *Argument Realization.* Cambridge, UK: Cambridge University Press.

Liu, Shixia, Wu, Yingcai, Wei, Enxun, Liu, Mengchen, and Liu, Yang. 2013. Storyflow: Tracking the Evolution of Stories. *IEEE Transactions on Visualization and Computer Graphics*, **19**(12), 2436–2445.

Mani, Inderjeet, and Pustejovsky, James. 2012. *Interpreting Motion: Grounded Representations for Spatial Language.* Oxford, NY: Oxford University Press.

Mathew, Thomas, and Katz, Graham E. 2009. Supervised Categorization for Habitual versus Episodic Sentences. In: *Sixth Midwest Computational Linguistics Colloquium.* Bloomington, IN: Indiana University Press.

Mittwoch, Anita. 1988. Aspects of English Aspect: On the Interaction of Perfect, Progressive and Durational Phrases. *Linguistics and Philosophy*, **11**, 203–54.

Moens, Marc, and Steedman, Mark. 1988. Temporal Ontology and Temporal Reference. *Computational Linguistics*, **14**, 15–28.

Narayanan, Srini. 1997. *Knowledge-Based Action Representations for Metaphor and Aspect (KARMA).* Ph.D. Thesis, Department of Computer Science, University of California at Berkeley.

O'Gorman, Tim, Wright-Bettner, Kristin, and Palmer, Martha. Richer Event Description: Integrating Event Coreference with Temporal, Causal and Bridging Annotation. Pages 47–56 of: Caselli, Tommaso, Miller, Ben, van Erp, Marieke, Vossen, Piek and Caswell, David (eds.), Proceedings of the 2nd Workshop on Computing News Storylines. Austin, TX: Association of Computational Linguistics.

Pesetsky, David. 1995. *Zero Syntax: Experiencers and Cascades.* Cambridge, MA: MIT Press.

Rothstein, Susan. 2004. *Structuring Events.* Oxford, UK: Blackwell.

Segers, Roxane, Rospocher, Marco, Vossen, Piek, et al. 2016. *The Event and Implied Situation Ontology (ESO): Application and Evaluation.* Pages 1463–1470 of: Calzolari, Nicoletta, Choukri, Khalid, Declerck, Thierry, et al. (eds.), *Proceedings of the Tenth International Conference on Language Resources and Evaluation (LREC 2016).* European Language Resources Association.

Shahaf, Dafna, Guestrin, Carlos, and Horvitz, Eric. 2012. Trains of Thought: Generating Information Maps. Pages 899–908 of: Egyed-Zsigmond, Elöd, Gripay, Yann, Favre, Cécile, and Largeron, Christine (eds.), *Proceedings of the 21st International Conference on World Wide Web.* New York: Association of Computing Machinery.

Siegel, Eric V., and McKeown, Kathleen R. 2001. Learning Methods to Combine Linguistic Indicators: Improving Aspectual Classification and Revealing Linguistic Insights. *Computational Linguistics*, **26**(4), 595–628.

Smith, Carlota. 1991. *The Parameter of Aspect.* Dordrecht, The Netherlands: Kluwer.

Talmy, Leonard. 1976. Semantic Causative Types. Pages 43–116 of: Shibatani, Masayoshi (ed.), *The Grammar of Causative Constructions*, Vol. 6. New York: Academic Press.

Talmy, Leonard. 1985. Lexicalization Patterns: Semantic Structure in Lexical Forms. Pages 57–149 of: Shopen, Timothy (ed.), *Language Typology and Syntactic Description: Grammatical Categories and the Lexicon*, Vol. 3. Cambridge, UK: Cambridge University Press.

Talmy, Leonard. 1988. Force Dynamics in Language and Cognition. *Cognitive Science*, **2**, 49–100.

van Erp, Marieke, Satyukov, Gleb, Vossen, Piek, and Nijssen, Marit. 2014. Discovering and Visualizing Stories in the News. Pages 3277–3282 of: Calzolari, Nicoletta, Choukri, Khalid, Declerck, Thierry, et al. (eds.), *Proceedings of the 9th Language Resources and Evaluation Conference (LREC2014)*. European Language Resources Association.

Vendler, Zeno. 1957. Verbs and Times. *The Philosophical Review*, **66**, 143–60.

Viberg, Ake. 1983. The Verbs of Perception: A Typological Study. *Linguistics*, **21**(1), 123–162.

Xue, Nianwen, and Zhang, Yuchen. 2014. Buy One Get One Free: Distant Annotation of Chinese Tense, Event Type, and Modality. Pages 1412–1416 of: Calzolari, Nicoletta, Choukri, Khalid, Declerck, Thierry, et al. (eds.), *Proceedings of the 9th International Conference on Languages Resources and Evaluation (LREC-2014)*. European Language Resources Association.

Zaenen, Annie. 1993. Unaccusativity in Dutch: Integrating Syntax and Lexical Semantics. Pages 129–161 of: Pustejovsky, James (ed.), *Semantics and the lexicon*. Dordrecht, The Netherlands: Kluwer Academic.

Zarcone, Alessandra, and Lenci, Alessandro. 2008. Computational Models of Event Type Classification in Context. Pages 1232–1238 of: Calzolari, Nicoletta, Choukri, Khalid, Maegaard, Bente, et al. (eds.), *Proceedings of the 6th International Conference on Language Resources and Evaluation (LREC 08)*. European Language Resources Association.

4

Extracting and Aligning Timelines

Mark A. Finlayson, Andres Cremisini, and Mustafa Ocal

Abstract. Understanding the timeline of a story is a necessary first step for extracting storylines. This is difficult, because timelines are not explicitly given in documents, and parts of a story may be found across multiple documents, either repeated or in fragments. We outline prior work and the state of the art in both timeline extraction and alignment of timelines across documents. With regard to timeline extraction, there has been significant work over the past 40 years on representing temporal information in text, but most of it has focused on temporal graphs and not timelines. In the past 15 years researchers have begun to consider the problem of extracting timelines from these graphs, but the approaches have been incomplete and inexact. We review these approaches and describe recent work of our own that solves timeline extraction exactly. With regard to timeline alignment, most efforts have been focused only on the specific task of cross-document event coreference (CDEC). Current approaches to CDEC fall into two camps: event–only clustering and joint event–entity clustering, with joint clustering using neural methods achieving state-of-the-art performance. All CDEC approaches rely on document clustering to generate a tractable search space. We note both shortcomings and advantages of these various approaches and, importantly, we describe how CDEC falls short of full timeline alignment extraction. We outline next steps to advance the field toward full timeline alignment across documents that can serve as a foundation for extraction of higher-level, more abstract storylines.

4.1 Introduction

Storylines rarely spring from a text fully formed, neatly and precisely laid out and clear for all to see. Rather, storylines come to us piecemeal, in dribs and drabs, often with multiple storylines intertwined. This is especially evident in news about current events, where a story may unfold across days, weeks, or even years, where specific texts (e.g., news articles written by journalists) often present in detail only the most recent part of the story or focus on one particular episode, with only quick reviews of prior events included for context. There are numerous processing steps that are necessary to reveal the actual storylines, including general syntactic preprocessing, entity detection, and event and temporal relation extraction (Seretan and Wehrli, 2009; Dinarelli and Rosset, 2011; Mirza, 2014). In this chapter we focus on two critical steps along the path to revealing storylines, namely, the extraction of *timelines* from texts and the *alignment* of those timelines with each other.

A timeline is a total ordering of the events and times in a text, possibly anchoring some time points to clock or calendar time and providing metric durations for some intervals. It is important to note that a timeline is not the same as a storyline. A *storyline* is a sequence of interrelated events that tells a specific story of interest, often with a plot or other narrative structure. A specific text might contain part or whole of any number of storylines (including none at all), and those storylines could appear in a wide variety of orders, fragments, or combinations. Indeed, the identity of a storyline is dependent to some degree on the reader, where the storyline might change depending on their goals or interests. In contrast, a *timeline* is a structure that organizes the events and times mentioned in a text into a global ordering. It is one step beyond the *temporal graph*, which captures the explicit temporal relationships mentioned or directly implied in the text.

In the timeline extraction and alignment work described in this chapter, we assume that we begin with three basic inputs that themselves have been extracted from a set of texts. First, we assume that we have the events and times mentioned in the texts; this step can be achieved using dedicated tools trained on specific annotated corpora such as TimeBank (Llorens et al., 2010). Second, we assume that we have the temporal relationships for each text, which again is a matter of TimeML parsing (Verhagen et al., 2007; UzZaman et al., 2013). Third, we assume that we have the entities and their roles with respect to events. Entity extraction is a well covered topic, and role assignment is covered by a semantic role labeler (SRL) or abstract meaning representation parsing (Johansson and Nugues, 2008; Foland and Martin, 2016).

Starting from these inputs, in the first half of this chapter (Section 4.2) we focus on timeline extraction, namely, taking a temporal graph that reflects directly expressed local orders and converting it into a set of timelines that expresses a global ordering. We first define the problem and then discuss the significant prior work in this area, which, unfortunately, is limited and does not completely solve the problem. We then describe our TimeLine EXtraction (TLEX) method, the most recent work on this problem, which solves the timeline extraction problem exactly, modulo the quality of the starting temporal graph.

With timelines in hand, we turn in the second half of the chapter to timeline alignment (Section 4.3). Timelines extracted from each individual text will need to be aligned globally and we concentrate here on the most well-addressed portion of the problem, that of cross-document event coreference (CDEC). We review the prior work and state of the art, identifying two main types of approaches: event-only clustering and joint event–entity clustering. We identify the pros and cons and point toward next steps.

We conclude the chapter by showing how these two different streams of work can be brought together (Section 4.4) and summarize the contributions (Section 4.5).

4.2 Extracting Timelines

A timeline gives a total ordering of events and times and is useful for a number of natural language understanding tasks. Unfortunately, timelines are rarely explicit in text and usually cannot be directly read off from the text itself. Instead, texts explicitly reveal only *partial* orderings of events and times. Such information can be used to construct a temporal graph by using a temporal representation language such as a temporal algebra or TimeML, as described below, through either automatic analyzers (e.g., Verhagen, 2005), manual annotation (e.g., Pustejovsky, Hanks et al., 2003), or some combination of the two.

There has been some prior work on extracting timelines from TimeML graphs, but these solutions are incomplete: they do not deal with all possible relations and result in output that can contain ordering errors, a natural result of using supervised machine learning. In contrast, we have showed in our TLEX approach that if we leverage prior work on temporal constraint problem solving and formulate timeline extraction as a *constraint satisfaction problem*, we can achieve a theoretically *exact* solution. Furthermore, in contrast to prior work, TLEX handles all possible temporal relations.

4.2.1 Prior Work in Timeline Extraction

Temporal Algebras

Allen (1983) proposed a calculus that defines 13 possible relations between time intervals, called Allen's interval algebra. Every interval has a starting time point (I^-) and an ending time point (I^+), and the start point comes strictly before the end point ($I^- < I^+$). Intervals can be related by disjunctive sets of 13 primitive temporal relations (e.g., BEFORE, AFTER, MEETS). Allen's algebra is especially useful for describing the temporal relationships expressed in text, and we can construct temporal graphs by representing events and times mentioned in the texts as intervals, with relationships expressed using Allen's framework.

Allen's algebra is a *qualitative temporal framework*. In a great deal of later work, Allen's conception of temporal algebras was extended to *quantitative* cases, such as simple temporal problems (STPs), temporal constraint satisfaction problems (TCSPs), disjunctive temporal problems (DTPs), and temporal networks with alternatives (TNAs; for a comprehensive review of the field of temporal reasoning, see Barták et al., 2014). These types of temporal frameworks allow precise reasoning about the temporal distance between time points as represented in the temporal graphs. Theorists have proved quite a number of formal results regarding both types of frameworks (Barták et al., 2014, section 2). While quite useful for planning and scheduling problems, quantitative frameworks are less useful for natural language text (especially narratives and news), which usually does not contain a great deal of precise metric temporal information.

Whether quantitative or qualitative, it is possible to *solve* a temporal graph, which means assigning specific time values (or at least integer order values) to every time point in the graph, which is the same as extracting a timeline.

Temporal Annotation in Language

The gap between formal representations such as Allen's algebra and actual real-world text is bridged by temporal annotation schemes. With regard to time expressions themselves, which include expressions of when something happened, how often something occurs, or how long something takes, researchers have developed a sequence of TIMEX annotation schemes (Ferro et al., 2001; Setzer, 2001; Pustejovsky, Castao et al., 2003). This allow the annotation of expressions such as *at 3 p.m.* (when), *every 2 days* (how often), or *for 1 hour* (how long). Because events are also involved in temporal relations, these approaches were extended into schemes for capturing both times and events. For example, the Translingual Information Detection, Extraction, and Summarization scheme (TIDES; Ferro et al., 2001) integrates TIMEX2 expressions as well as a scheme for annotating events. TIDES includes annotations for temporal expressions, events, and temporal relations. TIDES uses only six temporal relation types to represent the relationship between events; therefore, it gives only a limited view of temporal information from texts.

Deficiencies in TIDES led to the development of TimeML (Pustejovsky, Castao et al., 2003), another markup language for annotating temporal information, originally targeted at news articles. TimeML added facilities for representing not just Allen's temporal relations but added event coreference relations (IDENTITY), as well as aspectual relations and subordinating relations. Aspectual relations represent the relationship between an event and its parts and fall into five types: INITIATES, REINITIATES, TERMINATES, CULMINATES, and CONTINUES. Subordinating relations introduce event–event relationships of conditional, hypothetical, belief, assertion, or counterfactual nature. A TimeML annotation results in a TimeML graph where the nodes represent events, temporal intervals, and time points and edges represent temporal, aspectual, or subordinating TimeML links between nodes.

Limitations in TimeML led researchers to develop improved event annotation schemes. O'Gorman et al. (2016) proposed the richer event description (RED), which, like TimeML, annotates events, times, and temporal relationships but goes further by annotating associated entities and subevent relationships.[1] These additions provide a more integrated sense of how the events in documents relate to each other and allow the development of systems that learn rich relationships.

For different types of events and times, Reimers et al. (2016) proposed the event time annotation scheme, which adds a category of *punctual* events that lack start and end time points. This scheme also distinguishes singleday events and multiday events. Furthermore, unlike TimeML, the annotation scheme allows events that do not have explicit time expression to have a possible date range in a format of "before YYYY-MM-DD and after YYYY-MM-DD." Later, due to low inner annotator agreement on TimeML temporal relations, Ning et al. (2018) proposed the multiaxis annotation scheme where temporal relations are based on the start time point of events.

Although these recent annotation schemes attempted to overcome limitations of TimeML, we focus here on TimeML, because they are all supersets of TimeML, and lack significant data for evaluation.

Prior Approaches to Timeline Extraction

Kreutzmann and Wolter (2014) showed how to use AND-OR linear programming (LP) to solve *qualitative* (i.e., nonmetric) graphs, a set of which includes graphs represented in Allen's algebra. Similarly, Gantner et al. (2008) built the *Generic Qualitative Reasoner* to solve binary qualitative constraint graphs, which takes a calculus description and one or more constraint graphs as input

---

[1] See also Chapter 7.

and solves them using path consistency and backtracking. Although these provide approaches for solving qualitative temporal graphs, their methods cannot be applied directly to TimeML graphs because of subordinating relationships.

In contrast to these constraint-based approaches, other natural language processing researchers have applied machine learning to extract timelines. Following on earlier work by Mani et al. (2006), Do et al. (2012) developed a model to predict associations and temporal relations between pairs of temporal intervals. Combining integer linear programming (ILP) and a collection of local pairwise classifiers, they performed global inference to predict both event–time relations and event–event relations at the same time. Before applying the classifiers, they grouped same events by using event coreference and they showed that event coreference can increase timeline construction performance significantly. Their model attempts to predict both absolute time occurrence for each event in a news article, as well as temporal relations between neighboring events. Because they only look at neighbors, the timeline they extract is necessarily a reflection only of local ordering information. Furthermore, they trained on only three of Allen's temporal relations (BEFORE, AFTER, and OVERLAPS). Their system achieved an accuracy of 73%.

Kolomiyets et al. (2012) proposed a timeline extraction approach using temporal dependency structures over intervals (temporal dependency trees – TDTs – which are trees rather than graphs), again using only a subset of Allen's temporal relations. The main advantage of TDTs is that they can be straightforwardly computed using adapted dependency parsers. This approach took a sequence of event words as input and produced a TDT structure. Although they achieved 70% accuracy in event ordering, the approach only used six temporal relations – BEFORE, AFTER, INCLUDES, IS_INCLUDED, IDENTITY, OVERLAP. Additionally, we have shown that the TDT representation loses significant temporal information relative to temporal graphs (Ocal and Finlayson, 2020).

Finally, instead of using single learner, Chambers et al. (2014) proposed CAscading EVent Ordering architecture (CAEVO) for event ordering. CAEVO is a sieve-based architecture that blends multiple learners into a precision-ranked cascade of sieves. CAEVO contains 12 sieves. Each sieve proposes its labels, and CAEVO decides which label to add to the temporal graph using transitive closure. However, that method was demonstrated only with five relations – BEFORE, AFTER, INCLUDES, IS_INCLUDED, and SIMULTANEOUS – and thus excludes large portions of TimeML and results in roughly only F_1 of 0.501.

In addition to the fact that all of these systems had imperfect performance, in all cases the methods only consider intervals, rather than start and endpoints, and so lose much detailed temporal information.

4.2.2 TLEX: Extracting Exact Timelines

Although the machine learning–based methods mentioned above are useful in terms of generating partial orderings, they suffer from three major problems: they do not handle all possible temporal relations (including subordinating relations), they work only on intervals rather than time points, and their statistical approaches introduce noise into the final result.

In contrast to the above approaches, we designed TLEX, a method for extracting a set of exact timelines using all of the information available in a TimeML graph. TLEX achieves perfect accuracy modulo the correctness of an underlying TimeML graph. Like prior work in solving temporal constraint problems, TLEX checks the TimeML graph for consistency but goes further by automatically identifying inconsistent subgraphs, which allows them to be manually corrected. TLEX outputs one timeline for each temporally connected subgraph, including *subordinated* timelines, which represent possible, counter-factual, or conditional situations. These subordinated timelines are connected to the main timeline in a trunk-and-branch structure. We provide a formal argument for TLEX's correctness, as well as an experimental evaluation of TLEX using 385 manually annotated texts comprising 129,860 words across four corpora.

We illustrate TLEX's method using the following example. In this example, each event is underlined and given a numerical subscript for reference.

David's door is knocked$_1$, and he answered$_2$ it. As soon as he opened$_3$ the door, David's neighbor started complaining$_4$ about the noise. He was quickly bored$_5$, but realized$_6$ that if he said$_7$ something, his neighbor would be mad$_8$. So he continued$_9$ to listen$_{10}$.

TLEX takes the full TimeML graph as input, which is shown in Figure 4.1. TLEX first **partitions** the TimeML temporal graph into subgraphs internally connected only with temporal and aspectual links; each of these subgraphs will correspond to an individual timeline (either a *main* timeline or a *subordinated* timeline) and is connected to other subgraphs only via subordinating links. Figure 4.1 shows this partitioning with dashed lines.

TLEX next **transforms** each TimeML temporal subgraph to a temporal constraint graph. As we explained above, a temporal constraint graph is a graph where nodes are time points and edges are primitive temporal constraints

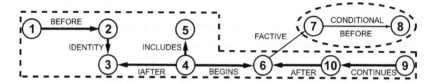

Figure 4.1 Visualization of the TimeML graph from the example. Numbers correspond to the events in the text, and arrows correspond to the temporal, aspectual, or subordinating links. The two temporally and aspectually connected subgraphs are separated by dashed lines, and links on the main timeline are bolded.

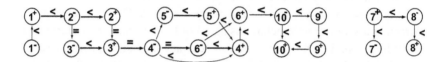

Figure 4.2 The two constraint graphs corresponding to the temporally and aspectually connected subgraphs shown in Figure 4.1. These are produced by replacing each node I with I^- and I^+ and replacing each temporal or aspectual link with the equivalent set of primitive temporal relationships.

such as $<$ and $=$. We assume that every node in the TimeML graph can be represented as an interval I with a starting time point (I^-) and an ending time point (I^+), related by the constraint $I^- < I^+$. Every temporal and aspectual links can then be rewritten as simple conjunctions of temporal primitive constraints. For example, we can rewrite A BEFORE B as $A^+ < B^-$ or A CULMINATES B as $(B^- < A^-) \land (A^+ = B^+)$. The temporal constraint graph for the example is shown in Figure 4.2.

TLEX next **solves** the temporal constraint graph, using off-the-shelf constraint solvers, to assign integers to interval start and endpoints. When we order the integers that are assigned for nodes, we will obtain the order of events and times, namely, the *timeline*. The timeline for the example is shown in Figure 4.3.

Barták et al. (2014) showed that if there is a solution that satisfies the temporal graph, then the graph must be consistent. If the constraint solver determines that there is no solution, then the TimeML graph must be inconsistent. When TLEX finds an inconsistent graph, it finds all relations that contribute to specific inconsistencies. TLEX merges any inconsistent subgraphs that share relations, and these subgraphs can then be given to annotators to fix those inconsistencies based on the texts.

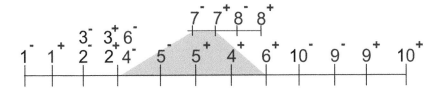

Figure 4.3 Visualization of the timeline extracted from Figure 4.2. The two subgraphs are arranged into main and subordinated timelines connected by a grey branch.

4.3 Aligning Timelines

Once we have timelines extracted from texts, the next problem is to align those timelines to provide a global, corpus-wide ordering. Though anchors to clock and calendar times facilitate such alignment, this information is normally sparse, especially in news and narrative. Aligning timelines thus requires inference of when different timelines refer to the same events. This task is called CDEC. Even perfect CDEC will not result in a full global alignment, however, because some events will not be mentioned in all timelines. Thus, timeline alignment also requires identification of overlapping but otherwise distinct events and time periods – or, at least, identification of indeterminacy of the available information.

Unfortunately, the field has not attacked the full timeline alignment problem. Rather, it has focused primarily on CDEC, and that is the work we will review here. The goal of CDEC is to assign every event mentioned in a corpus to exactly one set of event mentions, where all of the mentions refer to the same event. All existing approaches to CDEC have two steps: first, document clustering, followed by event clustering within each document cluster.

CDEC is not restricted exclusively to events that appear in different documents but rather applies to *all* events within a corpus, including those that appear within the same document. Aligning events within a document is a subtask of CDEC and is called within-document event coreference (WDEC). Although conceptually similar to CDEC, there are some differentiating practical considerations that merit discussion. Most CDEC systems include document information in their feature set when deciding coreference between events, which is not available for WDEC. Additionally, because a document clustering step is not necessary, WDEC reduces solely to event clustering. Importantly, determining pairwise event co-reference within document can actually be a more challenging task than cross-document coreferencing. For example, our reimplementation of the system of Cybulska and Vossen (2015) shows that whereas the pairwise event coreference classifier achieves an F_1 of 0.78 on cross-document event pairs, the same classifier achieves only 0.57 on within-document pairs.

4.3.1 Prior Work and State of the Art in CDEC

ECB and ECB+ Corpus

Most CDEC work has been evaluated on the EventCorefBank (ECB) and EventCorefBank+ (ECB+) corpora, with most using ECB+ because it is larger. ECB was the first corpus developed specifically for CDEC (Bejan and Harabagiu, 2010). It comprises 482 documents selected from GoogleNews, clustered into 43 topics, with each topic containing documents that discuss a specific event, such as the 2009 Indonesian earthquake or the 2008 riots in Greece over a teenager's death. The corpus is annotated using a "bag of events" and entities approach, where coreferring events are all placed into the same group along with their related entities but relationships between specific entities and events are not recorded. A limitation of this annotation scheme is that it makes it impossible to differentiate events based on their arguments.

ECB+ extends ECB with 500 articles (for a total of 982) that refer to similar but unrelated events across the same 43 topics (Cybulska and Vossen, 2014). For example, the topic with the 2009 Indonesian earthquake was expanded with texts referring to the 2013 Indonesian earthquake. These extra texts were marked with a different subtopic.

Initial Approaches

As noted, all extant CDEC systems begin with document clustering followed by event clustering. Most CDEC systems approach document clustering with off-the-shelf algorithms, and in the experimental setups used with the ECB+ corpus these algorithms tend to work quite well, though we discuss some subtleties in Section 4.3.2.

Early CDEC resolution systems used different approaches that were not carried into more recent work. Bejan and Harabagiu (2010) used a Bayesian approach that extends a Dirichlet process using a mixture model called the Chinese Restaurant Process to find the configuration of event clusters with greatest probability given the data. The authors use gold-standard document clusters but do not make use of gold-standard event annotations, using an event extractor developed in earlier work instead and augmenting the predicted events using a semantic parser. They tested their model on the ECB data set and achieved an overall performance of 0.52 CoNLL F_1. This is the only system that reports cross-validation results.

Chen and Ji (2009), in contrast, developed an approach that formulates WDEC as a spectral graph clustering problem. Although this system was tested on the ACE data set, which only includes WDEC annotations (not CDEC), its performance of 0.836 F-measure is potentially of interest to CDEC work.

Event-Only Clustering

Later approaches to CDEC subdivide into *event-only* clustering and *joint event–entity* clustering. Cybulska and Vossen (2015) described a conceptually straightforward, yet strong-performing event-only approach using three decision tree classifiers, one to predict whether two documents contain at least one coreferring event pair, one to generate WDEC clusters, and one for merging cross-document WDEC clusters (Cybulska and Vossen, 2015; Vossen and Cybulska, 2018). All of the classifiers were trained with features derived from pairs of "event templates," which comprise all event information within a unit of discourse organized into labeled slots (e.g. *action, human_participant*). The attractiveness of this approach lies in its conceptual uniformity and simplicity, essentially repeating the same process at different levels of granularity.

Kenyon-Dean et al. (2018) described a different event-only clustering approach that attempts to generate event embeddings for clustering within the hidden layer of a neural network. The paper does not specify whether document clustering was performed before CDEC or whether they used gold-standard labels. The authors trained a neural network with a single hidden layer to predict the event cluster of an event given its feature representation (e.g., *word2vec* embeddings). Because their interest was clustering and not classification, however, they constrained the training loss function in such a way as to produce more clusterable event embeddings in the model's hidden layer. As a final step, they used the event embeddings of test set events as input to an agglomerative clustering algorithm.

Joint Event–Entity Clustering

In contrast to event-only clustering, joint event–entity clustering attempts to resolve event and entity coreference concurrently, using information from either step to inform the decisions made by the other. Lu and Ng (2017) described a system that jointly learns (1) event trigger detection, (2) event anaphoricity, and (3) event coreference. They only performed WDEC and evaluated their model on the KBP 2016 English and Chinese data sets for event coreference. Their formulation makes explicit use of discourse information within the document to construct a conditional random field (CRF) that performs the classification. Given the vast conceptual differences between KBP 2016 and ECB+, it is difficult to compare results across the two data sets. However, Lu and Ng (2017) reported state-of-the-art performance on KBP 2016 at the time.

Lee et al. (2012) described a system that also performs document clustering before computing event and entity clustering. Instead of ingesting gold-standard event and entity labels, they used a publicly available system that performs nominal, pronominal, and verbal mention extraction. After extracting all candidate event or entity mentions, they made use of a publicly available within-document resolution system that applies a series of high precision deterministic rules to decide entity coreference. Using this initial clustering, they trained a linear regressor that predicts the quality of merging two clusters (where quality is defined as the number of correct pairwise links divided by the number of total pairwise links), merging clusters in decreasing order of predicted quality. They did not distinguish between events and entities at clustering time but rather performed cluster merges using features derived from the relationships between the mentions in two candidate clusters, relying heavily on an SRL. They used the ECB data set, adding a series of event and entity coreference annotations.

Barhom et al. (2019) described a joint entity–event clustering model that is the current state of the art on ECB+. This system performs document clustering using K-means and then uses gold-standard event trigger and entity annotations to generate vector embeddings for events and entities, including both character, word, and context embeddings (ELMo is used for the context embeddings; Peters et al., 2018). Together with these vectors the system uses a *dependency vector*, which is the concatenation of a set of vectors designed to capture interdependency between event and entity mentions. For entities, this set includes an embedding for the event head the entity modifies as well as the embeddings for the event heads of all coreferring events. For events, the set includes entity embeddings for each of four event roles (ARG0, ARG1, TMP, LOC) that combine the embedding for the modifying entity mention and the embeddings of all other entity mentions that corefer with the modifying entity. The system computes event and entity clusters iteratively, recomputing the dependency vectors as clusters are merged. They employed an agglomerative clustering algorithm furnished with two trained pairwise prediction functions that output the likelihood that two pairs of events or entities corefer.

4.3.2 Shortcomings of Current CDEC Approaches

Given that all existing CDEC systems use document clustering models to restrict the search space for event clustering, it is important to investigate the role played by errors in document clustering. Importantly, all ECB+ CDEC papers report near-perfect or perfect performance on document clustering on the same test set, topics 36–45 (Cybulska and Vossen, 2015; Kenyon-Dean et al., 2018; Barhom et al., 2019). For example, we confirmed the results reported in Barhom et al. (2019) on topics 36–45 by reimplementing their document clustering method. Yet when we use the same algorithm to perform fivefold cross-validation on document topic clusters of roughly the same size (1–9, 10–18, etc.) on different sections of the corpus, the approach showed performance of anywhere between 2 and 11 percentage points lower across a range of metrics, including homogeneity, completeness, V-measure, and the adjusted Rand index. It is highly likely that this variation in document clustering performance impacts final CDEC performance, because document clustering defines the search space for event clustering.

Only one CDEC paper reports cross-validated performance results, though on the earlier and smaller ECB corpus and using the gold-standard document clustering labels instead of a document clustering model (Bejan and Harabagiu, 2010). No ECB+ papers report on cross-validated CDEC performance.

4.3.3 Next Steps for CDEC

Table 4.1 compares performance from a selection of papers from the CDEC literature discussed above. We see a general upward trend in performance over time, with lower performance on ECB than on ECB+; this is of note because ECB+ was intended to be more difficult (Cybulska and Vossen, 2014). The significant performance gains made by Barhom et al. (2019) suggest that a joint event–entity clustering approach is a promising research direction. In fact, taking the joint approach to its logical conclusion suggests removing the document clustering step altogether and solving the entire task in one shot. Whether or not such an approach would be tractable on large corpora is an open question. Despite this, the performance achieved by Cybulska and Vossen (2015) is noteworthy, given that they described a conceptually less complex approach than that of Barhom et al. (2019). The performance discrepancies on pairwise event resolution classification within and a cross documents reported above suggest that furnishing the framework introduced

Table 4.1. *Performance comparison of selected papers*

Paper	Test set (ECB or ECB+)	Document clustering method	Summary of approach	Co-NLL F_1
Bejan and Harabagiu, 2010	Fivefold cross-validation	Gold labels	Bayesian	0.52
Lee et al., 2012	13-43	Expectation maximization–based	Joint event–entity	0.56
Kenyon-Dean et al., 2018	36-45 (+)	?	Event embedding	0.69
Cybulska and Vossen, 2015	36-45 (+)	Decision tree	Event features	0.73
Barhom et al., 2019	36-45 (+)	K-means	Joint event–entity	0.80

Co-NLL = Conference on Natural Language Learning.

by Cybulska and Vossen (2015) with a more sophisticated clustering technique might prove worthwhile. This was one motivation behind the work of Kenyon-Dean et al. (2018), who developed event embeddings specifically tuned for clustering, although they did not report performance improvement on the results of Cybulska and Vossen (2015). Possibly, the more straightforward feature vectors extracted by Cybulska and Vossen (2015) would prove easier to cluster.

In general, a more comprehensive study of how error propagates through the different subsystems, along with now-standard cross-validation experiments, would seem to be highly informative for future work. This could be at least partly achieved by researchers reporting the results of the subcomponents of their systems (e.g., document clustering, pairwise event classifiers).

4.4 Bringing It All Together

The motivation of combining timeline extraction and CDEC is the extraction of corpus-wide stories. Extracting timelines orders events and times from a single document, and CDEC identifies clusters of different descriptions of the same event but provides no information about the temporal ordering of the event clusters. Currently, almost all timeline extraction approaches focus on single documents, with most ingesting gold-standard WDEC annotations. Extracting a corpus-wide, cross-document event timeline requires merging these two tasks and tackling other as-yet-unaddressed problems. In particular, how do we align event sequences that are not shared between different timelines? CDEC at best provides individual points of alignment, leaving the alignment of interstitial intervals undetermined.

There has been at least one piece of work targeting this combined task: TimeLine, proposed by Minard et al. (2015), performs both CDEC and temporal relation extraction across an entire corpus. It builds a timeline for each text by anchoring the time expressions in that text and ordering events in the text. However, Minard et al.'s approach ignores the majority of TimeML relations and it only achieves 0.076 F_1 score, so clearly it is far from optimal.

Even if were are able to extract a corpus-wide timeline or timelines, this raises other deeper questions about what storylines are present in a corpus with multiple authors, sources, or perspectives. In particular, it is hardly inconceivable that a corpus may express multiple, even incompatible, stories. This is not a rare edge case: in our own studies we have found that even simple texts like folktales more often than not have multiple timelines. In the case of much more complex large-scale news corpora, where information evolves over time from potentially competing or unreliable sources, what does it mean, then, to extract a single storyline? Our representational schemes must admit and express these possibilities. Evaluating such corpus-wide-level storylines poses additional challenges. Obviously, comparison with human judgments is the gold standard, through either full manual annotation or sampling evaluations. But given that different stories might depend on individual perspectives or beliefs (one need only think of the current difficulties of dis- or misinformation in our current media ecosystem), the reliability of even human-provided storylines by which to judge automatic results is problematic.

4.5 Conclusion

We review the literature on both timeline extraction and timeline alignment and discussed the current state-of-the-art. Although there has been quite a bit of formal work on temporal representation and solving temporal constraint problems, the most recent approaches to timeline extraction have adopted a supervised machine learning paradigm which has fallen short. Our own state-of-the-art TLEX approach has demonstrated an exact solution to the problem, modulo the correctness of underlying temporal graph. For timeline alignment, we have focused specifically on the task of CDEC. We discuss the two main types of clustering approaches – event-only and joint event–entity – with latter systems achieving state-of-the-art performance. We outline several paths forward, noting that document clustering is a key step that has been hitherto not carefully examined. Despite recent improvements, CDEC is not yet fully solved, and even perfect performance on CDEC will not beget the medium-term goal of corpus-wide timeline alignment. Therefore, we are still some steps away from the ultimate goal of global, corpus-wide storyline extraction.

Acknowledgments The authors were supported by U.S. Office of Naval Research Grant N00014-17-1-2983 to Mark A. Finlayson.

References

Allen, James. 1983. Maintaining Knowledge about Temporal Intervals. *Communications of the ACM*, **26**(11), 832–843.

Barhom, Shany, Shwartz, Vered, Eirew, Alon, et al. 2019. Revisiting Joint Modeling of Cross-Document Entity and Event Coreference Resolution. *arXiv 1906.01753*.

Barták, R., Morris, R. A., and Venable, K. B. 2014. *An Introduction to Constraint-Based Temporal Reasoning.* Morgan & Claypool Publishers.

Bejan, Cosmin Adrian, and Harabagiu, Sanda. 2010. Unsupervised Event Coreference Resolution with Rich Linguistic Features. Pages 1412–1442 of: Hajič, Jan, Carberry, Sandra, Clark, Stephen, and Nivre, Joakim (eds.), *Proceedings of the 48th Annual Meeting of the Association for Computational Linguistics.*

Chambers, Nathanael, Cassidy, Taylor, McDowell, Bill, and Bethard, Steven. 2014. Dense Event Ordering with a Multi-pass Architecture. *Transactions of the Association for Computational Linguistics*, **2**, 273–284.

Chen, Zheng, and Ji, Heng. 2009. Graph-Based Event Coreference Resolution. Pages 54–57 of: Choudhury, Monojit, Hassan, Samer, Mukherjee, Animesh, and Muresan, Smaranda (eds.), *Proceedings of the 2009 Workshop on Graph-Based Methods for Natural Language Processing.*

Cybulska, Agata, and Vossen, Piek. 2014. Using a Sledgehammer to Crack a Nut? Lexical Diversity and Event Coreference Resolution. Pages 4545–4552 of: Calzolari, Nicoletta, Choukri, Khalid, Declerck, Thierry, et al. (eds.), *Proceedings of the 9th Language Resources and Evaluation Conference (LREC2014).*

Cybulska, Agata, and Vossen, Piek. 2015. "Bag of Events" Approach to Event Coreference Resolution. Supervised Classification of Event Templates. *International Journal of Computational Linguistics and Applications*, **6**(2), 11–27.

Dinarelli, Marco, and Rosset, Sophie. 2011. Models cascade for tree-structured named entity detection. Pages 1269–1278 of: *Proceedings of 5th International Joint Conference on Natural Language Processing.*

Do, Quang Xuan, Lu, Wei, and Roth, Dan. 2012. Joint Inference for Event Timeline Construction. Pages 677–687 of: Tsujii, Jun'ichi, Henderson, James, and Paşca, Marius (eds.), *Proceedings of the 2012 Joint Conference on Empirical Methods in Natural Language Processing and Computational Natural Language Learning (EMNLP-CoNLL'12).*

Ferro, L., Gerber, L., Mani, I., Sundheim, B., and Wilson, G. 2001. *TIDES Temporal Annotation Guidelines, ver. 1.0.2.* www.timeml.org/terqas/readings/ MTRAnnotationGuide_v1_02.pdf.

Foland, William, and Martin, James H. 2016. CU-NLP at SemEval-2016 Task 8: AMR Parsing Using LSTM-Based Recurrent Neural Networks. Pages 1197–1201 of: Bethard, Steven, Carpuat, Marine, Cer, Daniel, et al. (eds.), *Proceedings of the 10th International Workshop on Semantic Evaluation (SemEval-2016)*. San Diego, CA: Association for Computational Linguistics.

Gantner, Zeno, Westphal, Matthias, and Wölfl, Stefan. 2008. GQR – A Fast Reasoner for Binary Qualitative Constraint Calculi. Pages 24–29 of: Guesgen, Hans W., Ligozat, Gérard, and Rodriguez, Rita V. (eds.), *Proceedings of the AAAI'08 Workshop on Spatial and Temporal Reasoning*.

Johansson, Richard, and Nugues, Pierre. 2008. Dependency-Based Semantic Role Labeling of PropBank. Pages 69–78 of: Lapata, Mirella, and Ng, Hwee Tou (eds.), *Proceedings of the 2008 Conference on Empirical Methods in Natural Language Processing*.

Kenyon-Dean, Kian, Cheung, Jackie Chi Kit, and Precup, Doina. 2018. Resolving Event Coreference with Supervised Representation Learning and Clustering-Oriented Regularization. *arXiv 1805.10985*.

Kolomiyets, Oleksandr, Bethard, Steven, and Moens, Marie-Francine. 2012. Extracting Narrative Timelines as Temporal Dependency Structures. Pages 88–97 of: Li, Haizhou, Lin, Chin-Yew, Osborne, Miles, Lee, Gary Geunbae, and Park, Jong C. (eds.), *Proceedings of the 50th Annual Meeting of the Association for Computational Linguistics: Long Papers. Volume 1*. Association for Computational Linguistics.

Kreutzmann, Arne, and Wolter, Diedrich. 2014. Qualitative Spatial and Temporal Reasoning with AND/OR Linear Programming. Pages 495–500 of: Schaub, Torsten, Friedrich, Gerhard, and O'Sullivan, Barry (eds.), *Proceedings of the Twenty-first European Conference on Artificial Intelligence (ECAI'14)*.

Lee, Heeyoung, Recasens, Marta, Chang, Angel, Surdeanu, Mihai, and Jurafsky, Dan. 2012. Joint Entity and Event Coreference Resolution across Documents. Pages 489–500 of: Tsujii, Jun'ichi, Henderson, James, and Paşca, Marius (eds.), *Proceedings of the 2012 Joint Conference on Empirical Methods in Natural Language Processing and Computational Natural Language Learning (EMNLP-CoNLL 2012)*.

Llorens, Hector, Saquete, Estela, and Navarro-Colorado, Borja. 2010. TimeML Events Recognition and Classification: Learning CRF Models with Semantic Roles. Pages 725–733 of: Huang, Chu-Ren, and Jurafsky, Dan (eds.), *Proceedings of the 23rd International Conference on Computational Linguistics*.

Lu, Jing, and Ng, Vincent. 2017. Joint Learning for Event Coreference Resolution. Pages 90–101 of: Barzilay, Regina, and Kan, Min-Yen (eds.), *Proceedings of the 55th Annual Meeting of the Association for Computational Linguistics: Volume 1. Long Papers*.

Mani, Inderjeet, Verhagen, Marc, Wellner, Ben, Lee, Chong Min, and Pustejovsky, James. 2006. Machine Learning of Temporal Relations. Pages 753–760 of: Calzolari, Nicoletta, Cardie, Claire, and Isabelle, Pierre (eds.), *Proceedings of the 21st International Conference on Computational Linguistics and the 44th Annual Meeting of the Association for Computational Linguistics (ICCL-ACL'06).* Sydney, Australia.

Minard, Anne-Lyse, Speranza, Manuela, Agirre, Eneko, et al. 2015 (01). SemEval-2015 Task 4: TimeLine: Cross-Document Event Ordering. Pages 778–786 of: Nakov, Preslav, Zesch, Torsten, Cer, Daniel, and Jurgens, David (eds.), *Proceedings of SemEval-2015.*

Mirza, Paramita. 2014. Extracting Temporal and Causal Relations between Events. Pages 10–17 of: Kochmar, Ekaterina, Louis, Annie, Volkova, Svitlana, Boyd-Graber, Jordan, and Byrne, Bill (eds.), *Proceedings of the ACL 2014 Student Research Workshop.* Baltimore, MD: Association for Computational Linguistics.

Ning, Qiang, Wu, Hao, and Roth, Dan. 2018. A Multi-Axis Annotation Scheme for Event Temporal Relations. Pages 1318–1328 of: Gurevych, Iryna, and Miyao, Yusuke (eds.), *Proceedings of the 56th Annual Meeting of the Association for Computational Linguistics: Volume 1. Long Papers.* Melbourne, Australia: Association for Computational Linguistics.

Ocal, Mustafa, and Finlayson, Mark. 2020. Evaluating Information Loss in Temporal Dependency Trees. Pages 2148–2156 of: Calzolari, Nicoletta, Béchet, Frédéric, Blache, Philippe, et al. (eds.), *Proceedings of the 12th Language Resources and Evaluation Conference.* Marseille, France: European Language Resources Association.

O'Gorman, Tim, Wright-Bettner, Kristin, and Palmer, Martha. 2016. Richer Event Description: Integrating Event Coreference with Temporal, Causal and Bridging Annotation. Pages 47–56 of: Caselli, Tommaso, Miller, Ben, van Erp, Marieke, Vossen, Piek, and Caswell, David (eds.), *Proceedings of the 2nd Workshop on Computing News Storylines (CNS 2016).* Austin, TX: Association for Computational Linguistics.

O'Gorman, Tim, Wright-Bettner, Kristin, and Palmer, Martha. 2021. The Richer Event Description Corpus for Event-Event Relations. Pages 151–169 of: Caselli, Tommaso, Palmer, Martha, Hovy, Eduard, and Vossen, Piek (eds), *Computational Analysis of Storylines: Making Sense of Events.* Cambridge University Press.

Peters, Matthew E., Neumann, Mark, Iyyer, Mohit, et al. 2018. Deep Contextualized Word Representations. *arXiv CoRR 1802.05365.*

Pustejovsky, James, Castao, José, Ingria, Robert, et al. 2003. TimeML: Robust Specification of Event and Temporal Expressions in Text. In: Bos, Johan, and Koller, Alexander (eds.), *Fifth International Workshop on Computational Semantics (IWCS-5).*

Pustejovsky, James, Hanks, Patrick, Saurí, Roser, et al. 2003. The TimeBank Corpus. Pages 647–656 of: Archer, Dawn, Rayson, Paul, Wilson, Andrew, and McEnery, Tony (eds.), *Proceedings of Corpus Linguistics Conference.* Lancaster, UK.

Reimers, Nils, Dehghani, Nazanin, and Gurevych, Iryna. 2016. Temporal Anchoring of Events for the TimeBank Corpus. Pages 2195–2204 of: Erk, Katrin, and Smith, Noah A. (eds.), *Proceedings of the 54th Annual Meeting of the Association for Computational Linguistics: Volume 1. Long Papers.* Berlin.

Seretan, Violeta, and Wehrli, Eric. 2009. Multilingual Collocation Extraction with a Syntactic Parser. *Language Resources and Evaluation,* **43**(1), 71–85.

Setzer, Andrea. 2001. *Temporal Information in Newswire Articles: an Annotation Scheme and Corpus Study.* Ph.D. Thesis, University of Sheffield.

UzZaman, Naushad, Llorens, Hector, Derczynski, Leon, et al. 2013. SemEval-2013 Task 1: TempEval-3: Evaluating Time Expressions, Events, and Temporal Relations. Pages 1–9 of: Manandhar, Suresh, and Yuret, Deniz (eds.), *Second Joint Conference on Lexical and Computational Semantics (*SEM), Volume 2: Proceedings of the Seventh International Workshop on Semantic Evaluation (SemEval 2013).* Atlanta: Association for Computational Linguistics.

Verhagen, Marc. 2005. Temporal Closure in an Annotation Environment. *Language Resources and Evaluation*, **39**(5), 211–241.

Verhagen, Marc, Gaizauskas, Robert, Schilder, Frank, et al. 2007. Semeval-2007 Task 15: Tempeval Temporal Relation Identification. Pages 75–80 of: Agirre, Eneko, Màrquez, Lluís, and Wicentowski, Richard (eds.), *Proceedings of the Fourth International Workshop on Semantic Evaluations (SemEval-2007).* Prague, Czech Republic.

Vossen, Piek, and Cybulska, Agata. 2018. Identity and Granularity of Events in Text. Pages 501–522 of: Costa-jussà, M. R., and Fonollosa, J. A. R. (eds.), *Lecture Notes in Computer Science*, Vol. 9624. Berlin: Springer.

5

Event Causality

Paramita Mirza

Abstract. A crucial aspect of understanding and reconstructing narratives is identifying the underlying causal chains, which explain why certain things happened and make a coherent story. In order to build such causal chains, or *causelines* (see Chapter 6), we need to identify causal links between events in the story, which may be expressed explicitly as well as understood implicitly using commonsense knowledge. This chapter reviews research efforts on the automated extraction of such event causality from natural language text. It starts with a brief review of existing causal models in psychology and psycholinguistics as a building block for understanding causation. These models are useful tools for guiding the annotation process to build corpora annotated with causal pairs. I then outline existing annotated resources, which are used to build and evaluate automated causality extraction systems. I focus on summarizing research efforts on automatic extraction systems for identifying causality between events triggered by lexical items: for instance, extracting a causal link between *hugged* and *felt* in 'He hugged her tight because he felt grateful'. Most extraction systems rely on the presence of explicit causal connectives such as *because*. However, causality between events may be expressed implicitly through adjacency in discourse. Furthermore, circumstantial events surrounding the causal complex are rarely expressed with language as they are part of human common sense. Therefore, discovering causal common sense is also important to fill the gaps in the causal chains, and I discuss existing work in this line of research.

5.1 Introduction

An important part of understanding text, narratives in particular, arises from understanding whether and how two events are related semantically. For instance, when given a sentence 'He hugged her tight because he felt grateful for her help', humans understand that there are three events, indicated by the words 'hugged', 'felt grateful' and '(her) help', and that the *helping* event results in him *feeling grateful*, which in turn leads to the *hugging* event, establishing a causal chain among them. Besides being important components of discourse understanding, automatic extraction of event causality and causal reasoning are important for various downstream tasks such as question answering, decision support and future event prediction given a chain of past events, among others.

As a starting point, we should first consider a definition of *causation* in the general sense. It is commonly agreed in philosophical and psychological literature that (1) causation is a relation between two events – *cause* and *effect*; (2) causation has a temporal dimension – the cause must precede the effect; and (3) causation is counterfactual: if the cause had not occurred, the effect would not have occurred either.

It is important to note that causation exists as a psychological principle for understanding the world independent of language, even though language can be used to talk about causation (Neeleman and van de Koot, 2012). Consider our previous example, 'He hugged her tight because he felt grateful'. As humans we understand that the *hugging* event is indeed triggered by him *feeling grateful*. However, it would not happen if certain conditions were not in place or certain events did not happen, for instance, both of them feel comfortable with hugging each other, they stand in close proximity, his arms were free and so on. Such a *mental model* (Neeleman and van de Koot, 2012) or *causal complex* (Hobbs, 2005) contains fine-grained information of eventualities (events or states) whose happening or holding entails that the effect will happen, and therefore, it cannot be trivially conveyed with a single linguistic expression.

When we intend to use knowledge about causal relations between events to reason formally about causation, we need to consider which eventualities are in or out of the causal complex for a particular effect; meanwhile, for language understanding and determining lexical semantics between concepts, it is often sufficient to distinguish eventualities that deserve to be called *causes* for a resulting event or state (Hobbs, 2005).

In this chapter I will first focus on the second inquiry, i.e., on understanding whether there exists a *causal relation* encoded in certain linguistic expressions, in terms of *causes* and resulting *effects*. I will start with a brief overview of existing attempts in the psychology field to model causation, which are useful for guiding causal annotation endeavours. I will also summarize available resources annotated with causal relations, followed by research efforts on automated extraction of event causality that leverage such resources. I will then discuss existing work on discovering causal common sense, which is important for constructing causal chains, taking into account triggering and enabling factors in the causal complex for an effect to happen.

5.2 Modelling Causal Relations

Counterfactual Model: The first inquiry previously mentioned, related to determining which eventualities are in or out of the causal complex, leads one to examine counterfactuals (Hobbs, 2005). According to the *counterfactual model* (Lewis, 1973), an event C is a cause of an event E if and only if it holds true that if C had not occurred, E would not have occurred. Considering our example where someone felt grateful and hugged his partner as a result, the situation is causal because if he had not felt grateful, he would not have hugged her.

There are several problems of the counterfactual model pointed out in Wolff (2007). One critical problem is that it might consider noncausal factors as causal (Wolff and Song, 2003; Neeleman and van de Koot, 2012). For instance, if both of his arms had not been free to move (or the extreme case, if he had not been born), then he would not have hugged her. Another issue with the counterfactual model is *overdetermination* (Sloman, 2005; Wolff, 2007). Consider an example where he hugged her not only because he felt grateful but also because he missed her presence. Based on the counterfactual principle, neither should be considered a cause because if he had not felt grateful, he would still have hugged her. To conclude, although counterfactual thinking can influence the causal reasoning, i.e., distinguishing eventualities that are in and out of causal complex, causal relationships cannot be reduced to counterfactual conditionals (Wolff, 2007).

Probabilistic Causation: Probabilistic causation designates a group of theories that aim to characterize the relationship between *causes* and *effects* using the tools of *probability theory* (Hitchcock, 2018). The central idea behind these theories is that causes *raise* the probabilities of their effects, which can be expressed formally using conditional probability:

$$P(E|C) > P(E|\neg C), \tag{5.1}$$

meaning that the probability that E occurs, given that C occurs, is higher than the probability that E occurs given that C does not occur (e.g., Reichenbach, 1956; Suppes, 1970).

The *probabilistic contrast model* (Cheng and Novick, 1991) introduces the notion of *covariation*, $\Delta P = P(E|C) - P(E| \neg C)$, which is computed over a *focal set*, i.e., a set of events implied by the context E. When ΔP is greater than some (empirically determined) criterion, there should be a causal attribution to event C. In the case of event C constantly appearing in a focal set, leading to division by zero in computing the probability of the effect in the absence of event C, the causal status of such an event can only be determined by events in other focal sets, i.e., event C is (1) an *enabling condition* if it does co-vary with the effect in another focal set – namely, a set of events selected under another context, but (2) causally irrelevant if it does not co-vary with the effect in any other focal sets. Furthermore, this model distinguishes two main types of causal relationships: positive contrasts specify *facilitatory* causes (e.g., smoking *causes* cancer), whereas negative contrasts specify *inhibitory* causes (e.g., antioxidants *prevent* cancer).

The causation models based on probabilistic theory have a problem in establishing causal relationships on the basis of a single observation, because reliable probabilities depend on multiple observations (Tenenbaum and Griffiths, 2001). In the case of understanding causal relationships between events in natural language texts, the models are only applicable when we have sufficient explicitly correlated events. Such correlated events can be mined from large collections of narratives (e.g., news corpora); however, the reporting bias commonly present in news may distort the account of causation.

Dynamics Model: Another major approach towards causation involves *physicalist models*, which are built upon the assumption that causation can be described in terms of physical quantities such as energy, momentum, impact forces, chemical forces and electrical forces, among others. The *dynamics model* (Wolff and Song, 2003; Wolff et al., 2005; Wolff, 2007) is one of the prominent ones, which is based on Talmy's *force dynamic* account on causality (Talmy, 1988).

According to the dynamics model, causation involves interactions between two main entities: an *affector* and a *patient*. An affector is the entity that *acts on* a patient. The concept of causation, along with its related concepts, is captured in terms of three dimensions: (1) the patient tendency for the result; (2) the presence of concordance between the affector and the patient; and (3) the occurrence of the result (Wolff and Song, 2003). Table 5.1 shows the representation of CAUSE, ENABLE and PREVENT concepts by the dynamics model.

In a CAUSE situation, such as 'Strong wind caused the bridge to collapse', the tendency of the bridge (patient) is not to collapse (result), but the strong wind (affector) does not act in concordance with the tendency, and the result

Table 5.1. *Causality concepts represented by the dynamics model*

	Patient tendency for result	Affector–patient concordance	Occurrence of result
CAUSE	No	No	Yes
ENABLE	Yes	Yes	Yes
PREVENT	Yes	No	No

occurs. Meanwhile, in an ENABLE situation, as in 'Vitamin B enables the body to digest food', the tendency of the body (patient) is to digest food and Vitamin B (affector) acts in concordance, assisting the tendency, and the result occurs.

The dynamics model was tested by linking it with natural language; participants were tasked to sort 23 verbs expressing causality into groups according to the verbs' similarity to each other (Wolff and Song, 2003). The result indicated that these verbs fell into the three causal categories predicted by the model.

5.3 Causal Annotation in Natural Language Text

Natural language displays a great range of devices to express causal relations, including causative verbs such as *break* or *kill*, which express some contributing factors causing some entities to become *broken* or *dead*, prepositions such as *due to*, as well as discourse connectives such as *because* or *since* (Waldmann et al., 2017). In this section I will focus on attempts to annotate causal relations between different units of discourse (e.g., clauses, verbal events). I will expand on causative verbs later in Section 5.5, because such verbs implicitly encode causal commonsense knowledge.

Existing annotation schemes for causal relations can be generally distinguished into two approaches related to different discourse units used: *text spans* and *lexical units*. With the first approach, causation in 'He hugged her tight because he felt grateful' is annotated between *He hugged her tight* and *he felt grateful*, whereas *hugged* and *felt* are causally connected with the second approach.[1] Table 5.2 summarizes available resources annotated with causal relations.

---

[1] With the exception of PropBank (Palmer et al., 2005) that focuses on predicate–argument relations. Text spans denoting the reasons for an action are annotated as causal arguments (ARGM-CAU) of a lexical predicate, as in 'They [*moved* PREDICATE] to London [*because of the baby* ARGM-CAU]'.

Table 5.2. *Resources annotated with causal relations*

Corpus	Size (no. of documents)	Discourse unit	No. of causal pairs
PDTB (Prasad et al., 2008)	2,159	Text span	6,289
BECauSE 2.0 (Dunietz et al., 2017)	119	Text span	1,634
SemEval-2007 (Girju et al., 2007)	–	Nominal	114
Do et al. (2011)	20	ACE event	414
Bethard et al. (2008)	556	TimeML event	271
Causal-TimeBank (Mirza and Tonelli, 2014)	183	TimeML event	318
CaTeRS (Mostafazadeh et al., 2016b)	320	TimeML event	488

Text Spans: The Penn Discourse Treebank (PDTB) corpus (Prasad et al., 2008) addresses the annotation of discourse relations that hold between exactly two text spans as arguments, which can be phrases, clauses or sentences. Such semantic relations are expressed either explicitly via lexical items (e.g., *because*) or implicitly via adjacency in discourse. In PDTB, the CAUSE relation is classified as a subtype of CONTINGENCY. Out of 102 known explicit discourse markers (e.g., *and, in contrast*), 28 explicitly mark causal relations (e.g., *as a result, consequently*). In addition to explicit markers, open-ended markers such as *This may help explain why* were also considered and annotated as *AltLex* relations. Among 6,289 annotated causal pairs, 2,099 are explicit and 273 contain an AltLex, and the rest are implicit causation (Hidey and McKeown, 2016).

The BECauSE 2.0 corpus (Dunietz et al., 2017) adopts the annotation scheme of PDTB but with a focus on annotating any form of *causal language* presented in the text with explicit lexical triggers. Each causal annotation consists of *cause* and *effect* spans, as well as a *causal connective* (e.g., *because of* or *opens the way for*). In addition to the distinction between positive causation (FACILITATE) and inhibitory causation (INHIBIT), three types of causation were considered: CONSEQUENCE (e.g., '[*They moved to London $_{effect}$*] **because of** [*the baby $_{cause}$*]'); MOTIVATION (e.g., '[*Their old apartment was too small $_{cause}$*], **so** [*they moved to London $_{effect}$*]'); and PURPOSE (e.g., '[*They moved to London $_{effect}$*] **so that** [*they could have a bigger house $_{cause}$*]').

The corpus comprises a total of 1,803 sentences expressing causation, of which 1,634 sentences contain both cause and effect arguments.

Lexical Units: The *SemEval-2007* shared task on *Classification of Semantic Relations between Nominals* (Girju et al., 2007) gives access to a corpus containing nominal causal relations, among other semantic relations considered in the task. A nominal is defined as a noun or a noun phrase, excluding named entities and complex noun phrases (e.g., *the engine of the lawn mower*). Textual data was collected via wild-card search patterns; for instance, with '* cause *' as a query. The CAUSE–EFFECT relation is then annotated as true between e_1 and e_2 in sentences such as 'Happiness and [*laughter $_{e_1}$*] can cause [*wrinkles $_{e_2}$*]'.

Several works focus on annotating causal relations between *events* triggered by lexical units, following either *TimeML* (Pustejovsky et al., 2003) or *ACE* (Linguistic Data Consortium, 2005) annotation schemes for modelling events. Both TimeML and ACE define an event as *something that happens/occurs* or *a state that holds true*, which can be expressed by a verb, a noun, an adjective, as well as a nominalization either from verbs or from adjectives. However, both event models are designed for different purposes, hence resulting in different annotation of events. In addition to basic features of events existing in both models (tense, aspect, polarity and modality), ACE events have more complex structures involving *event arguments*, which can be either *event participants* or *event attributes* (location and time).[2] Though all events in TimeML are annotated, only 'interesting' events falling into a set of particular types and subtypes are annotated in ACE.

ACE Events: The event model adopted in Do et al. (2011) for identifying event causality is a simplification of the ACE events, in which only the subjects and objects of a *predicate* – a word triggering the presence of an event – are taken into account as *event arguments*, if any. Both verbal and nominal predicates were considered, allowing the detection of causality between *verb–verb*, *verb–noun* and *noun–noun* triggered event pairs. Event arguments were automatically extracted via dependency parsing. In order to evaluate their approach, they developed an evaluation corpus by collecting 20 news articles from CNN and annotating the causal pairs using two simple notions for

---

[2] Similar predicate–argument structures are found in FrameNet (Baker et al., 1998), which systematically describes semantic frames. FrameNet also captures relationships between frames, including, among others, *Precedes* and *Is Preceded by*, capturing temporal ordering, and *Is Causative of*, expressing causality.

causality (*C*): (1) the *cause* should temporally precede the *effect*, and (2) the *effect* occurs because the *cause* occurs. In the case where the existence of causation is debatable, they annotate the pairs with *relatedness* (*R*) indication. Evaluated on 10 documents, the annotators agreed on 67% of 248 distinct event pairs having *C* + *R* relations. However, they only agreed on 58% event pairs for having *C* relation, highlighting the difficulty of distinguishing causally related events. In total, 492 *C* + *R* and 414 *C* relation annotations were obtained.

TimeML Events: Bethard et al. (2008) utilized an existing event extraction system for identifying TimeML events in the Penn Treebank corpus (Marcus et al., 1993) and then annotated 1,000 pairs of events conjoined with the conjunction *and*. The extracted event pairs were annotated with both temporal and causal relations in parallel. For causal relations, the authors investigated two annotation guidelines, with the latter shown to be more robust: (1) identifying NECESSARY and SUFFICIENT events based on the counterfactual model and (2) choosing between CAUSAL vs NO-REL by paraphrasing the word *and* with, for instance, *and as a result* vs *and independently*, respectively. The second guideline is relatively simple for annotators, but agreement is only moderate (kappa of 0.556), in part because there are both causal and noncausal readings of such connective phrases.

Mirza and Tonelli (2014) augmented the TimeBank corpus (Pustejovsky et al., 2006) taken from the TempEval-3 shared task (UzZaman et al., 2013) – containing gold annotated TimeML events, temporal information and ordering – with causal information. The annotators relied on explicit *causal signals* (marked as CSIGNAL) to identify *causal relations* (annotated with CLINK, analogous to TLINK for temporal relations in TimeML) between events. A CLINK was established between two events when one of the considered causal constructions was identified, including, among others (Mirza and Tonelli, 2014; Mirza et al., 2014), expressions containing CSIGNALs such as 'Its shipments [*declined* EFFECT] **as a result of** a [*reduction* CAUSE] in inventories' and periphrastic constructions involving verbs associated with Cause, Enable and Prevent relations listed in Wolff and Song (2003), as exemplified in 'The [*blast* CAUSE] **caused** the boat to [*heel* EFFECT] violently'. The total number of annotated CLINKs in the resulting Causal-TimeBank corpus (Mirza and Tonelli, 2014) is 318, with Dice's coefficient of 0.73 on a subset of five documents.

The CaTeRS annotation scheme (Mostafazadeh et al., 2016b) looked at causality between events more from a commonsense reasoning standpoint rather than linguistic markers. The authors annotated 320 stories from the ROCStories Corpus (Mostafazadeh et al., 2016a) with events and semantic relations, both temporal and causal. The semantic relation annotation was initiated with deciding whether one of nine causal relation types (combinations of CAUSE, ENABLE, PREVENT and CAUSE_TO_END relations with valid temporal relations such as BEFORE and OVERLAP) occur, followed by choosing one of existing temporal relation types (BEFORE, OVERLAP, CONTAIN, IDENTITY) when no causality was detected. For instance, given a sentence 'It was [*raining* e_1] so hard that it prevented me from [*going* e_2] to school', a PREVENT–OVERLAP relation is established between e_1 and e_2.[3] There are overall 488 causal links, with CAUSE–BEFORE being the most frequent type, and moderate agreement of the semantic link annotation in general (kappa of 0.49).

5.4 Extracting Event Causality

Understanding discourse relations that are expressed in natural language texts is important for downstream natural language processing applications such as question-answering and decision-making support systems. Recognizing causal relations in particular is necessary to reconstruct a causal chain of events as part of story or narrative understanding. Existing annotated resources for causal relations allow us to consider automatic approaches for identifying causation in natural language texts, both as training data to build machine learning models and as evaluation benchmarks to measure the performance of the automatic methods.

Even though there exists a body of work on the extraction of causal relations between nominals (e.g., Dasgupta et al., 2018), as well as work leveraging the PDTB corpus for the automatic detection of discourse relations in general (e.g., Pitler and Nenkova, 2009; Liu and Li, 2016) or causal relations specifically (e.g., Hidey and McKeown, 2016), in this section I will focus only on automatic extraction systems developed for identifying causality between *events* triggered by lexical items, for each event model previously discussed in Section 5.3, using the corresponding annotated data.

ACE Event Causality: Do et al. (2011) explored a minimally supervised approach by devising a causality measure in terms of *cause–effect association (CEA)* between two events e_i and e_j, which takes into account the *pointwise mutual information* (PMI) between (1) event predicates, (2) the predicate of

---

[3] This example illustrates the temporal implications of causation, in which the *cause* start before the *effect*; however, there is no restriction on their relative ending, allowing the OVERLAP relation to happen.

an event and the arguments of the other event, and (3) event arguments. Furthermore, they leveraged the interactions between event causality and discourse relation predictions through a global inference procedure, which can be formalized via an integer linear programming (ILP) framework as a constraint optimization problem (Roth and Yih, 2004). One introduced constraint is related to the types of predicted discourse connectives (e.g., CAUSE, CONDITION) that are allowed to enclose a causal event pair. Evaluated on the evaluation corpus they built, mentioned in Section 5.3, the system achieves a performance of 41.7% F1-score on extracting causality between events.

TimeML Event Causality: Bethard and Martin (2008) built a classification model for extracting causal relations using a subset of the annotated corpus of parallel temporal and causal relations described in Section 5.3. They used 697 out of 1,000 event pairs to train a support vector machine (SVM) classifier using both syntactic and semantic features and used the rest for evaluating the system, resulting in a 37.1% F1-score. The performance of the causal relation classifier is significantly boosted to a 52.4% F1-score by additionally exploiting gold-standard temporal labels as features. Rink et al. (2010) performed textual graph classification using the same event causality corpus built by Bethard and Martin (2008), leveraging syntactic features as well as the hypernym chain for the senses resulting from word sense disambiguation. Following Bethard and Martin (2008), they also made use of manually annotated temporal relation types as a feature to build the classification model. This results in a 57.9% F1-score, a 15 percentage point increase compared with the system without the additional feature of temporal relations. However, the system proposed by Bethard and Martin (2008) for automatically extracting temporal links yields only a 49% F1-score. Hence, it is highly likely that leveraging automatically extracted temporal labels as features will show no benefit and propagate errors instead.

Mirza and Tonelli (2016) proposed a hybrid approach for the extraction and classification of both temporal and causal relations between events from English documents, which are pre-annotated with TimeML events and temporal expressions. They developed CATENA (CAusal and TEmporal relation extraction from NAtural language texts), which consists of two main modules, one for temporal and the other for causal; both modules rely on a *sieve-based architecture* introduced in Chambers et al. (2014) for event ordering, in which the remaining unlabelled pairs – after running a rule-based component and/or a transitive reasoner – are fed into a supervised classifier.

In the causal module, the rule-based (RB) sieve is responsible for identifying causal constructions involving *affect* and *link* verbs presented in

Mirza and Tonelli (2014), as well as *periphrastic causative* verbs associated with Cause, Enable and Prevent listed in Wolff and Song (2003), which are further expanded using the Paraphrase Database (PPDB) by Ganitkevitch et al. (2013). The machine-learned (ML) sieve is a linear SVM classifier leveraging various features including syntactic and semantic features, event attributes and features related to temporal and causal signals, which are also extended with PPDB phrases.

The authors made use of the Causal-TimeBank corpus (see Section 5.3) to train the supervised classifier and additionally annotated 20 TempEval-3-platinum documents (UzZaman et al., 2013) with causal links as the evaluation set, following the same annotation schemes and guidelines. Whereas the data-driven ML sieve achieves only an 18.2% F1-score, the combination of RB and ML sieves yields a 62.2% F1-score, a 4.3 percentage point increase compared with the standalone RB sieve, with the ML sieve contributing to boosting the recall of the highly precise RB sieve (recall moves up from 42.3% to 53.8%).

The low performance of the ML module is mostly due to dependency parsing mistakes, especially for long sentences. For instance, a causal link was established between *acquire* and *respond* in 'StatesWest Airlines, Phoenix, Ariz., said it [*withdrew* EFFECT] its offer to [*acquire*] Mesa Airlines **because** the Farmington, N.M., carrier didn't [*respond* CAUSE] to its offer . . .' instead of between *withdrew* and *respond*, as a result.

Explicit vs Implicit Causal Signals: Another issue of the ML sieve in CATENA is the difficulty in disambiguating signals such as *and* and *since*. As previously mentioned above, Bethard and Martin (2008) and Rink et al. (2010) tackled this specific problem of classifying event pairs conjoined with the conjuction *and*, resulting in only 52.4% and 57.9% F1-scores respectively with the help of gold-annotated temporal labels. One possible explanation for the low performance is that a data-driven approach for this particular task would require sufficient training data of causal event pairs in order to uncover causal common sense; for example, that feeling grateful may be one of the reasons for hugging someone. Discovering such causal common sense will also be beneficial for identifying causal relations when there are no markers at all, which are more common in natural language texts (e.g., 62% of causal pairs in the PDTB corpus are of implicit nature). I will discuss existing efforts in this line of research of discovering causal common sense in the following section.

5.5 Causal Commonsense Discovery

Discovering causal common sense is crucial for recognising latent causation that is implicitly present in natural language text; for instance, to notice the causal relations between 'helped' and 'hugged' events in 'She helped him a lot. He hugged her gratefully'. As humans we understand that we would feel thankful if someone helped us, and feeling thankful often leads to hugging the person who helped us. Furthermore, it is important to note that we can only hug someone when that person is in close proximity to us. Such background knowledge is a necessity for an automatic method to be able to reconstruct and to reason about causal chains among events, taking into account triggering and enabling factors that persist in the causal complex for the causation to hold. In this section, I will discuss several attempts on building a repository of causal common sense to serve its purposes.

Causative Verbs: Causative verbs were briefly mentioned in Section 5.3 and were defined as verbs that implicitly encode states resulting from some events and contributing factors (Neeleman and van de Koot, 2012; Waldmann et al., 2017). For example, the verb 'break' in 'Mary broke the vase' may express 'some event involving Mary was the cause of the vase becoming broken'. Such linguistic representation of causative verbs can be characterized as $[\ldots x \ldots]_{e_1}$ CAUSE $[[\ldots y \ldots]_s]_{e_2}$, which denotes 'event e_1 involving entity x was the cause of event e_2 of entity y becoming in state s'. Note that there is no universal agreement among linguists regarding the representation of causative verbs (see, for instance, the discussion in Neeleman and van de Koot, 2012). Further accounts on causative verbs related to (in)direct causation and resultative contructions (as in 'John hammered the metal flat') were discussed in Waldmann et al. (2017).

In VerbNet (Kipper et al., 2008), causative verbs may be identified via semantic frames of some verb classes (e.g., BREAK-45.1), in which semantic predicates CAUSE(AGENT, E) and *state*(RESULT(E), PATIENT) are present; *state* denotes semantic predicates in VerbNet related to the resulting states, such as DEGRADATION_MATERIAL_INTEGRITY for BREAK-45.1. In FrameNet (Baker et al., 1998), we may assume that verbs belonging to CAUSE_* frames, such as CAUSE_TO_FRAGMENT or CAUSE_TEMPERATURE_CHANGE, are causative verbs.

Event Causality: A few resources on word/frame semantics such as WordNet (Fellbaum, 1998), FrameNet (Baker et al., 1998) and VerbOcean (Chklovski and Pantel, 2004) provide information about causal relations between lexical units that can be realized as events. However, they suffer from limited coverage due to having been manually constructed, or due to the semi-automatic approach adopted on highly implicit nature of language.

Riaz and Girju (2013) focused on the identification of causal relations in verb pairs. For example, *kill–arrest* has a higher likelihood of encoding causation than *build–maintain*. They relied on the unambiguous discourse markers *because* and *but* to automatically collect training instances of causal and non-causal event pairs, respectively. By utilising a set of metrics capturing causal associations, which exploit information available from a large number of unlabeled verb pairs, the result is a knowledge base of causal associations of verbs (KB_c). In KB_c, roughy 10K verb pairs are categorized as *Strongly Causal* (S_c), *Ambiguous* (A_c) and *Strongly Non-causal* ($S_{\neg c}$), based on the likelihood of causality encoded by the pairs, assuming uniform distribution across three categories.

One limitation of prior work in event causality is that it has primarily focused on newswire, limiting the causal understanding to newsworthy events, instead of everyday events such as human activities in general. Hu et al. (2017) explored unsupervised methods for modelling causality to learn event relations from blogs (topically focused on *camping*) and movie scene descriptions (excluding dialogues), resulting in high-quality causal pairs (e.g., ⟨*person, pack up*⟩ → ⟨*person, go home*⟩). Over 80% of pairs were indeed judged as causal by human annotators. The authors relied on the *Causal Potential* (CP) measure, based on Suppes' probabilistic account of causation (Suppes, 1970), to assess the causal relation between events. Subsequent work by Hu and Walker (2017) further explored four different types of *narrative causality* presenting in film scene descriptions, including PHYSICAL (*A* physically causes *B*), MOTIVATIONAL (*A* happens with *B* as a motivation), PYSCHOLOGICAL (*A* brings about emotions expressed in *B*) and ENABLING (*A* enables *B*).

ATOMIC[4] (Sap et al., 2019) introduced a commonsense repository for everyday events, causes and effects. Recall our example event earlier 'He hugged her tight'. By querying ATOMIC with 'PersonX hugs PersonY tight' we obtained the following as results: (1) *Causes of PersonX* (e.g., 'Because PersonX wanted to show their love and level of care'), (2) *Attributes of PersonX* (e.g., 'PersonX is seen as emotional'), (3) *Effects on PersonX* (e.g., 'As a result, PersonX feels happy') and (4) *Effects on others* (e.g., 'As a result, others feel loved').

---

[4] https://mosaickg.apps.allenai.org/

The ATOMIC repository was built through answering questions about an event with regards to *If–Then* knowledge, collected via crowdsourcing. The scheme distinguishes nine different relations belonging to three types of *If–Then* relations: *if-Event-then-Mental-State*, *if-Event-then-Event* and *if-Event-then-Persona*. Around 24K common *event phrases* were extracted for the annotation from various corpora, including stories, books, Google Ngrams and Wiktionary idioms. Considered as events are verb phrases with a verb predicate and its argument like 'drinks coffee in the morning'. For a more general representation of events, tokens referring to people were replaced with a `Person` variable; e.g., 'PersonX drinks coffee in the morning'. The resulting knowledge graph of ATOMIC contains over 300K nodes.

Recent progress in training deep contextualized language models using large-scale text corpora (e.g., BERT by Devlin et al., 2019) gives rise to explorations beyond extractive methods as an avenue for discovering commonsense knowledge. COMmonsEnse Transformers (COMET; Bosselut et al., 2019) was proposed to learn to generate novel commonsense tuples by leveraging such language models, given existing tuples in ATOMIC as a seed set of knowledge. Evaluated on 100 sampled events, this approach yields 56.5% precision (at 10) of generated inferences that are scored by human judges as being plausible or not. Anecdotal examples of generated causal pairs include 'As a result, PersonX gets fat' for 'PersonX eats red meat'. Though this is an interesting approach for discovering causal commonsense pairs, the plausibility of the generated tuples depends a lot on the textual corpus used to train the language model, which could suffer from the reporting bias.

Event Circumstantiality. Commonsense knowledge about causes and effects of strongly causal links is not sufficient to reconstruct coherent causal chains as we need to take into account all triggering and enabling factors in the causal complex of a given narrative. For instance, in order to *hug* someone, that person must *be in close proximity* as a precondition. Vossen et al. (see Chapter 6) adopt a broader class of event relations comprising causality, enablement, prevention and entailment – termed *circumstantiality*. The Circumstantial Event Ontology (CEO; Segers et al., 2018) was proposed to capture such a wide range of circumstantial relations. Events are circumstantially related if there exist shared properties in the pre, during, and post situations. As an example, the property 'fire exist true' could tie a circumstantial relation from *ceo:Arson* to *ceo:ExtinguishingFire* because the presence of fire is a post situation of an arson event and a pre situation of a fire-extinguishing event. The ontology consists of 223 event classes of which 189 are fully modeled with pre, during and post situations.

5.6 Conclusions

In this chapter, I have discussed research endeavours in identifying causal chains, or *causelines*, in order to understand and reconstruct coherent stories in narratives. Such causal chains can be constructed from identifying causal links between events presented in a narrative. Causal expressions in natural language texts may contain explicit causal markers, which are identifiable by automated extraction systems. I have reviewed existing work on causal extraction systems, which leverage language resources annotated with causal relations. I have listed several such corpora using different annotation schemes, guided by existing causal models in psychology and psycholinguistic that I have summarized briefly in the beginning of this chapter.

However, causation in language is more commonly expressed implicitly via adjacency in discourse. In this case, existing data-driven causal relation extraction systems are lacking in discovering the underlying causal links, due to limited training data available. Furthermore, circumstantial events surrounding the causal complex are rarely expressed with language as they are part of human common sense. Hence, discovering causal common sense is crucial to fill the gaps in the causal chains and the causal complex. I have discussed existing work in this line of research of causal commonsense discovery.

References

Baker, Collin F., Fillmore, Charles J., and Lowe, John B. 1998. The Berkeley FrameNet Project. Pages 86–90 of: *Proceedings of the 17th International Conference on Computational Linguistics: Volume 1*. Montreal, QC, Canada: Association for Computational Linguistics.

Bethard, Steven, and Martin, James H. 2008. Learning Semantic Links from a Corpus of Parallel Temporal and Causal Relations. Pages 177–180 of: Moore, Johanna D., Teufel, Simone, Allan, James, and Furui, Sadaoki (eds.), *Proceedings of ACL'08: HLT, Short Papers*. Columbus, OH: Association for Computational Linguistics.

Bethard, Steven, Corvey, William, Klingenstein, Sara, and Martin, James H. 2008. Building a Corpus of Temporal-Causal Structure. In: Calzolari, Nicoletta, Choukri, Khalid, Maegaard, Bente, et al. (eds.), *Proceedings of LREC'08*. Marrakech, Morocco: European Language Resources Association (ELRA).

Bosselut, Antoine, Rashkin, Hannah, Sap, Maarten, Malaviya, Chaitanya, Celikyilmaz, Asli, and Choi, Yejin. 2019. COMET: Commonsense Transformers for Automatic Knowledge Graph Construction. Pages 4762–4779 of: Korhonen, Anna, Traum, David, and Màrquez, Lluís (eds.), *Proceedings of the 57th Annual Meeting of the Association for Computational Linguistics*. Florence, Italy: Association for Computational Linguistics.

Chambers, Nathanael, Cassidy, Taylor, McDowell, Bill, and Bethard, Steven. 2014. Dense Event Ordering with a Multi-pass Architecture. *Transactions of the Association for Computational Linguistics*, **2**, 273–284.

Cheng, Patricia W., and Novick, Laura R. 1991. Causes versus Enabling Conditions. *Cognition*, **40**(1–2), 83–120.

Chklovski, Timothy, and Pantel, Patrick. 2004. VerbOcean: Mining the Web for Fine-Grained Semantic Verb Relations. Pages 33–40 of: Lin, Dekang, and Wu, Dekai (eds.), *Proceedings of the 2004 Conference on Empirical Methods in Natural Language Processing*. Barcelona, Spain: Association for Computational Linguistics.

Dasgupta, Tirthankar, Saha, Rupsa, Dey, Lipika, and Naskar, Abir. 2018. Automatic Extraction of Causal Relations from Text Using Linguistically Informed Deep Neural Networks. Pages 306–316 of: Komatani, Kazunori, Litman, Diane, Yu, Kai, et al. (eds.), *Proceedings of the 19th Annual SIGdial Meeting on Discourse and Dialogue*. Melbourne, Australia: Association for Computational Linguistics.

Devlin, Jacob, Chang, Ming-Wei, Lee, Kenton, and Toutanova, Kristina. 2019. BERT: Pre-training of Deep Bidirectional Transformers for Language Understanding. Pages 4171–4186 of: Burstein, Jill, Doran, Christy, and Solorio, Thamar (eds.), *Proceedings of the 2019 Conference of the North American Chapter of the Association for Computational Linguistics: Human Language Technologies, Volume 1 (Long and Short Papers)*. Minneapolis, MN: Association for Computational Linguistics.

Do, Quang, Chan, Yee Seng, and Roth, Dan. 2011. Minimally Supervised Event Causality Identification. Pages 294–303 of: Barzilay, Regina, and Johnson, Mark (eds.), *Proceedings of the 2011 Conference on Empirical Methods in Natural Language Processing*. Edinburgh: Association for Computational Linguistics.

Dunietz, Jesse, Levin, Lori, and Carbonell, Jaime. 2017. The BECauSE Corpus 2.0: Annotating Causality and Overlapping Relations. Pages 95–104 of: Schneider, Nathan, and Xue, Nianwen (eds.), *Proceedings of the 11th Linguistic Annotation Workshop*. Valencia, Spain: Association for Computational Linguistics.

Fellbaum, Christiane (ed.). 1998. *WordNet: An Electronic Lexical Database*. Cambridge, MA: MIT Press.

Ganitkevitch, Juri, Van Durme, Benjamin, and Callison-Burch, Chris. 2013. PPDB: The Paraphrase Database. Pages 758–764 of: Vanderwende, Lucy, Daumé III, Hal, and Kirchhoff, Katrin (eds.), *Proceedings of the 2013 Conference of the North American Chapter of the Association for Computational Linguistics: Human Language Technologies*. Atlanta, GA: Association for Computational Linguistics.

Girju, Roxana, Nakov, Preslav, Nastase, Vivi, Szpakowicz, Stan, Turney, Peter, and Yuret, Deniz. 2007. SemEval-2007 Task 04: Classification of Semantic Relations between Nominals. Pages 13–18 of: Agirre, Eneko, Màrquez, Lluís, and Wicentowski, Richard (eds.), *Proceedings of the Fourth International Workshop on Semantic Evaluations (SemEval-2007)*. Prague, Czech Republic: Association for Computational Linguistics.

Hidey, Christopher, and McKeown, Kathy. 2016. Identifying Causal Relations Using Parallel Wikipedia Articles. Pages 1424–1433 of: *Proceedings of the 54th Annual Meeting of the Association for Computational Linguistics (Volume 1: Long Papers)*. Berlin: Association for Computational Linguistics.

Hitchcock, Christopher. 2018. Probabilistic Causation. In: Zalta, Edward N. (ed.), *The Stanford Encyclopedia of Philosophy*. Metaphysics Research Lab, Stanford University.

Hobbs, Jerry R. 2005. Toward a Useful Concept of Causality for Lexical Semantics. *Journal of Semantics*, **22**, 181–209.

Hu, Zhichao, and Walker, Marilyn. 2017. Inferring Narrative Causality between Event Pairs in Films. Pages 342–351 of: Jokinen, Kristiina, Stede, Manfred, DeVault, David, and Louis, Annie (eds.), *Proceedings of the 18th Annual SIGdial Meeting on Discourse and Dialogue*. Saarbrücken, Germany: Association for Computational Linguistics.

Hu, Zhichao, Rahimtoroghi, Elahe, and Walker, Marilyn. 2017. Inference of Fine-Grained Event Causality from Blogs and Films. Pages 52–58 of: Caselli, Tommaso, Miller, Ben, van Erp, Marieke, et al. (eds.), *Proceedings of the Events and Stories in the News Workshop*. Vancouver: Association for Computational Linguistics.

Kipper, Karin, Korhonen, Anna, Ryant, Neville, and Palmer, Martha. 2008. A Large-Scale Classification of English Verbs. *Language Resources and Evaluation*, **42**(1), 21–40.

Lewis, David. 1973. Causation. *The Journal of Philosophy*, **70**(17), 556–567.

Linguistic Data Consortium. 2005. *ACE (Automatic Content Extraction) English Annotation Guidelines for Events*.

Liu, Yang, and Li, Sujian. 2016. Recognizing Implicit Discourse Relations via Repeated Reading: Neural Networks with Multi-Level Attention. Pages 1224–1233 of: Su, Jian, Duh, Kevin, and Carreras, Xavier (eds.), *Proceedings of the 2016 Conference on Empirical Methods in Natural Language Processing*. Austin, TX: Association for Computational Linguistics.

Marcus, Mitchell P., Marcinkiewicz, Mary Ann, and Santorini, Beatrice. 1993. Building a Large Annotated Corpus of English: The Penn Treebank. *Computational Linguistics*, **19**(2), 313–330.

Mirza, Paramita, and Tonelli, Sara. 2014. An Analysis of Causality between Events and Its Relation to Temporal Information. Pages 2097–2106 of: Tsujii, Junichi, and Hajic, Jan (eds.), *Proceedings of COLING 2014, the 25th International Conference on Computational Linguistics: Technical Papers*. Dublin, Ireland: Dublin City University and Association for Computational Linguistics.

Mirza, Paramita, and Tonelli, Sara. 2016. CATENA: CAusal and TEmporal Relation Extraction from NAtural Language Texts. Pages 64–75 of: Matsumoto, Yuji, and Prasad, Rashmi (eds.), *Proceedings of COLING 2016, the 26th International Conference on Computational Linguistics: Technical Papers*. Osaka, Japan: The COLING 2016 Organizing Committee.

Mirza, Paramita, Sprugnoli, Rachele, Tonelli, Sara, and Speranza, Manuela. 2014. Annotating Causality in the TempEval-3 Corpus. Pages 10–19 of: Kolomiyets, Oleksandr, Moens, Marie-Francine, Palmer, Martha, Pustejovsky, James, and Bethard, Steven (eds.), *Proceedings of the EACL 2014 Workshop on Computational Approaches to Causality in Language (CAtoCL)*. Gothenburg, Sweden: Association for Computational Linguistics.

Mostafazadeh, Nasrin, Grealish, Alyson, Chambers, Nathanael, Allen, James, and Vanderwende, Lucy. 2016b. CaTeRS: Causal and Temporal Relation Scheme for Semantic Annotation of Event Structures. Pages 51–61 of: Palmer, Martha, Hovy, Ed, Mitamura, Teruko, and O'Gorman, Tim (eds.), *Proceedings of the Fourth Workshop on Events*. San Diego, California: Association for Computational Linguistics.

Mostafazadeh, Nasrin, Chambers, Nathanael, He, Xiaodong, Parikh, Devi, Batra, Dhruv, Vanderwende, Lucy, Kohli, Pushmeet, and Allen, James. 2016a. A Corpus and Cloze Evaluation for Deeper Understanding of Commonsense Stories. Pages 839–849 of: Knight, Kevin, Nenkova, Ani, and Rambow, Owen (eds.), *Proceedings of the 2016 Conference of the North American Chapter of the Association for Computational Linguistics: Human Language Technologies*. San Diego, CA: Association for Computational Linguistics.

Neeleman, Ad, and van de Koot, Hans. 2012. The Linguistic Expression of Causation. Pages 20–51 of: *The Theta System: Argument Structure at the Interface*. Oxford: Oxford University Press.

Palmer, Martha, Gildea, Daniel, and Kingsbury, Paul. 2005. The Proposition Bank: An Annotated Corpus of Semantic Roles. *Computational Linguistics*, **31**(1), 71–106.

Pitler, Emily, and Nenkova, Ani. 2009. Using Syntax to Disambiguate Explicit Discourse Connectives in Text. Pages 13–16 of: Su, Keh-Yih, Su, Jian, Wiebe, Janyce, and Li, Haizhou (eds.), *Proceedings of the ACL-IJCNLP 2009 Conference Short Papers*. Suntec, Singapore: Association for Computational Linguistics.

Prasad, Rashmi, Dinesh, Nikhil, Lee, Alan, Miltsakaki, Eleni, Robaldo, Livio, Joshi, Aravind, and Webber, Bonnie. 2008. The Penn Discourse TreeBank 2.0. In: Calzolari, Nicoletta, Choukri, Khalid, Maegaard, Bente, et al. (eds.), *Proceedings of the Sixth International Conference on Language Resources and Evaluation (LREC'08)*. Marrakech, Morocco: European Language Resources Association.

Pustejovsky, James, Castao, José, Ingria, Robert, et al. 2003. TimeML: Robust Specification of Event and Temporal Expressions in Text. Pages 28–34 of: Maybury, Mark T. (ed.), *New Directions in Question Answering*. AAAI Press.

Pustejovsky, James, Littman, Jessica, Saurí, Roser, and Verhagen, Marc. 2006. *TimeBank 1.2 Documentation*. Technical Report, Brandeis University.

Reichenbach, Hans. 1956. *The Direction of Time*. Dover Publications.

Riaz, Mehwish, and Girju, Roxana. 2013. Toward a Better Understanding of Causality between Verbal Events: Extraction and Analysis of the Causal Power of Verb–Verb Associations. Pages 21–30 of: Eskenazi, Maxine, Strube, Michael, Di Eugenio, Barbara, and Williams, Jason D. (eds.), *Proceedings of the SIGDIAL 2013 Conference*. Metz, France: Association for Computational Linguistics.

Rink, Bryan, Bejan, Cosmin Adrian, and Harabagiu, Sanda M. 2010. Learning Textual Graph Patterns to Detect Causal Event Relations. In: *FLAIRS Conference*.

Roth, Dan, and Yih, Wen-tau. 2004. A Linear Programming Formulation for Global Inference in Natural Language Tasks. Pages 1–8 of: *Proceedings of the Eighth Conference on Computational Natural Language Learning (CoNLL-2004) at HLT-NAACL 2004*. Boston: Association for Computational Linguistics.

Sap, Maarten, LeBras, Ronan, Allaway, Emily, et al. 2019. ATOMIC: An Atlas of Machine Commonsense for If–Then Reasoning. In: *Proceedings of AAAI'19*.

Segers, Roxane, Caselli, Tommaso, and Vossen, Piek. 2018. The Circumstantial Event Ontology (CEO) and ECB+/CEO: An Ontology and Corpus for Implicit Causal Relations between Events. In: Calzolari, Nicoletta, Choukri, Khalid, Cieri, Christopher, et al. (eds.), *Proceedings of the Eleventh International Conference on Language Resources and Evaluation (LREC 2018)*. Miyazaki, Japan: European Language Resources Association.

Sloman, Steven. 2005. *Causal Models: How People Think about the World and Its Alternatives*.

Suppes, Patrick. 1970. *A Probabilistic Theory of Causality*. Amsterdam: North-Holland Publishing Co.

Talmy, Leonard. 1988. Force Dynamics in Language and Cognition. *Cognitive Science*, **12**(1), 49–100.

Tenenbaum, Joshua B., and Griffiths, Thomas L. 2001. Structure Learning in Human Causal Induction. Pages 59–65 of: Leen, T., Dietterich, T., and Tresp, V. (eds.), *Structure Learning in Human Causal Induction*, Vol. 13. MIT Press.

UzZaman, Naushad, Llorens, Hector, Derczynski, Leon, et al. 2013. SemEval-2013 Task 1: TempEval-3: Evaluating Time Expressions, Events, and Temporal Relations. Pages 1–9 of: Manandhar, Suresh, and Yuret, Deniz (eds.), *Second Joint Conference on Lexical and Computational Semantics (*SEM), Volume 2: Proceedings of the Seventh International Workshop on Semantic Evaluation (SemEval 2013)*. Atlanta, GA: Association for Computational Linguistics.

Vossen, Piek, Caselli, Tommaso, and Segers, Roxane. 2021. A Narratology-based Framework for Storyline Extraction. Pages 130–147 of: Caselli, Tommaso, Palmer, Martha, Hovy, Eduard, and Vossen, Piek (eds), *Computational Analysis of Storylines: Making Sense of Events*. Cambridge University Press.

Waldmann, Michael R., Solstad, Torgrim, and Bott, Oliver. 2017. *Causality and Causal Reasoning in Natural Language*.

Wolff, Phillip. 2007. Representing Causation. *Journal of Experimental Psychology: General*, **136**(1), 82–111.

Wolff, Phillip, Klettke, Bianca, Ventura, Tatyana, and Song, Grace. 2005. Expressing Causation in English and Other Languages. Pages 29–48 of: *Categorization Inside and Outside the Laboratory: Essays in Honor of Douglas L. Medin. APA Decade of Behavior Series*. Washington, DC: American Psychological Association.

Wolff, Phillip, and Song, Grace. 2003. Models of Causation and the Semantics of Causal Verbs. *Cognitive Psychology*, **47**(3), 276–332.

6

A Narratology-Based Framework for Storyline Extraction

Piek Vossen, Tommaso Caselli, and Roxane Segers

Abstract. Stories are a pervasive phenomenon of human life. They also represent a cognitive tool to understand and make sense of the world and of its happenings. In this contribution we describe a narratology-based framework for modeling stories as a combination of different data structures and to automatically extract them from news articles. We introduce a distinction among three data structures (timelines, causelines, and storylines) that capture different narratological dimensions, respectively chronological ordering, causal connections, and plot structure. We developed the Circumstantial Event Ontology (CEO) for modeling (implicit) circumstantial relations as well as explicit causal relations and create two benchmark corpora: ECB+/CEO, for causelines, and the Event Storyline Corpus (ESC), for storylines. To test our framework and the difficulty in automatically extract causelines and storylines, we develop a series of reasonable baseline systems.

6.1 Introduction

We experience life as a story developing to the good or to the bad, in which specific events form turning points. We also tell such stories about (other) people; for example, through books, news, and blogs. Stories, as they are commonly understood, are more than *chronologically ordered* sequences of events. In a story, we typically select certain events and not others. One factor that determines this selection is the causal relation that we focus on to *explain* why things happened. Another factor is that we see events from a *perspective* that is reflected in our framing; e.g., focusing on the victim or those responsible. A consequence of this is that stories can be labeled as boring, interesting, exciting, informative, among others. Storytelling creates unique narrative objects in which temporal, explanatory, and perspective relations are mixed. A text thus represents a complex relation between the temporal order of events (a *timeline*); their causal, or explanatory, connections (a *causeline*); and the way in which these relations are framed and reported, taking one event as the turning point; that is, the event with high impact to the framed participants. Other events may be related to this turning point as preceding and explaining (or triggering) its occurrence, or following and being its consequence, and together form a *storyline*. Typically, such turning points are presented as the climax to which stories develop over time, as is proposed in narratological frameworks (Bal, 1997).

Our contributions can be summarized as follows:

- We present a formal model for such storylines, encompassing the notions of timeline, causeline, and storyline as measurable and quantifiable properties of events (Section 6.2).
- We derive two complementary annotation schemes from this model and apply these to news data, resulting in two new benchmark corpora for causelines and storylines (Section 6.3);
- We carry out a set of experiments using various approaches to extract causelines and storylines and evaluate these against the benchmark corpora (Section 6.4).

6.2 A Narratology-Grounded Framework for Storylines Identification

Storytelling is a pervasive human activity dealing with streams of information, selecting the relevant aspects and discarding irrelevant ones. The outcome of the storytelling processes are best defined as *narrative objects*, or simply narratives. We create narratives for reasoning over and understanding changes and to facilitate decision-making processes accordingly (Bruner, 1990; Boyd, 2009; Gottschall, 2012). Narratives qualify as a specific type of discourse only if certain conditions are met (Forster, 1956; Bal, 1997; Mani, 2012), namely:

- they contain a set of events (fictional or real);
- they have participants (i.e., actors) involved in the events;
- they give rise to a chronologically and logically ordered sequence of the events involved;
- they contain a *focalizer* (Bal, 1997), or a perspective from which the narrative is told.

According to these conditions, the single mention of an event (e.g., a killing, an election, or a greeting) is not a narrative per se. The core distinguishing

Figure 6.1 Plot structure representation.

property of narratives from other types of discourse is the combination of *chronologically* and *logically* ordered sequence of events. Narratology frameworks label a chronologically sequence of events as *fabula*, or story, and a logically ordered sequence of events as **plots**. Quoting Forster (1956), a text like "*The king died and then the queen died*" cannot be fully qualified as a narrative because the focus is only on the chronological order of the events (i.e., the *fabula*). On the other hand, a text like "*The king died and then the queen died of grief*" is understood as a narrative because, in addition to the chronological order of the events (i.e., the *fabula*) there is an *explanatory* relation connecting them, in particular, the fact that the queen died *because* of the grief *caused by* the death of the king, her husband. In other words, it instantiates a plot.

Plots make explicit "why" things happen, rather then just telling "how" and "when." The focus is on connecting relevant event sequences in terms of explanatory relations, rather than simply chronological ones, as *fabulae* (stories) do. The logical plot may be realized in various ways in a narrative resulting in a *plot structure*. A plot structure is a complex entity composed by three elements, as illustrated in Figure 6.1.

- Exposition: the introduction of the actors and the settings (e.g., the location).
- Predicament: the set of problems or struggles that the actors have to go through. It is composed by three elements: (i) *rising action*, the event(s) that increases the tension created by the predicament; (ii) *climax*, the event(s) that create the maximal level of tension; and (iii) *falling action*, the event(s) that resolve the climax and lower the tension. The climax event can be seen as the turning point around which the narrative develops.
- Extrication: which refers to the "end" of the predicament and indicates the ending.

Within narratology, the notions of narrative, *fabula*, plot, and plot structure are closely related and partly overlap. In our model, these notions (*fabula*, plot, and plot structure) find their equivalent in three data structures. In particular, given a narrative document, the *fabula* matches a *timeline* (i.e., a set of temporally anchored and chronologically ordered events); the plot corresponds to a *causeline*, defined as a set of circumstantial relations or, in other words, loose and strict causal relations, explicitly and implicitly expressed; and, finally, the plot structure is converted into a *storyline*, a set of (pairwise) relations between events that expresses the perspective with which the narrative is reported and how the events are connected (i.e., the rising and falling relations) to reach a turning point (i.e., a climax).

These data structures are deeply interrelated to each other, where one entails the other, in particular: a timeline is always entailed by a causeline, and a causeline is always entailed by a storyline. A further aspect to stress is that causelines and storylines are complementary data structures. Causelines makes the "why" between pairs of events explicit, whereas the storylines highlight the relevance of the events to identify a set of preconditions, a turning point, and a set of consequences.

More formally, given a timeline $l \in L$ for a specific period of time, we define a storyline S as n-tuples T, E, R, P such that

$$\mathbf{T}imepoints = (t_1, t_2, \ldots, t_n)$$

$$\mathbf{E}vents = (e_1, e_2, \ldots, e_n)$$

$$\mathbf{R}elations = (r_1, r_1, \ldots, r_n)$$

$$\mathbf{P}erspectives = (p_1, p_1, \ldots, p_n).$$

T consists of an ordered set of points in time; E is a set of events; R is a set of explanatory relations between events, subsuming causelines; and P is a set of perspectives on the events. Perspectives express the likelihood of an event e to be a climax event. Each e in E is related to a t in T. A storyline, S, can be expressed as a function, F, that finds the most plausible set of plot relations across the timelines $l \in L$ of a text, given timepoints, events, and perspectives, such that

$$S = argmax(F(l)|T, E, P)$$

$$F(l) = \sum_{i,j=1}^{n} C(r, e_i, e_j).$$

The function F sums the connectivity C of explanatory relations in R given a chronologically ordered sequence of events ($l \in L$) with respect to a (candidate) climax event. A storyline will result in that sequence of chronologically ordered events with maximum connectivity score.

To better illustrate the differences and connections between the theoretical notions and the data structures, consider the following example, extracted from the Event Coreference Bank+ Corpus (ECB+; Cybulska and Vossen, 2014). We have marked in bold all event mentions, as defined in ECB+, and illustrate the three data structures:

1. Police **say**$_{e1}$ that on Saturday around 11:30 p.m. Kimani Gray was **standing**$_{e2}$ outside his home with five other young men before **splitting off**$_{e3}$ when he **noticed**$_{e4}$ two plainclothes officers in an unmarked car. After he "**adjusted**$_{e5}$ his waistband and continued to **act**$_{e6}$ in a suspicious manner," officials **say**$_{e7}$ the cops **got out**$_{e8}$ of their car and **approached**$_{e9}$ Gray – who allegedly **turned**$_{e10}$ toward them with a loaded .38-caliber revolver in hand. The 30-year-old sergeant and 26-year-old **fired**$_{e11}$ 11 shots [...].

- *timeline*: [NOW] → includes → **say**$_{e1}$; **say**$_{e1}$ → before → **say**$_{e7}$; **say**$_{e1}$ → after → [Saturday around 11:30 p.m.]; [Saturday around 11:30 p.m.] → includes → **standing**$_{e2}$; **standing**$_{e2}$ → before → **splitting off**$_{e3}$; **splitting off**$_{e3}$ → simultaneous → **noticed**$_{e4}$; **adjusted**$_{e5}$ → before → **got out**$_{e8}$; **act**$_{e6}$ → before → **got out**$_{e8}$; **got out**$_{e8}$ → before → **approached**$_{e9}$; **approached**$_{e9}$ → simultaneous → **turned**$_{e10}$; **turned**$_{e10}$ → before → **fire**$_{e11}$;
- *causelines*: **act**$_{e6}$ → circumstantial → **approached**$_{e9}$; **splitting off**$_{e3}$ → circumstantial → **noticed**$_{e4}$; **turned**$_{e10}$ → circumstantial → **fire**$_{e11}$
- *storyline*: **noticed**$_{e4}$ → rising_action → **splitting off**$_{e3}$ → rising_action → **adjusted**$_{e5}$ → rising_action → **act**$_{e6}$ → rising_action → **approached**$_{e9}$ → rising_action → **turned**$_{e10}$ → rising_action → **fire**$_{e12[climax]}$;

In example 1, the timeline reflects the temporal order and anchoring of all events mentioned in the narrative. Each event mention is associated with a temporal expression (e.g., [NOW]; [Saturday around 11:30 p.m.]) or directly temporally related to each other. Every event mention is present, even those that do not contribute to the plot or the plot structure (e.g., **say**$_{e1}$ and **say**$_{e7}$). On the other hand, the multiple causelines retain only the events that express a circumstantial relation; i.e., those events for which we can identify some loose causal relation. Finally, the storyline extends (as in this case) or inherits causelines and makes explicit additional explanatory relations (using rising actions only in this case) that may lead to a (candidate) climax event (i.e., $fire_{e_1}2$). Each rising action in example 1 provides a meaningful (explanatory) connection (i.e., an explanation) between event pairs, contributing to understanding why the chronologically following event occurred and how the sequence of events led to the occurrence of the climax event ($fire_{e_1}2$).

If after the main event $fire_{e_1}2$ the narrative mentions consequences, such as dying and protests, these will be related as falling actions, making it a turning point of the climax.[1]

Being able to properly distinguish and reconstruct these three data structures is essential to extracting and identifying storylines from documents in a principled way. Furthermore, this framework calls for the development of appropriate solutions, according to the specific data structure that is targeted. In the remainder of this chapter we will show how the framework has been translated with respect to data sets and corpora, focusing on causelines and storylines. As for timelines, we adopt an established annotation framework based on ISO-TimeML (Pustejovsky et al., 2010) and its extensions (Cassidy et al., 2014; O'Gorman et al., 2016).[2]

6.3 From Theory to Data: Annotating Causelines and Storylines

We translated our framework into two different annotation schemes, one for causelines and the other for storylines, and applied it to news data. The annotation process has been used as an empirical validation of the components of the model, resulting in two new benchmark corpora.

6.3.1 Modeling Causelines

Causelines address a specific type of explanatory relations in narratives, namely, reasons why events happened. Causality is the most clear semantic relation that may provide such explanations. However, causality is also

---

[1] For this topic, other news articles that were published later report on the riots following the shooting, in which case these riots are the climax and firing at the boy is a rising event, and damage, looting, and arrests are the consequences of the riots.
[2] For a detailed overview about timeline extraction, see Chapter 4.

a debated relation, and causes often remain vague or implicit in stories (see Chapter 5 for an overview on causality and automatic approaches to causal relation extraction.). Building on Ikuta et al. (2014), we therefore use the umbrella term *circumstantiality* to capture a broad range of weak and strong relations, including causality, enablement, prevention, and entailment. These relations differ from strict causal relations in that the consequence is not logically necessary but (culturally or empirically) expected, made possible or explained by backward presupposition; e.g., *you crossed the streets and therefore you were hit by a truck*. As a sum, circumstantial relations make explicit why one event enabled the next event, to facilitate the understanding of a narrative. Causelines are then simply sequences of event mentions connected by circumstantial relations.

Previous work has modeled circumstantial relations in very different ways. A first notable contribution is The Penn Discourse Treebank (PDTB; Prasad et al., 2008). In their framework, contingency relations give rise to a hierarchy, including causality, enablement, and condition. Annotation is conducted at the level of discourse segments and not the level of event mentions, which unfortunately makes it impossible to know the actual pairs of events involved. Chklovski and Pantel (2004) and Hu et al. (2013, 2017) targeted contingency relations directly for pairs of events. Although they used different methods (e.g., lexical patterns vs. statistical association measures, such as pointwise mutual information or causal potential), they still only identified general contingency relations between verbs, ignoring the specific context of occurrence in a document. These systems produce databases of pairs of events (i.e., verbs) that stand in a contingency relation. Other initiatives such as CaTeRS (Mostafazadeh et al., 2016), Causal TimeBank (Mirza et al., 2014), and BeCauSE 2.0 (Dunietz et al., 2017) target only a specific subset of relations; i.e., only causal relations expressed through certain causal connectives. A different approach and take on causality is addressed in the richer event description (RED) corpus (Ikuta et al., 2014; O'Gorman et al., 2016), where annotators are free to make causal inferences even in absence of particular connectives.

In our work, we extend previous approaches in two major aspects. First, we target "circumstantial" relations between pairs of events, thus requiring event mentions in documents to be our minimal annotation units. Secondly, we extend the annotations to also include other types of relations such as such as enablement, prevention, and entailment, even in the absence of explicit textual markers.

To capture such a wide range of (possibly implicit) circumstantial relations, we make use of the Circumstantial Event Ontology (CEO).[3] CEO (Segers et al., 2018) models circumstantial relations through *shared properties* of the event classes. A circumstantial relation is defined as a relation that holds between event classes, where an event of class A may give rise to another event of class B if properties resulting from the happening of A form preconditions to enable the happening of B. For instance, the class "ceo:Shooting" allows for a semantic circumstantial relation with the class "ceo:Impacting," because they both share the property of translocation of an object from location X to Y, the former as the outcome of the event (postcondition) and the latter as a condition to take place (precondition). Modeling these event properties provides a means to chain logically related events and their shared participants within and across documents. With respect to existing ontologies (SUMO; Niles and Pease, 2001) and lexicons (FrameNet; Baker et al., 1998; and WordNet; Fellbaum, 1998), CEO formalizes event knowledge and relations at the most abstract level rather than for specific lexical items and concepts. The axioms in CEO do not define (lexical) concepts exhaustively but capture only the minimally implied properties that reflect the change.

CEO consists of 223 event classes, of which 189 are fully modeled with pre, during, and postsituations. We defined 92 binary properties and 29 unary properties. In total, 189 unique situation rules were defined that consist of 192 binary situation rule assertions and 264 unary rule assertions. All classes are mapped to FrameNet frames (265 mappings) and SUMO classes (195 mappings) and the CEO roles to FrameNet elements (265 mappings).

We enriched the ECB+ corpus, originally annotated for event coreference (Cybulska and Vossen, 2014), with circumstantial relations, resulting in the ECB+/CEO corpus.[4] We extracted 22 CEO-compliant topics (508 articles) that cover calamities such as earthquakes, murders, hijacks, and arsons and automatically added event mentions by means of a compliant state-of-the art system (Caselli and Morante, 2018).[5] After this, two trained annotators completed the markup of the circumstantial relations between events, as well as coreference relations for all automatically generated event mentions not yet covered in the ECB+ corpus.[6] Annotators were asked to connect pairs of calamity events with a circumstantial link if one event could be used to explain the occurrence of the other.

---

[3] github.com/cltl/CEO-Ontology
[4] For more details, readers are referred to the work of Segers et al. (2018)
[5] The system achieves 0.8187 F1-score for event trigger detection on the TempeEval-3 test set.
[6] If two event mentions are coreferential, they also denote the same concept and share the same participants, time, and location.

In total, 3,038 new event instances expressing calamities were annotated, with 3,448 new event coreference sets and 2,244 circumstantial links. On average, every ECB+/CEO article contains about 7 new coreference sets and about 5 different circumstantial relations. Inter-annotator agreement has been measured with Cohen's kappa on a subset of 21 articles, reaching $\kappa = 0.76$.

6.3.2 Modeling Storylines

Models for understanding narratives mainly focused on fictional texts (Rumelhart, 1975; Lehnert, 1981; Mani, 2012). Research on storyline extraction from nonfictional data is limited. The majority of this work models storylines as a topic clustering task of documents over time (Allan, 2002; Becker et al., 2011; Kawamae, 2011; Binh Tran et al., 2013; Aggarwal, 2014). Shahaf and Guestrin's (2010) seminal work, on the other hand, was the first to argue that clustering is not sufficient and emphasizes that coherence is the defining aspect of storylines. They proposed to generate storylines as coherent chains of documents. However, their storylines do not reflect the unfolding of a specific event in the world but rather structure a document collection as two connecting dots; i.e., its beginning and end documents. Other work targets the problem as a temporal summarization task (Huang and Huang, 2013) or as a joint distribution over locations, entities (organizations and persons), keywords (event mentions), and a set of topics (Zhou et al., 2016). Chambers and Jurafsky (2009, 2010) introduced a new representation format, called narrative event chains, based on unsupervised learning from news stories. Their assumption is that narrative coherence is reflected in events sharing coreferring protagonists. Each chain is essentially an entity-centric timeline rather than a storyline.

Following our model, we created the Event Storyline Corpus (ESC; Caselli and Vossen, 2016, 2017). Similar to ECB+/CEO, we built on top of ECB+ and added storyline interpretations as an extra annotation layer, called a *plot link*. Plot link relations are used to connect only events that actively contribute to the expression of a storyline matching the internal components of the plot structure: rising action(s), climax, and falling action(s).

Plot relations are directional relations, involving a source, S_e, and a target event, T_e. Their annotation is conducted in a two-step approach: first, identify all eligible pairs of events that can express a plot relation and then classify each relation with one of the following values: rising_action or falling_action.

We did not explicitly annotate the climax event. We assume that climax events can be indirectly derived from the annotated pairs as those events toward which most rising and falling events point, either directly or indirectly. They should come out as the natural turning points, where the direction of the plot changes from rising to falling.

Plot links are compatible with other discourse annotation initiatives, namely, PDTB. In many cases a plot relation can be mapped to other categories such as "background," "narration," or "reason." However, plot links differ from such frameworks because they mainly aim at capturing the perspective of a narrative to connect to (one or multiple) climax events. Secondly, the binary values of the relation values reduce the complexity of the annotation process. Finally, plot relations highlight event–event relations at a microlevel of the discourse dimension.

The ESC v1.2 corpus has been realized by merging together experts and crowdsourced annotation (Caselli and Inel, 2018). It is composed of 258 documents grouped into 22 topics/stories, 6,315 event mentions, and 6,383 plot links. `rising_action` relations amount to 3,160, and 3,225 are the `falling_action` relations. Expert annotation was conducted by two trained annotators and spanned both intra- and intersentence levels (interannotator agreement with Cohen's kappa on a subset of 44 articles is $\kappa = 0.62$). The evaluation of the crowd data (i.e., spammer removal and data quality) has been conducted by applying the CrowdTruth disagreement-aware methodology (Aroyo and Welty, 2014, 2015). The manually annotated data (both experts and crowd) at mention level can be expanded using the event coreference chains in ECB+, thus increasing the number of plot relations.

6.4 Validating Causelines and Extracting Storylines

To obtain insight into our claims about causelines and storylines, we ran a set of experiments using different systems on both ECB+/CEO and ESC v1.2.

As a baseline system (bl), we simply assume that events in the sequential order of mentioning in a text also express a circumstantial and/or a plot relation.

To use CEO, we developed the CEO-Pathfinder module[7] that reads the ontology and a CEO lexicon. The lexicon was derived from the ECB+/CEO annotations and has 655 words manually mapped unambiguously to a CEO class. The CEO-Pathfinder module looks up every mention of an event from the corpus in the lexicon and obtains its corresponding CEO class. Next, it compares the pre-, during, and post-situation assertions of pairs of CEO classes to see whether there is a match such that a post- or during situation assertion

[7] https://github.com/cltl/ceopathfinder

of *ceo:Class1* is the pre-situation assertion of *ceo:Class2*. We check the events in both orders. If a single property matches, we assume that there is a valid circumstantial relation and/or a plot relation. The current implementation does not check whether the situations apply to the corresponding referents of the participants as defined in the ontology.

The CEO-Pathfinder has the option to assume a hidden event between pairs to bridge pre- and postconditions. For example, *shooting* may require *hitting* as an event before explaining *injuring*. To consider the pair *shooting* and *injuring* to be circumstantial, the CEO-Pathfinder scans the ontology for any potential event that may follow *shooting* to enable *injuring*. We experimented with two levels of intermediate events: (i) one intermediate (hidden) event (*ceo1*) and (ii) two intermediate (hidden) events (*ceo2*).

To better assess the performance of CEO, we compare it with three other variants. First, we reuse FBK-PRO (Mirza and Tonelli, 2014) as integrated in the NewsReader platform (Vossen et al., 2016) and extract all explicitly marked causal relations. Secondly, we use *narrative chains* (Chambers and Jurafsky, 2009) as a resource to determine circumstantial and plot relations. For any event pair in the evaluation data, we create a relation if the pairs occur in that order in any narrative chain. Finally, we implement a system that exploits causal relations from FrameNet (Baker et al., 1998). For each pair of events it checks whether any of the associated FrameNet frames stand in a *Causative_of* or *Inchoative_of* relation according to FrameNet 1.7. We use the FrameNet lexicon to obtain all possible frames associated with the words listed in the evaluation data as events.

Summing up the different systems:

- **bl**: Baseline system that assumes that the order of mentioning two events in the text reflects a circumstantial/plot relation.
- **ceo**: Two events only have a circumstantial/plot relation if there is a property match across post-, during-, and preconditions.
- **ceoi1**: The same as **ceo** except that it may assume another event as a hidden bridge between two events.
- **ceoi2**: The same as **ceo** except that there can be two other events as a hidden bridge.
- **fbkcl**: Events are connected through a circumstantial/plot relation if there is an explicit causal relation detected by the FBK-PRO system.
- **fn**: Events are connected through a circumstantial/plot relation if there is an explicit causal relation in FrameNet.
- **nc**: Events are connected through a circumstantial/plot relation if they are listed together in a narrative chain.

Table 6.1. *Causelines: P, R, and F1 scores on ECB+/CEO*

System	Same sentence only			Full text		
	P	**R**	**F1**	**P**	**R**	**F1**
bl	0.775	**0.799**	**0.786**	0.248	**1.000**	0.397
ceo	0.881	0.107	0.191	0.576	0.300	0.394
ceoi1	0.872	0.208	0.337	0.485	0.421	0.451
ceoi2	0.874	0.284	0.429	0.442	0.488	**0.464**
fn	0.879	0.022	0.043	0.647	0.110	0.188
fbkcl	**0.898**	0.027	0.052	**0.794**	0.038	0.073
nc	0.760	0.016	0.031	0.468	0.044	0.080

Results for causelines are illustrated in Table 6.1. We provide the precision (P), recall (R), and harmonic mean (F1) for pairs of mentions observed in the same sentence and across the complete document. In the latter case, all mention pairs are candidates, which we expect to give the highest recall and lowest precision. For the events in the same sentence, we expect the highest precision and lowest recall. For FrameNet and explicit causal relations detected by FBK-PRO, we expect high precision and low recall as well. All scores have been computed by taking into account automatic expansion of the annotated data to include event coreference.

Not surprising, the results reflect our predictions. The baseline obtains the best results when building circumstantial relations using only events in the same sentence, although the highest precision is provided by using FBK-PRO (*0.898*), followed by CEO without hidden events and FrameNet. Narrative chains (nc) lag behind. On the other hand the CEO approaches have 10 times higher recall than the other non-baseline approaches. Also remarkable, CEO with intermediate hidden events (ceo1 and ceo2) hardly suffer in precision but double the recall.

Recall gets maximized at the cost of precision when event pairs are extended beyond the sentence level. In the full-text scenario, the baseline has 100% recall but the other approaches also increase in recall, showing that a substantial number of circumstantial relations holds across events mentioned in different sentences. In the full-text scenario, CEO (ceo2) gives the best F1 score (*0.464*). Because CEO can still gain from recall by improving the lexical coverage while there is no potential gain for the baseline, we expect the CEO approach to exceed the baseline in the future.

Table 6.2 reports the scores for storylines with CEO-Pathfinder, using P, R, and F1. Similar to causelines, we have expanded the set of event pairs using

Table 6.2. *Storylines: P, R, and F1 scores on ESC v1.2 test data*

Models	Same sentence only			Full test		
	P	R	F1	P	R	F1
bl	0.276	**0.327**	**0.292**	0.174	**0.984**	**0.291**
ceo	0.313	0.006	0.011	0.181	0.021	0.038
ceo1	0.302	0.013	0.024	0.190	0.047	0.075
ceo2	0.349	0.021	0.040	0.204	0.072	0.107
fn	0.563	0.002	0.004	0.328	0.008	0.017
fbkcl	**0.774**	0.005	0.010	**0.512**	0.009	0.018
nc	0.104	0.002	0.003	0.111	0.003	0.006

available annotations for event coreference. According to our model, we expect that all systems should results in lower scores (in absolute terms) when applied to the storyline data set.

As the results show, all approaches, including the baseline (bl), have lower scores, in general. FBK-PRO remains the system that still obtains the best precision but with extremely low recall. Recall is actually the weakest aspect of storyline extraction. We interpret this as cues concerning (i) lack of coverage of the lexicons used in CEO-Pathfinder (i.e., CEO lexicon, FrameNet lexicon, and narrative chains) and, most importantly, (ii) the different nature of relations with respect to causelines. Although we assume that storylines entail causelines, storylines are built on rising and falling relations, which are not captured by causelines.

We compared the annotated events pairs with the lexicons to obtain more insight into their coverage. The lexicon annotated with CEO classes has a coverage of 77.71%, whereas FrameNet has a coverage of 45.46% and narrative chains 13.13%, where the latter lexicons do not include inflected forms. Early experiments with embeddings show that lexical coverage of the CEO lexicon can easily be expanded to 86.79% considering the top 30 most similar words.

6.5 Conclusion

In this chapter we present a formal model for storylines based on ideas from narratology. We show how theoretical notions such as story, plot, and plot structure can be translated into three corresponding data structures, namely, timelines, causelines, and storylines.

Our work is ongoing and there are a number of directions we plan to follow. Currently, the two corpora are released separately. Because both annotations are based on ECB+, it makes sense to combine them and release them as one corpus. To detect circumstantial relations, we can also combine the resources that are available: CEO, FrameNet, SUMO, WordNet, and narrative chains. This will increase the recall and, through voting, possibly also the precision. Because recall seems to be the main bottleneck, it is worthwhile to use unsupervised methods to expand the resources; e.g., through word embeddings, clustering, and topic detection. If unsupervised methods can also provide training data, e.g., finding news articles on similar events, we could experiment with end-to-end systems that do not rely on gold annotations of events, participants, time expressions, coreference relations. Such end-to-end systems are more challenging not only because of possible error propagation but also because it is more difficult to decide which events are relevant and which ones are not. So far we addressed mostly *semantic* relations between events, but news articles also contain *episodic* relations that are specific for that particular incident; e.g., the fact that it was raining that day. Knowledge-based approaches cannot predict episodic relations. We may have to learn these from large quantities of news articles on similar incidents. Finally, we experimented so far only with extracting the causeline and storyline from each single document separately. The ECB+ corpus lends itself to cross-document extraction as well. A future work will be to combine the causelines and storylines from separate documents into a single causeline and storyline across documents that report on the same incident.

References

Aggarwal, Charu C. 2014. Mining Text and Social Streams: A Review. *SIGKDD Explorations*, **15**(2), 9–19.

Allan, James. 2002. Introduction to Topic Detection and Tracking. Pages 1–16 of: Allan, James (ed.), *Topic Detection and Tracking*. Boston: Springer.

Aroyo, Lora, and Welty, Chris. 2014. The Three Sides of CrowdTruth. *Journal of Human Computation*, **1**, 31–34.

Aroyo, Lora, and Welty, Chris. 2015. Truth Is a Lie: Crowd Truth and the Seven Myths of Human Annotation. *AI Magazine*, **36**(1), 15–24.

Baker, Collin F., Fillmore, Charles J., and Lowe, John B. 1998. The Berkeley FrameNet Project. Pages 86–90 of: *Proceedings of the 17th International Conference on Computational Linguistics. Volume 1*. Association for Computational Linguistics.

Bal, Mieke. 1997. *Narratology: Introduction to the Theory of Narrative*. University of Toronto Press.

Becker, Hila, Naaman, Mor, and Gravano, Luis. 2011. Beyond Trending Topics: Real-World Event Identification on Twitter. *ICWSM*, **11**(2011), 438–441.

Binh Tran, Giang, Alrifai, Mohammad, and Quoc Nguyen, Dat. 2013. Predicting Relevant News Events for Timeline Summaries. Pages 91–92 of: *Proceedings of the 22nd International Conference on World Wide Web*. ACM.

Boyd, Brian. 2009. *On the Origin of Stories*. Harvard University Press.

Bruner, Jerome S. 1990. *Acts of Meaning*. Vol. 3. Harvard University Press.

Caselli, Tommaso, and Inel, Oana. 2018. Crowdsourcing StoryLines: Harnessing the Crowd for Causal Relation Annotation. Pages 44–54 of: Caselli, Tommaso, Miller, Ben, van Erp, Marieke, et al. (eds.), *Proceedings of the 2018 Events and Stories in the News Workshop (EventStory 2018)*. Santa Fe, NM: Association for Computational Linguistics.

Caselli, Tommaso, and Morante, Roser. 2018. Systems' Agreements and Disagreements in Temporal Processing: An Extensive Error Analysis of the TempEval-3 Task. In: Calzolari, Nicoletta, Choukri, Khalid, Cieri, Christopher, et al. (eds.), *Proceedings of the Eleventh International Conference on Language Resources and Evaluation (LREC 2018)*. Miyazaki, Japan: European Language Resources Association.

Caselli, Tommaso, and Vossen, Piek. 2016. The Storyline Annotation and Representation Scheme (StaR): A Proposal. Pages 67–72 of: Caselli, Tommaso, Miller, Ben, van Erp, Marieke, Vossen, Piek, and Caswell, David (eds.), *Proceedings of the 2nd Workshop on Computing News Storylines (CNS 2016)*. Austin, TX: Association for Computational Linguistics.

Caselli, Tommaso, and Vossen, Piek. 2017. The Event StoryLine Corpus: A New Benchmark for Causal and Temporal Relation Extraction. Pages 77–86 of: Caselli, Tommaso, Miller, Ben, van Erp, Marieke, et al. (eds.), *Proceedings of the Events and Stories in the News Workshop*. Vancouver: Association for Computational Linguistics.

Cassidy, Taylor, McDowell, Bill, Chambers, Nathanael, and Bethard, Steven. 2014. An Annotation Framework for Dense Event Ordering. Pages 501–506 of: Toutanova, Kristina, and Wu, Hua (eds.), *Proceedings of the 52nd Annual Meeting of the Association for Computational Linguistics: Volume 2. Short Papers*. Baltimore, MD: Association for Computational Linguistics.

Chambers, N., and Jurafsky, D. 2010. A Database of Narrative Schemas. In: Calzolari, Nicoletta, Choukri, Khalid, Maegaard, Bente, et al. (eds.), *Proceedings of the 9th Language Resources and Evaluation Conference (LREC2010)*.

Chambers, Nathanael, and Jurafsky, Dan. 2009. Unsupervised Learning of Narrative Schemas and Their Participants. Pages 602–610 of: Su, Keh-Yih, Su, Jian, Wiebe, Janyce, and Li, Haizhou (eds.), *Proceedings of the Joint Conference of the 47th Annual Meeting of the ACL and the 4th International Joint Conference on Natural Language Processing of the AFNLP: Volume 2*. Association for Computational Linguistics.

Chklovski, Timothy, and Pantel, Patrick. 2004. VerbOcean: Mining the Web for Fine-Grained Semantic Verb Relations. Pages 33–40 of: Lin, Dekang, and Wu, Dekai (eds.), *Proceedings of the 2004 Conference on Empirical Methods in Natural Language Processing*. Barcelona, Spain: Association for Computational Linguistics.

Cybulska, Agata, and Vossen, Piek. 2014. Using a Sledgehammer to Crack a Nut? Lexical Diversity and Event Coreference Resolution. In: Calzolari, Nicoletta, Choukri, Khalid, Declerck, Thierry, et al. (eds.), *Proceedings of the 9th Language Resources and Evaluation Conference (LREC2014)*.

Dunietz, Jesse, Levin, Lori, and Carbonell, Jaime. 2017. The BECauSE Corpus 2.0: Annotating Causality and Overlapping Relations. Pages 95–104 of: Schneider, Nathan, and Xue, Nianwen (eds.), *Proceedings of the 11th Linguistic Annotation Workshop*. Valencia, Spain: Association for Computational Linguistics.

Fellbaum, Christiane (ed.). 1998. *WordNet: An Electronic Lexical Database*. MIT Press.

Finlayson, Mark A., Cremisini, Andreas, and Ocal, Mustafa. 2021. Extracting and Aligning Timelines. Pages 91–109 of: Caselli, Tommaso, Palmer, Martha, Hovy, Eduard, and Vossen, Piek (eds), *Computational Analysis of Storylines: Making Sense of Events*. Cambridge University Press.

Forster, Edward Morgan. 1956. *Aspects of the Novel*. Harcourt.

Gottschall, Jonathan. 2012. *The Storytelling Animal: How Stories Make Us Human*. Houghton Mifflin Harcourt.

Hu, Zhichao, Rahimtoroghi, Elahe, Munishkina, Larissa, Swanson, Reid, and Walker, Marilyn A. 2013. Unsupervised Induction of Contingent Event Pairs from Film Scenes. Pages 369–379 of: Yarowsky, David, Baldwin, Timothy, Korhonen, Anna, Livescu, Karen, and Bethard, Steven (eds.), *Proceedings of the 2013 Conference on Empirical Methods in Natural Language Processing*. Seattle, WA: Association for Computational Linguistics.

Hu, Zhichao, Rahimtoroghi, Elahe, and Walker, Marilyn. 2017. Inference of Fine-Grained Event Causality from Blogs and Films. Pages 52–58 of: Caselli, Tommaso, Miller, Ben, van Erp, Marieke, et al. (eds.), *Proceedings of the Events and Stories in the News Workshop*. Vancouver: Association for Computational Linguistics.

Huang, Lifu, and Huang, Lian'en. 2013. Optimized Event Storyline Generation Based on Mixture-Event-Aspect Model. Pages 726–735 of: Yarowsky, David, Baldwin, Timothy, Korhonen, Anna, Livescu, Karen, and Bethard, Steven (eds.), *Proceedings of the 2013 Conference on Empirical Methods in Natural Language Processing*. Seattle, WA: Association for Computational Linguistics.

Ikuta, Rei, Styler, Will, Hamang, Mariah, O'Gorman, Tim, and Palmer, Martha. 2014. Challenges of Adding Causation to Richer Event Descriptions. Pages 12–20 of: Mitamura, Teruko, Hovy, Eduard, and Palmer, Martha (eds.), *Proceedings of the Second Workshop on EVENTS: Definition, Detection, Coreference, and Representation*. Baltimore, MD: Association for Computational Linguistics.

Kawamae, Noriaki. 2011. Trend Analysis Model: Trend Consists of Temporal Words, Topics, and Timestamps. Pages 317–326 of: *Proceedings of the Fourth ACM International Conference on Web Search and Data Mining*. ACM.

Lehnert, Wendy G. 1981. Plot Units and Narrative Summarization. *Cognitive Science*, **5**(4), 293–331.

Mani, Inderjeet. 2012. Computational Modeling of Narrative. *Synthesis Lectures on Human Language Technologies*, **5**(3), 1–142.

Mirza, Paramita, Sprugnoli, Rachele, Tonelli, Sara, and Speranza, Manuela. 2014. Annotating Causality in the TempEval-3 Corpus. Pages 10–19 of: Kolomiyets, Oleksandr, Moens, Marie-Francine, Palmer, Martha, Pustejovsky, James, and Bethard, Steven (eds.), *Proceedings of the EACL 2014 Workshop on Computational Approaches to Causality in Language (CAtoCL)*. Gothenburg, Sweden: Association for Computational Linguistics.

Mirza, Paramita, and Tonelli, Sara. 2014. An Analysis of Causality between Events and Its Relation to Temporal Information. Pages 2097–2106 of: Tsujii, Junichi, and Hajic, Jan (eds.), *Proceedings of COLING 2014, the 25th International Conference on Computational Linguistics: Technical Papers*. Dublin, Ireland: Dublin City University and Association for Computational Linguistics.

Mostafazadeh, Nasrin, Grealish, Alyson, Chambers, Nathanael, Allen, James, and Vanderwende, Lucy. 2016. CaTeRS: Causal and Temporal Relation Scheme for Semantic Annotation of Event Structures. Pages 51–61 of: Palmer, Martha, Hovy, Ed, Mitamura, Teruko, and O'Gorman, Tim (eds.), *Proceedings of the Fourth Workshop on Events*. San Diego, CA: Association for Computational Linguistics.

Niles, Ian, and Pease, Adam. 2001. Towards a Standard Upper Ontology. Pages 2–9 of: *Proceedings of the International Conference on Formal Ontology in Information Systems. Volume 2001*. FOIS '01. New York: Association for Computing Machinery.

O'Gorman, Tim, Wright-Bettner, Kristin, and Palmer, Martha. 2016. Richer Event Description: Integrating Event Coreference with Temporal, Causal and Bridging Annotation. Pages 47–56 of: Caselli, Tommaso, Miller, Ben, van Erp, Marieke, Vossen, Piek, and Caswell, David (eds.), *Proceedings of the 2nd Workshop on Computing News Storylines (CNS 2016)*. Austin, TX: Association for Computational Linguistics.

Prasad, Rashmi, Dinesh, Nikhil, Lee, Alan, et al. 2008. The Penn Discourse TreeBank 2.0. In: Calzolari, Nicoletta, Choukri, Khalid, Maegaard, Bente, et al. (eds.), *Proceedings of the Sixth International Conference on Language Resources and Evaluation (LREC'08)*. Marrakech, Morocco: European Language Resources Association.

Pustejovsky, James, Lee, Kiyong, Bunt, Harry, and Romary, Laurent. 2010. ISO-TimeML: An International Standard for Semantic Annotation. In: *Proceedings of the Seventh International Conference on Language Resources and Evaluation (LREC'10)*. European Language Resources Association.

Rumelhart, David E. 1975. Notes on a Schema for Stories. Pages 211–236 of: Bobrow, Daniel G., and Collins, Allan (eds.), *Representation and Understanding*. San Diego, CA: Morgan Kaufmann.

Segers, Roxane, Caselli, Tommaso, and Vossen, Piek. 2018. The Circumstantial Event Ontology (CEO) and ECB+/CEO: An Ontology and Corpus for Implicit Causal Relations between Events. Pages 4585–4592 of: Calzolari, Nicoletta, Choukri, Khalid, Cieri, Christopher, et al. (eds.), *Proceedings of the Eleventh International Conference on Language Resources and Evaluation (LREC 2018)*. Miyazaki, Japan: European Language Resources Association.

Shahaf, Dafna, and Guestrin, Carlos. 2010. Connecting the Dots between News
    Articles. Pages 623–632 of: *Proceedings of the 16th ACM SIGKDD International
    Conference on Knowledge Discovery and Data Mining*. ACM.
Vossen, Piek, Agerri, Rodrigo, Aldabe, Itziar, et al. 2016. NewsReader: Using
    Knowledge Resources in a Cross-Lingual Reading Machine to Generate More
    Knowledge from Massive Streams of News. *Knowledge-Based Systems*, **110**,
    60–85.
Zhou, Deyu, Xu, Haiyang, Dai, Xin-Yu, and He, Yulan. 2016. Unsupervised Storyline
    Extraction from News Articles. Pages 3014–3021 of: *Proceedings of the Twenty-
    Fifth International Joint Conference on Artificial Intelligence*. New York: AAAI
    Press.

PART TWO

Connecting the Dots

Resources, Tools, and Representations

7

The Richer Event Description Corpus for Event–Event Relations

Tim O'Gorman, Kristin Wright-Bettner, and Martha Palmer

Abstract. A variety of approaches exist for annotating temporal and event information in text, but it has been difficult to compare and contrast these different corpora. The Richer Event Description (RED) corpus, as an ambitious annotation of temporal, causal, and coreference annotation, provides one point of comparison for discussing how different annotation decisions contribute to the timeline and causal chains which define a document. We present an overview of how different event corpora differ and present new methods for studying the impact of these temporal annotation decisions upon the resulting document timeline. This focuses on illuminating the contribution of three particular sources of information – event coreference, causal relations with temporal information, and long-distance temporal containment – to the actual timeline of a document. By studying the impact of specific annotation strategies and framing the RED annotation in the larger context of other event–event relation annotation corpora, we hope to provide a clearer sense of the current state of event annotation and of promising future directions for annotation.

7.1 Introduction

A crucial element of understanding any narrative or news report is an understanding of the timeline of events. This remains a difficult challenge for natural language processing (NLP) systems. However, although many different corpora have been build to handle temporal topics, there is still no consensus regarding the annotation of event-centric information such as temporal relations, causal chains, or event coreference. Though major advances have been made in formalizing markup languages for characterizing temporal relations (Pustejovsky, Castano et al., 2003; Pustejovsky, et al., 2010), there is less consensus on when to apply such labels, leading to large practical differences between corpora. There are also many temporally adjacent topics that might provide temporal information when annotated, including event coreference (Bejan and Harabagiu, 2010; Lee et al., 2012), temporal relations (Pustejovsky, Hanks et al., 2003), modal or veridicality annotations (Saurí and Pustejovsky, 2009), annotations of the narrative structure or plot links of a documents (see Chapter 6), or annotations of causal relations and chains within a document.

As the number of possible event–event pairs explodes as the size of documents increases, it is generally considered impractical to annotate all possible relations; thus, event–event relations corpora are differentiated by the different strategies they use to define the subsets of those possible relations that should be considered during annotation. The Richer Event Description (RED; Ikuta et al., 2014; O'Gorman et al., 2016) corpus was created to be an ambitious annotation of a wide variety of temporal information. It exemplifies one kind of approach to that problem, in which annotation focuses on informative temporal containment relations, augmented by a range of local temporal order, causal relations, and event coreference annotations. This strategy used in RED differs from the recent trend toward dense locally windowed annotations of temporal order (Chambers et al., 2014; Ning et al., 2018; Vashishtha et al., 2019).

This work provides two primary contributions. It reframes the role of RED annotation in the larger context of different event–event relations corpora and presents a case study regarding how to make actual comparisons between such event–event relation corpora. It is hoped that this comparison will provide a launching point for the design of future approaches to temporal and event-related annotation corpora and better inform groups attempting to use this information. We suggest that evaluating corpora in terms of their actual contribution to an estimated timeline is an objective way of making these comparisons and may help to provide more empirical ways to evaluate event–event relations corpora.

7.2 A Comparison of Event Annotation Choices

Rather than discussing these characteristics in a vacuum, we compare the RED annotations to other annotations of event coreference and event–event relations, often having many layers of annotation applied to the same raw text. One of the earliest annotations of event information is that of Time-Bank (Pustejovsky, Hanks et al., 2003), also augmented with fine-grained annotation of modality (Saurí and Pustejovsky, 2009), dense annotation of temporal relations (TB-Dense; Chambers et al., 2014), and causal relations (Mirza et al., 2014). The Universal Decompositional Semantics annotated temporal relations (Vashishtha et al., 2019) over the English Web Treebank (EWT) corpus, which also had annotations of event factuality (Rudinger et al., 2018) and genericity (Govindarajan et al., 2019). A third major group of annotations is applied over the Event Coreference Bank (ECB+) corpus, containing both event coreference (Cybulska and Vossen, 2014) and the Event Storylines Corpus (Caselli and Vossen, 2017). We also compare to the CATERS (Mostafazadeh et al., 2016) and THYME (Styler et al., 2014) annotations, which apply temporal annotations over short texts and clinical notes, respectively. These corpora provide context to ground RED annotations within the larger space of possible annotation decisions.

7.2.1 Detection of Events and Their Features

Though there is wide disagreement regarding which event–event relations to annotate, there is much more agreement regarding what constitutes an event and the general types of features that those events might be annotated with.

Most event-based approaches handle all events and eventualities, as in the TimeML guidelines, which define events as "situations that happen or occur". This encompasses not only verbs but also timeline-relevant nouns, adjectives, and multiword expressions. Approaches vary in how much they annotate semantically light verbs such as auxiliaries and in how to handle agent-denoting nominalizations such as "prisoner" or "murderer".

A larger source of difference regarding what qualifies as an event comes from corpora that only annotate events when they fit into a particular ontology of interest. Such corpora (Song et al., 2015; Hong et al., 2016; Araki et al., 2018) thus would label a mention "sale" as an event only if the ontology cares about a category such as "transaction event". Wide-coverage event ontologies (such as Richer Event Ontology [REO]; see Chapter 2) may also capture all events in a document, and some approaches (Pustejovsky, Castano et al., 2003; Caselli and Vossen, 2017) annotate all events with event types by using coarse-grained event types, distinguishing broad categories such as mental state events.

Frameworks also differ in what features are annotated on those events (features sometimes applied during such an "event detection" phase), such as tense, modality, and genericity. Coarse-grained distinctions for these categories can often be applied using small sets of three to four labels. For example, the RED annotation provides coverage of the minimal set of distinctions for each such category – distinguishing modality/genericity with for features (ACTUAL, HYPOTHETICAL, GENERIC, and UNCERTAIN/HEDGED), along with positive or negative polarity. RED also marks the speech time relation – whether a

Table 7.1. *Different definitions events and tense and modality features*

Corpora	Event Definitions	Tense/ Event Time	Modality/ Polarity	Genericity	Event Types	Filter by Types
RED	all	✓	✓	binary		no
UDS-T	verbs+adj.	✓	✓	✓		no
TimeBank	all	✓	✓		some	no
THYME	all	✓	✓			no
ECB/ESC	all	✓	✓	✓	some	no
ERE/RPI	all		binary	binary	ACE	yes
CaTers	all				TRIPS	yes

RED = Richer Event Description; UDS-T = Universal Decompositional Semantics–Temporal; THYME = Temporal Histories of Your Medical Events; ESC = Event Storylines Corpus; ECB = Event Coreference Bank; ERE = Entity Relations and Events; RPI = Hong et al. (2016); CaTeRS = Causal and Temporal Relation Scheme.

given event is *before*, *after*, or *overlap*s with document time, including a special category of *before/overlap* for present prefect forms such as *"I have been writing for weeks"* – in a manner similar to other speech time annotations (Pustejovsky and Stubbs, 2011; Styler et al., 2014). Other annotation approaches use fine-grained or even continuous scales for aspect (Croft et al., 2016), event factuality (Saurí and Pustejovsky, 2009; Rudinger et al., 2018; Vigus et al., 2019), or genericity (Govindarajan et al., 2019).

RED annotates all eventualities, without any filtering based on ontology, so that all events in a document are annotated. This annotation therefore captures a superset of the events that one might need for a particular event–event relations task and with basic representations of most of the features one may want to find for those events.

7.2.2 When to Annotate Temporal Relations

The fundamental question to be resolved in temporal annotation is *when* to annotate the temporal relationship between two events. Because it is generally agreed that individually considering every possible event–event pair in a document is impractical, the fundamental question of temporal annotation has been how to define a set of constraints that can limit the number of relations considered to a tractable quantity.

One source of these constraints is to only annotate explicit temporal relations, signaled by temporal adpositions or adverbs (such as *before* or *since*) or other grammatical signals such as aspect marking. Such an approach is one

criteriona applied by RED and by other corpora such as TimeBank (Pustejovsky, Hanks et al., 2003) both label such relations and label the explicit signal
itself. However, only marking such explicit relations would not be sufficient to
capture the timeline of a document.

Beyond those clear-cut explicit relations, one set of strategies for annotating
temporal relations is to have annotators view a full document and to select only
a subset of salient temporal relations that the annotators decide to label. One
approach to this is to emphasize only labeling informative temporal relations –
those that would provide the most information about the underlying timeline
(Pustejovsky and Stubbs, 2011) – by focusing upon hierarchical *containment*
relations ("includes" in Allen interval relations), because if one can cluster
events into larger macroevents, most event–event orderings can be inferred
from simply knowing the order of those larger events. RED follows that
narrative of containment-based annotations.

Such annotations have the advantage of capturing the most salient and useful labels but the disadvantage of providing a partial annotation of only these
informative relations (Ning et al., 2019). Recently, many other annotations
have defined more deterministic rules for which relations to consider – such
as a window of adjacent sentences – and consider all event–event pairs that
match such a deterministic heuristic (Chambers et al., 2014; Ning et al., 2018;
Vashishtha et al., 2019). Such approaches have computational advantages,
simplifying the hard task of detecting relationships into a simpler task of
classifying them.

A third such strategy is to limit the space of possible relations using a
temporal dependency approach (Kolomiyets et al., 2012; Zhang and Xue,
2018), where each event is only linked to a single other temporally related
event. Zhang and Xue (2018) found the temporal link to another event that
provides the most specific information about the current event.

An important factor in these different strategies is that they vary in how, if
ever, they can capture long-distance temporal relationships. Explicit marking
of temporal order is usually limited to adjacent sentences, and "dense" annotations of temporal order tend to have constrained windows of annotation.[1]
However, the container-based approaches such as RED can mark relations
over long distances, both between events and by marking containment between
temporal expressions and contained events. RED also provides methods for
marking long-distance temporal relations through an additional constraint
discussed in the next section – adding temporal relations labels to causal

---

[1] One exception to this is Hong et al. (2016), which attempts a largely pairwise annotation of
events between documents.

relationships, which are marked whenever an event clearly causes or enables another event. This provides a relatively limited set of contexts where a long-distance relation might be annotated, allowing annotations such as RED to tie together other unconnected sections of text.

7.2.3 Temporal Relations Covered

Despite the dramatic differences regarding when to annotate a temporal relation, there are not pursuantly dramatic differences regarding the actual inventories of temporal labels utilized by different annotation schemes. Though temporal inventories differ slightly from group to group, they naturally tend to be a subset of the Allen temporal interval relations (Allen, 1983). TimeML (Pustejovsky, Castano et al., 2003) established a set of approaches to annotate a subset of those intervals, and many later documents followed the same approach. Such annotations differ minimally in how they treat a small set of less frequent relations – whether to mark SIMULTANEOUS relations, to mark BEGINS-ON and ENDS-ON relations, and whether to encode aspectual – i.e., ALINK – relations. REO (see Chapter 2) has borrowed these basic temporal labels from RED in order to capture prototypical sequences of events for generic complex events.

Table 7.2 illustrates the temporal inventories for a number of these annotation frameworks. The most important deviation in this framework is not RED (which marks a conventional inventory of relations derived from TimeML) but rather Universal Decompositional Semantics–Temporal (UDS-T; Vashishtha et al., 2019), which relates events using a *continuous* representation of event

Table 7.2. *Temporal relation inventories, extending table from Mostafazadeh et al. (2016)*

Corpus	Before/ After	Meets	Overlap	Finishes/ End-on	Starts/ Begins-on	Contains/ Includes	Equals/ Identity
Allen	✓	✓	✓	✓	✓	✓	
RED	✓		✓	✓	✓	✓	✓
THYME	✓		✓	✓	✓	✓	✓
TimeML	✓	✓		✓	✓	✓	✓
CaTeRS	✓		✓			✓	✓
ESC	✓		✓			✓	

RED = Richer Event Description; THYME = Temporal History of Your Medical Events; CaTeRS = Causal and Temporal Relation Scheme; ESC = Event Storylines Corpus.

spans using two slider bars. Such an annotation can be reduced to the same information modeled in the other temporal relation inventories but adds useful continuous information about how the start and end points relate to each other, beyond what is captured by discrete temporal interval labels.

7.2.4 Event Coreference and Non-temporal Relations

RED augments temporal annotation with causal annotations (Ikuta et al., 2014), subtyping the temporal BEFORE and OVERLAP relations with casual counterparts into BEFORE/CAUSE, OVERLAP/CAUSE, BEFORE/PRECONDITION, and OVERLAP/PRECONDITION. Other annotations have also combined temporal and causal annotations (Mirza et al., 2014; Mostafazadeh et al., 2016).

Another class of nontemporal information is the subtyping of temporal CONTAINS relations into those that are purely temporal and those that express an event–subevent link – expressed in RED as CONTAINS-SUBEVENT. Being able to distinguish subevents can be important in the transition from pure temporal structure to an understanding of events and scripts. This is not unique to RED, because such links are annotated in Glavaš et al. (2014) and annotated within events of interest in Araki et al. (2014). However, the RED annotations are the largest such annotations of these subevent labels that we know of and may provide a useful starting point for script learning and characterization of larger events.

Finally, RED marks event coreference relations and partial coreference links (such as set/subset relations). Knowing whether two events are coreferent during a temporal information pass has useful implications for the larger representation of a document, because it allows annotators to avoid redundantly marking a given temporal relation multiple times in a document. RED also annotated set/member relations – such as between a class of events (as in a generalization) and individual instances. Hong et al. (2016) annotated not only event coreference and set/member but a long tail of other nontemporal event–event relations, such as subevent–subevent, member–member, and recurrence relations. The Event StoryLines Corpus (Caselli and Vossen, 2017) also provides explanatory PLOT LINK annotations, which similarly can be viewed as providing temporal information.

7.2.5 Actual Annotation Methods

There are two ongoing issues with event–event relation corpora that are fundamentally at odds: how to make annotations provide large amounts of scalable training data and how to provide extremely high-quality annotations.

The RED corpus provides one method of addressing the quality issue, by focusing on providing high-quality annotations through double annotation and adjudication of event detection and event feature annotations, only annotating temporal relations on top of the cleaned, adjudicated events. Such an approach minimizes the propagation of errors caused by low-level disagreements, such as the span of an event or whether to interpret a given event as generic or negated. By attempting to address such disagreements early in annotation, the RED annotations are as coherent as possible.

The RED approach differs from decompositional approaches, in which many different annotators provide annotations of event features or event–event relations with fine-grained or even continuous representations. Such approaches can be viewed as providing less coherent annotations (lacking such adjudication) but may offset that lack of coherence with richer information about the range of labels provided by different annotators.

7.2.6 Summarizing the Role of RED in Event Corpora

Tables 7.1, 7.2, and 7.3 show how different annotation approaches vary in their annotation decisions. One can see that more directly through example (1), which illustrates the events annotated in RED. One can see that all

Table 7.3. *Comparison of event–event relation annotations*

Corpora	Local Temp. Order	Long-distance Containment	Causal Relations	Plot Relations	Event Coreference
RED	salient	✓	✓		✓
TimeBank	salient	✓			
TB-Dense	all pairwise				
UDS-T	most pairwise				
Ning et al.	most pairwise				
ECB	plot-relevant		✓	✓	✓
CaTers	salient		✓		
THYME	salient	✓			

RED = Richer Event Description; TB-Dense = TimeBank Dense; UDS-T = Universal Decompositional Semantics–Temporal; ECB = Event Coreference Bank; THYME = Temporal Histories of Your Medical Events; CaTeRS = Causal and Temporal Relation Scheme.

eventualities – including pronouns such as *it* – are annotated as events. In RED, all such events also are annotated, in this case, as being BEFORE speech time and being of modality ACTUAL:

(1) Gadhafi's **[visit]** to Italy **[continued]** that process of **[emergence]** from international **[isolation]**. But **[it]** also drew **[protests]**, including at La Sapienza university, where Gadhafi was **[addressing]** a group of few hundred students.

We can see from such an example the kinds of relations that are captured as RED-style annotation through explicit and local temporal links such as aspectual marking and containment relations (CONTAINS-SUBEVENT):

	continued	CONTINUES	emergence
(2)	isolation	ENDS-ON	emergence
	visit	CONTAINS-SUBEVENT	addressing

The same sentences in RED would also receive event coreference and causal relations annotation for other events:

	it	OVERLAP/PRECONDITION	protests
(3)	visit	COREFERENCE	it
	visit	OVERLAP/CAUSES	continued

More dense annotations would get human judgments for other relations beyond these, including pairs such as (visit, emergence), (continued, isolation), or (isolation, protests).

One cluster of annotation approaches, typified by RED or TimeBank (Pustejovsky, Castano et al., 2003; O'Gorman et al., 2016), is one in which annotation is applied by experts over an entire document by selectively labeling informative event–event relations. Such an approach to annotation is naturally compatible with capturing long-distance relations, because the annotators are attempting to craft a representation of the entire timeline using those relations, but limits the density of annotation.

Those approaches differ from the more recent trend of annotation in which corpora are annotated with dense, and often decompositional, temporal relations annotations – providing labels for all possible event–event relations, modulo some set of constraints (Chambers et al., 2014; Ning et al., 2018; Vashishtha et al., 2019).

This characterization into those two prototypical approaches to temporal annotation also allows us to highlight the exceptions to this characterization.

Table 7.4. *Summarization of corpora*

Prototypically dense/decompositional	Vashishtha et al. (2019); Chambers et al. (2014); Ning et al. (2018)
Edge cases	Short texts (Mostafazadeh et al., 2016) unconstrained (Hong et al., 2016; Minard et al., 2016), temp dependencies (Kolomiyets et al., 2012; Zhang and Xue, 2018), storylines-focused (Caselli and Vossen, 2017)
Prototypically hierarchical/expert-annotated	Pustejovsky, Hanks et al. (2003); O'Gorman et al. (2016); Styler et al. (2014); Glavaš et al. (2014)

For example, whereas individually examining all possible event pairs tends to naturally require constraints to only consider event-pairs in neighboring sentences, approaches that filter by event ontologies can examine all event–event pairs (Hong et al., 2016) because that filtering reduces the total number of events. Other exceptions are those in which there are other constraints on which relations to annotate, such as constraining relations to match temporal dependencies (Kolomiyets et al., 2012; Zhang and Xue, 2019) or narrative structure (Caselli and Vossen, 2017).

This characterization of these different annotations, summarized in Table 7.4, shows that an important ongoing question for the future of event–event relations corpora is to understand the actual impact of these annotation decisions. We therefore highlight relations that are captured by RED but not currently annotated in any of the dense, decompositional approaches and propose methods for measuring the impact of such annotation decisions in terms of their contribution of information about the actual timeline of events.

7.2.7 Corpus Size Comparisons

We note that many of these corpora provide meaningfully large sets of annotated data, but none are overwhelmingly large. Table 7.5 illustrates the general size of the RED released corpus and of an additional corpus of RED data annotated for the DARPA Active Interpretation of Disparate Alternatives (AIDA) program. Though annotations are often measured in terms of the number of relations annotated, we might count or omit the presence of temporal links to the document time – a simple but informative feature for determining a timeline. Counts including those links are included parenthetically in the last column. Such counts reveal the importance of generating connections

Table 7.5. *Size of RED and other temporal corpora; relations include causal and plot relations*

	Events	Times	Event Clusters	Tokens	Relations (w/ DocTime)
RED (2016 release)	8,731	1,127	2,390	54,287	4,969 (13,700)
RED-AIDA	3,639	354	1,801	21,438	1,735 (5,374)
all RED	12,370	1,481	4,191	75,725	6,704 (19,074)
TimeBank (v1.2)	7,935	1,414		61,418	6,418
ECB (v0.9)	7,275	1,297	7,671		(12,423)
TB-Dense	1,729	289			(12,715)
UDS-T	32,302			254,830	70,368
Hong et al. (2016)	863				25,610
Ning et al. (2019)	1,300				3,572

ECB = Event Coreference Bank; TB-Dense = TimeBank Dense; UDS-T = Universal Decompositional Semantics–Temporal.

between annotations such as RED and the larger dense corpora such as UDS-T (Vashishtha et al., 2019) or TimeBank-Dense (Chambers et al., 2014).

7.3 Long-Distance Relations in RED: Contains, Causality, and Coreference

As noted in Sections 7.2.2 and 7.2.4, there are three ways in which temporal information between events separated by a long distance might be marked in RED annotations:

1. Two events are linked by long-distance containment relations (CONTAINS and CONTAINS/SUBEVENT).
2. Two events are linked by a causal relation (because causal relations also capture temporal order).
3. Two events are linked through event coreference, thus allowing temporal transitive closure to infer relations between events linked to those events.

This first focus on containment follows prior discussions of narrative container approaches (Pustejovsky and Stubbs, 2011; Styler et al., 2014), which emphasize the use of CONTAINS (and CONTAINS-SUBEVENT) relations, asking annotators to link an event to the most specific containing span whenever possible. Such larger containing events may have subevents scattered across large distances in some situations, such as when events described in the headline have subevents throughout the article (as in example (4)) or where specific events are part of a larger situation that is unfolding (as in example (5)):

(4) **PROTESTS** AS CITY COLLEGE CLOSES A STUDENT CENTER ...
    (10 sentences). ... A protester was **arrested**. [PROTESTS CONTAINS-SUBEVENT arrested]

(5) **FOCUS** TURNS TO THREE SUSPECTS IN BELGIAN DIAMOND
    ROBBERY ... (5 sentences). ... Investigators said Bertoldi's arrival in Geneva after the theft had provided a critical breakthrough in the **inquiry**. [Inquiry CONTAINS-SUBEVENT focus]

Similarly, causal annotations are annotated at any distance. Example (6) illustrates one such longer-distance causal link, wherein the event of leaving office is preceded by, and caused by, the later mentions "beat" event, itself a subevent of the 2010 elections:

(6) Skelton ... served as the chairman of House Armed Services Committee from 2007 until **leaving** office.... (6 sentences) ... Rep. Vicky Hartzler, the Republican who **beat** Skelton and still holds the seat, received support from many Tea Part [beat BEFORE/CAUSE leaving]

Such causal links can be inferred by annotators over long distances. Though allowing annotators to mark any kind of temporal ordering relations over a long distance of text might entail a vast collection of possible temporal order relations, the set of causal relations is much more limited in a text and thus provides more tractable long-distance relations.

7.4 Studying RED Impact on Event Ordering

We do not want to simply make generalizations about which kinds of relations may carry meaningful information without attempting to quantify that impact. However, such a measure is complicated for temporal annotations, because there is no single agreed-upon target of annotation. Instead, temporal annotations provide statements about the partial order of events and might only be truly evaluated against a true timeline of events. Thus, we suggest one way of approaching the evaluation of temporal annotation is to do just that: given a rich way of representing a total order of events in a timeline and a way of estimating that total order based on a given annotation, we can simply compare the correlation between the two (in this case, using Spearman's rank-order correlation).

We present one simple route toward a richer representation of the timeline, relying upon the observation that annotations such as RED are somewhat orthogonal to annotations such as TimeBank-Dense or UDS-T in which an emphasis is placed on dense, exhaustive annotation between adjacent sentences. Merging the contributions of different annotation schemes can naturally provide more information than would be practical to annotate in a single annotation pass and provides some separation between the assumptions of any one annotation and how you examine its results. Such an approach has some similarities to generation of timelines from TimeML outputs (see Chapter 4).

As a pilot of this, we implement RED-style event annotation on four documents in the development set of the English Web Treebank (Bies et al., 2012), the corpus also used for UDS-T annotations (Vashishtha et al., 2019). Because the UDS-T annotations take a dramatically different strategy toward the annotation of temporal information (as discussed in Section 7.2.2), we suggest that the union of the two annotations can be highly informative regarding the entire temporal structure of the document. UDS-T annotations are a crowdsourced annotation of event–event pairs within the same sentence or adjacent sentences, where annotators use two sliding scales to mark the relationships between the event spans, allowing a much more nuanced and continuous annotation than that illustrated by discrete labeling of the traditional temporal relationships. Though that annotation also involved event duration annotation, we do not leverage it here; it would naturally be relevant for extensions of this work.

We merge the RED annotations with the UDS-T annotations by aligning events according to their spans and then adding event–event relations to the graph until none are left, converting temporal relations into statements about order relations between the start and end points of each span. We treat this as a somewhat random process – because assertions about how events are ordered may contradict each other, we randomly select the order of relations to add and do not add relations that contradict existing information. We repeat this process many times for a given set of temporal information, so that we get a set of N timelines that are mostly compatible with the annotation provided. We generated such a temporal graph 50 times for each condition and kept the 10 event orders with the largest transitive closure.

Such an approach provides a more formal way to examine the idea motivating annotations such as RED of focusing on "highly informative" relations such as containment and allows one to measure how much redundancy exists between different annotation approaches. We compare the timelines generated by the union of RED and UDS-T documents to those produced when one

Table 7.6. *Correlation between timelines sampled using all data sources and timelines after certain annotations are removed*

Which timelines to compare	File1	File2	File3	File4	Avg. Δ
All vs All	0.211	0.292	0.185	0.261	
Remove RED DocTimeRel	0.223	0.193	0.167	0.222	−0.036
Remove Coref/Causation/Contains	0.228	0.289	0.162	0.229	−0.010
Remove Coref	0.247	0.283	0.171	0.248	0
Remove Causation	0.226	0.296	0.152	0.242	−0.008
Remove Contains	0.202	0.262	0.191	0.220	−0.019
RED only	0.271	0.177	0.137	0.228	−0.034
UDS-T only	0.146	0.199	0.115	0.209	−0.070

RED = Richer Event Description; UDS-T = Universal Decompositional Semantics–Temporal.

omits various pieces of information to study the impact of those individual annotations on the overall understanding of a document timeline. Table 7.6 illustrates, for each such condition, average Spearman's rank-order correlation between the orders (because we generate 10 timelines for each, this is an average of 100 comparisons).

The results of Table 7.6 illustrate the highly variable nature of this approach (most notable that even the correlation between the same merged set of annotations is often quite far from the 1.0 you would expect from an identical set of events) but still serves to show in general terms the impact of different annotation components on a final temporal ordering. Most notable, one can see the extent to which the two annotations provide different information about the document and have much more information than either approach alone. Moreover, one can see that the largest impact from RED annotations is the simple use of links to document time, which provide a simple grounding of each event into the correct general part of the timeline and may be especially useful for events with few other temporal relations. One can also see that of the discussed ways of getting long-distance temporal relations, the annotation with the most impact is that of the temporal containment relations.

7.5 Conclusions

The RED formalism remains one of the most comprehensive forms of event–event relation annotations. However, it is one point within an increasingly large landscape of different temporal relations corpora. We illustrate here a deeper focus on RED-style annotations of temporal relationships in text and illustrate the value of such a richly annotated event-centric corpus.

The evaluation results presented here illustrate a very preliminary way of evaluating such corpora. By attaining rich representations of event orderings and measuring the contribution of annotations to that order, we suggest that one may better study which kinds of annotations are actually informative and which annotations may provide little information. These results also highlight which aspects of RED annotation go beyond what is captured by many other corpora in which dense, local annotations are used. These aspects, such as long-distance temporal containment relations or relationships to speech time, point to important phenomena that researchers building future temporal annotations might consider.

References

Allen, James. 1983. Maintaining Knowledge about Temporal Intervals. *Communications of the ACM*, **26**(11), 832–843.

Araki, Jun, Liu, Zhengzhong, Hovy, Eduard, and Mitamura, Teruko. 2014. Detecting Subevent Structure for Event Coreference Resolution. Pages 4553–4558 of: Calzolari, Nicoletta, Choukri, Khalid, Declerck, Thierry, et al. (eds.), *Proceedings of the Ninth International Conference on Language Resources and Evaluation (LREC'14)*. Reykjavik, Iceland: European Language Resources Association.

Araki, Jun, Mulaffer, Lamana, Pandian, Arun, et al. 2018. Interoperable Annotation of Events and Event Relations across Domains. Pages 10–20 of: Bunt, Harry (ed.), *Proceedings 14th Joint ACL–ISO Workshop on Interoperable Semantic Annotation*. Santa Fe, NM: Association for Computational Linguistics.

Bejan, Cosmin Adrian, and Harabagiu, Sanda. 2010. Unsupervised Event Coreference Resolution with Rich Linguistic Features. Pages 1412–1422 of: *Proceedings of the 48th Annual Meeting of the Association for Computational Linguistics*.

Bies, Ann, Mott, Justin, Warner, Colin, and Kulick, Seth. 2012. English Web Treebank. Philadelphia: Linguistic Data Consortium.

Caselli, Tommaso, and Vossen, Piek. 2017. The Event StoryLine Corpus: A New Benchmark for Causal and Temporal Relation Extraction. Pages 77–86 of: Caselli, Tommaso, Miller, Ben, van Erp, Marieke, et al. (eds.), *Proceedings of the Events and Stories in the News Workshop*. Vancouver: Association for Computational Linguistics.

Chambers, Nathanael, Cassidy, Taylor, McDowell, Bill, and Bethard, Steven. 2014. Dense Event Ordering with a Multi-pass Architecture. *Transactions of the Association for Computational Linguistics*, **2**, 273–284.

Croft, William, Pešková, Pavlína, and Regan, Michael. 2016. Annotation of Causal and Aspectual Structure of Events in RED: A Preliminary Report. Pages 8–17 of: Palmer, Martha, Hovy, Ed, Mitamura, Teruko, and O'Gorman, Tim (eds.), *Proceedings of the Fourth Workshop on Events*. Austin, TX: Association for Computational Linguistics.

Cybulska, Agata, and Vossen, Piek. 2014. Using a Sledgehammer to Crack a Nut? Lexical Diversity and Event Coreference Resolution. Pages 4545–4552 of: Calzolari, Nicoletta, Choukri, Khalid, Declerck, Thierry, et al. (eds.), *Proceedings of the 9th Language Resources and Evaluation Conference (LREC2014)*.

Glavaš, Goran, Šnajder, Jan, Kordjamshidi, Parisa, and Moens, Marie-Francine. 2014. HiEve: A corpus for Extracting Event Hierarchies from News Stories. Pages 3678–3683 of: Calzolari, Nicoletta, Choukri, Khalid, Declerck, Thierry, et al. (eds.), *Proceedings of 9th Language Resources and Evaluation Conference*. European Language Resources Association.

Govindarajan, Venkata Subrahmanyan, Van Durme, Benjamin, and White, Aaron Steven. 2019. Decomposing Generalization: Models of Generic, Habitual, and Episodic Statements. *Transactions of the Association for Computational Linguistics*, **7**, 501–517.

Hong, Yu, Zhang, Tongtao, Horowit-Hendler, Sharone, Ji, Heng, O'Gorman, Tim, and Palmer, Martha. 2016. Building a Cross-document Event–Event Relation Corpus. Pages 1–6 of: Friedrich, Annemarie, and Tomanek, Katrin (eds.), *Proceedings of LAW X – The 10th Linguistic Annotation Workshop*.

Ikuta, Rei, Styler, Will, Hamang, Mariah, O'Gorman, Tim, and Palmer, Martha. 2014. Challenges of Adding Causation to Richer Event Descriptions. Pages 12–20 of: Mitamura, Teruko, Hovy, Ed, and Palmer, Martha (eds.), *Proceedings of the Second Workshop on EVENTS: Definition, Detection, Coreference, and Representation*. Baltimore, MD: Association for Computational Linguistics.

Kolomiyets, Oleksandr, Bethard, Steven, and Moens, Marie-Francine. 2012. Extracting Narrative Timelines as Temporal Dependency Structures. Pages 88–97 of: *Proceedings of the 50th Annual Meeting of the Association for Computational Linguistics: Long Papers. Volume 1*. Association for Computational Linguistics.

Lee, Heeyoung, Recasens, Marta, Chang, Angel, Surdeanu, Mihai, and Jurafsky, Dan. 2012. Joint Entity and Event Coreference Resolution across Documents. Pages 489–500 of: *Proceedings of the 2012 Joint Conference on Empirical Methods in Natural Language Processing and Computational Natural Language Learning (EMNLP-CoNLL 2012)*.

Minard, Anne-Lyse, Speranza, Manuela, Urizar, Ruben, et al. 2016. MEANTIME, the NewsReader Multilingual Event and Time Corpus. Pages 4417–4422 of: Calzolari, Nicoletta, Choukri, Khalid, Declerck, Thierry, et al. (eds.), *Proceedings of the Tenth International Conference on Language Resources and Evaluation (LREC 2016)*. Portorož, Slovenia: European Language Resources Association.

Mirza, Paramita, Sprugnoli, Rachele, Tonelli, Sara, and Speranza, Manuela. 2014. Annotating Causality in the TempEval-3 Corpus. Pages 10–19 of: Kolomiyets, Oleksandr, Moens, Marie-Francine, Palmer, Martha, Pustejovsky, James, and Bethard, Steven (eds.), *Proceedings of the EACL 2014 Workshop on Computational Approaches to Causality in Language (CAtoCL)*. Gothenburg, Sweden: Association for Computational Linguistics.

Mostafazadeh, Nasrin, Grealish, Alyson, Chambers, Nathanael, Allen, James, and Vanderwende, Lucy. 2016. CaTeRS: Causal and Temporal Relation Scheme for

Semantic Annotation of Event Structures. Pages 51–61 of: Palmer, Martha, Hovy, Ed, Mitamura, Teruko, and O'Gorman, Tim (eds.), *Proceedings of the Fourth Workshop on Events*. San Diego: Association for Computational Linguistics.

Ning, Qiang, He, Hangfeng, Fan, Chuchu, and Roth, Dan. 2019. Partial or Complete, That's the Question. Pages 2190–2200 of: *Proceedings of the 2019 Conference of the North American Chapter of the Association for Computational Linguistics: Human Language Technologies, Volume 1 (Long and Short Papers)*.

Ning, Qiang, Wu, Hao, and Roth, Dan. 2018. A Multi-axis Annotation Scheme for Event Temporal Relations. Pages 1318–1328 of: *Proceedings of the 56th Annual Meeting of the Association for Computational Linguistics: Volume 1. Long Papers*. Melbourne, Australia: Association for Computational Linguistics.

O'Gorman, Tim, Wright-Bettner, Kristin, and Palmer, Martha. 2016. Richer Event Description: Integrating Event Coreference with Temporal, Causal and Bridging Annotation. Pages 47–56 of: Caselli, Tommaso, Miller, Ben, van Erp, Marieke, Vossen, Piek, and Caswell, David (eds.), *Proceedings of the 2nd Workshop on Computing News Storylines (CNS 2016)*. Austin, TX: Association for Computational Linguistics.

Pustejovsky, James, and Stubbs, Amber. 2011. Increasing Informativeness in Temporal Annotation. Pages 152–160 of: Ide, Nancy, Meyers, Adam, Pradhan, Sameer, and Tomanek, Katrin (eds.), *Proceedings of the 5th Linguistic Annotation Workshop*. Portland, OR: Association for Computational Linguistics.

Pustejovsky, James, Hanks, Patrick, Saurí, Roser, et al. 2003. The TimeBank Corpus. Pages 647–656 of: Archer, Dawn, Rayson, Paul, Wilson, Andrew, and McEnery, Tony (eds.), *Proceedings of Corpus Linguistics Conference*. Lancaster, UK.

Pustejovsky, James, Castano, José, Ingria, Robert, et al. 2003. TimeML: Robust Specification of Event and Temporal Expressions in Text. AAAI Technical Report SS-03-07.

Pustejovsky, James, Lee, Kiyong, Bunt, Harry, and Romary, Laurent. 2010. ISO-TimeML: An International Standard for Semantic Annotation. In: *Proceedings of the Seventh International Conference on Language Resources and Evaluation (LREC'10)*. European Language Resources Association.

Rudinger, Rachel, White, Aaron Steven, and Van Durme, Benjamin. 2018. Neural Models of Factuality. Pages 731–744 of: *Proceedings of the 2018 Conference of the North American Chapter of the Association for Computational Linguistics: Human Language Technologies: Volume 1. Long Papers*. New Orleans, LA: Association for Computational Linguistics.

Saurí, Roser, and Pustejovsky, James. 2009. FactBank: A Corpus Annotated with Event Factuality. *Language Resources and Evaluation*, **43**(3), 227–268.

Song, Zhiyi, Bies, Ann, Strassel, Stephanie, et al. 2015. From Light to Rich ERE: Annotation of Entities, Relations, and Events. Pages 89–98 of: Hovy, Ed, Mitamura, Teruko, and Palmer, Martha (eds.), *Proceedings of the 3rd Workshop on EVENTS at the NAACL-HLT*.

Styler, William F., IV, Bethard, Steven, Finan, Sean, et al. 2014. Temporal Annotation in the Clinical Domain. *Transactions of the Association for Computational Linguistics*, **2**, 143–154.

Vashishtha, Siddharth, Van Durme, Benjamin, and White, Aaron Steven. 2019. Fine-Grained Temporal Relation Extraction. Pages 2906–2919 of: *Proceedings of the*

57th Annual Meeting of the Association for Computational Linguistics. Florence, Italy: Association for Computational Linguistics.

Vigus, Meagan, Van Gysel, Jens E. L., and Croft, William. 2019. A Dependency Structure Annotation for Modality. Pages 182–198 of: Xue, Nianwen, Croft, William, Hajic, Jan, et al. (eds.), *Proceedings of the First International Workshop on Designing Meaning Representations*. Florence, Italy: Association for Computational Linguistics.

Zhang, Yuchen, and Xue, Nianwen. 2018. Structured Interpretation of Temporal Relations. In: Calzolari, Nicoletta, Choukri, Khalid, Cieri, Christopher, et al. (eds.), *Proceedings of the Eleventh International Conference on Language Resources and Evaluation (LREC-2018)*. Miyazaki, Japan: European Languages Resources Association.

Zhang, Yuchen, and Xue, Nianwen. 2019. Acquiring Structured Temporal Representation via Crowdsourcing: A Feasibility Study. Pages 178–185 of: Mihalcea, Rada, Shutova, Ekaterina, Ku, Lun-Wei, Evang, Kilian, and Poria, Soujanya (eds.), *Proceedings of the Eighth Joint Conference on Lexical and Computational Semantics (* SEM 2019)*.

8

Low-Resource Event Extraction via Share-and-Transfer and Remaining Challenges

Heng Ji and Clare Voss

Abstract. Event extraction aims to find *who did what to whom, when,* and *where* from unstructured data. Over the past decade, research in event extraction has made advances in three waves. The first wave relied on supervised machine learning models trained from a large amount of manually annotated data and manually crafted features. The second wave eliminated this method of feature engineering by introducing deep neural networks with distributional semantic embedding features but still required large annotated data sets. This chapter provides an overview of a third wave with a *share-and-transfer* framework, which further enhances the portability of event extraction by transferring knowledge from a high-resource setting to another low-resource setting, reducing the need there for annotated data (see Figure 8.1). We describe three low-resource settings: a new domain, a new language, or a new data modality. The first *share* step of our approach is to construct a *common structured semantic representation space* into which these complex structures can be encoded. Then, in the *transfer* step of the approach, we can train event extractors over these representations in high-resource settings and apply the learned extractors to target data in the low-resource setting. We conclude the chapter with a summary of the current status of this new framework and point to remaining challenges and future research directions to address them.

8.1 Introduction

An event is a specific incident or situation that can be described as indicating *who did what to whom, when,* and *where*. Understanding events and communicating about them to other people are both fundamental human activities. However, it is typically more challenging to remember event-related information than entity-related information. For example, most people in the United States will know the named entity that is the answer to the question

163

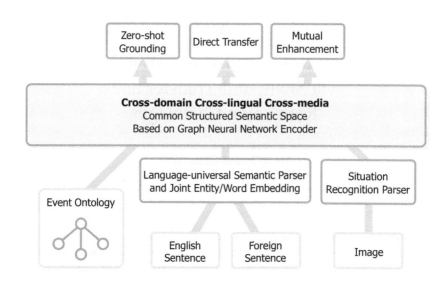

Figure 8.1 Share-and-transfer approach overview.

"Who was the president of United States in 2010?" but very few people would be able to recall all of the event information needed to answer the question "Who died from coronavirus?" Event extraction is the task that outputs essential elements of information about events in support of downstream applications, such as question-answering and timeline-based summaries.

The task of event extraction, as originally defined in natural language processing research, entails first identifying *event triggers* (the words or phrases that most clearly express event occurrences) and their *arguments* (the words or phrases for participants in those events) in unstructured texts and then classifying these phrases, respectively, for their types and roles. Situated at the end of the information extraction (IE) pipeline, event extraction represents the most complex component task. Recognizing the different forms in which an event may be expressed, distinguishing events of different types, and finding the arguments of an event are all challenging aspects of this task. Traditional event extraction techniques have focused on extracting events for only a limited set of predefined types from English text documents. However, users of event extraction systems now want to analyze event information from a much wider variety of sources, across

(1) *multiple domains*, where events may be tracked on different time-scales and expressed at different levels of specificity or abstraction, while providing users nonetheless with additional essential elements of information for reasoning about both old (known) and new scenarios;

(2) *multiple languages*, where certain relations and events of primary interest to a given community are reported predominantly in the low-resource language found in sources available to that community; and

(3) *multiple media*, where the content in visual modalities (such as images, videos) may reveal activities or identities of event participants not explicitly described in another modality (such as text or speech).

The most successful approaches to event extraction, originating in the first wave of IE research, have been based on supervised learning with hand-crafted symbolic features (Grishman et al., 2005; Ahn, 2006; Ji and Grishman, 2008; Liao and Grishman, 2011; Huang and Riloff, 2012; Riedel et al., 2009; Poon and Vanderwende, 2010; Li et al., 2013, 2014; Venugopal et al., 2014; Yang and Mitchell, 2016). More recently, in the second wave of IE, the systems with best results have been those augmented with distributional embedding features (Y. Chen et al., 2015, 2018; Nguyen and Grishman, 2015, 2016, 2018; Nguyen et al., 2016; Hong et al., 2018; Liu et al., 2018).

These approaches, however, incorporate domain-specific and language-specific information into their models and thus are costly to port beyond their original settings; they require substantial amounts of new annotations for retraining to a new domain or a new language. Compared to other tasks within IE pipelines, such as Name Tagging, the annotations needed for retraining models for Relation and Event Extraction are more costly; they require both structured data annotations and a rich label space. Publicly available, gold-standard annotations for event extraction exist for only a few languages and a limited number of event types (e.g., 33 event types defined in ACE[1] for English, Chinese, and Arabic). As a result, event extraction is substantially more challenging when conducted in underresourced settings with little or no annotated data. In this chapter, we examine three such settings: a new domain, a new language, and a new data modality (image in this chapter) respectively.

In the sections to follow, we present an overview of a new event extraction paradigm based on transferable neural network learning techniques that leverage existing, manually constructed schemas and annotations for a small set of seen[2] information concepts (e.g., types). Modeled as a bottom-up discovery problem, the idea is to "share-and-transfer": first, by combining symbolic and distributional embedding representations of the extracted information derived from source training data and encoding these via deep neural networks into one shared continuous semantic space and then by learning the extraction

---

[1] ACE was the Automatic Content Extraction Program (Doddington et al., 2004).
[2] Here *seen* means seen during training.

models over this space from source data and applying the learned extractors to target data. In this way, knowledge of how to extract the event structures with their types and argument roles from a high-resource setting is transferred; i.e., becomes available for recognizing unseen content in a low-resource setting.

8.2 Approach Overview

One of the challenges of traditional machine learning has been that models built for one task or domain typically suffer with degraded performance when later applied to new distinct tasks or domains. The models, though perhaps highly accurate within their training (source) domain or task, nonetheless require rebuilding from scratch when the relevant feature space distribution for new (target) data changes.

The objective of our "share-and-transfer" approach is to address the cross-domain, cross-lingual, and cross-modal challenges of porting the development of an event extractor from its source setting (domain, language, or modality) over which it was trained with plenty of annotated data to a new target setting (domain, language, or modality) for which there is little or no annotated data.

Informally, we describe our approach as leveraging annotated source data from a high-resourced setting, to enable building models for a low-resourced or no-resource target setting. For the share phase, we start by identifying the range of needed source-side data that, once transformed, will serve as the basis for a structured semantic space that will be common to – i.e., be a shared space for – both the source and target representations. We use the ample original source-side data and their transformed representations in the common space to train the event extractors. By virtue of having (i) constructed the shared space so that it would hold both source and target structures and (ii) trained the extractors over that space, we then run the grounding or transfer phase, (iii) applying these extractors to the target data, once transformed, to obtain the events on the target side.

For each of the settings, the key questions pertaining to the construction of such a common semantic space and the transfer, are

1. Which types of source data and other resources are used in constructing the common space?
2. What types of structured semantic information are used in training for grounding or transfer by way of the common space?
3. How is target data processed for event extraction?

In answer to 1, our approach to representation learning for extraction tasks in low-resource settings starts with data sources of structured knowledge that are already or that can be transformed into graph structures and all of which are either available or can be automatically derived by computational tools in high-resource settings from (i) semantic or conceptual networks, such as ontologies; (ii) linguistic representations of text data, such as semantic parse trees; and (iii) recent, novel computational representations of image data, such as situation graphs.

Then these sources, in answer to 2 – as features and graph structures that capture structured semantic information from an ontology or parser output on text or images – are encoded into low-dimensional embeddings by way of techniques based on deep learning and nonlinear dimensionality reduction. We describe the ways in which recent methods for embedding individual nodes and (sub)graphs within these sources are transformed as input to shared convolutional neural networks (CNNs) or graph-based convolutional neural networks (GCNs) for learning transfer functions. The learned functions preserve their semantic information in constructing a common structured semantic space for each type of transfer setting we consider.

In answer to 3, the target data sets (text or image) from the low-resource setting are transformed, by way of embeddings and neural network encoders, into their vector representations situated in the common semantic space.

The next section provides the descriptions of the transformations of text-based multidomain and multilingual source-side data, respectively, in Sections 8.3.1 and 8.3.2. Following these descriptions, the section shifts to detailing the more complex transformations of multimodal data in Section 8.3.3. The transformations for the construction of common semantic spaces in each of these three settings take place in advance of the transfer phase that will be described in Section 8.4.

8.3 Share: Construction of Common Semantic Space

Traditional methods of processing and understanding unstructured texts have mainly relied on symbolic semantics. For example, to extract the "attacker" of a military attack event from a text passage, there needs to be a way to feed the series of symbolic representations for the words and their relations in each sentence into a knowledge network. The sentence might include a verb that indicates the attack event; a noun phrase in subject position for the candidate attacker entity, which may be a person; etc. The symbolic feature engineering to automate the process of determining which words or phrases in each sentence will fill which part or parts of an event structure is costly; it requires substantial linguistic expertise and time.

In recent years, the incorporation of distributional semantic representations in natural language processing tasks has been a notable game changer. The inspiration for distributional semantics comes from an observation made long ago, now referred to as the distributional hypothesis (Harris, 1954): linguistic items with similar distributions have similar meanings. This hypothesis, together with the advent of dense-vector embeddings for encoding words into a common vector space, has been so successful in monolingual tasks that this combination has led to further research to determine how such spaces might also be used for other applications. One such example has been extracting information from unstructured texts in multiple languages by inducing cross-lingual word embeddings for two or more languages in the same vector space. The success of these applications derives from the mathematical relations between embeddings, specifically where constructed vectors for translations and words with similar meanings are geometrically close in the shared cross-lingual vector space. As described in Section 8.3.1, our approach takes this methodology further, generalizing it so that *structured* content of semantic relations within events is preserved in extended embeddings of a shared vector space. That space, when constructed with embeddings for gold-standard relation and event annotations from high-resource languages (e.g., English), then supports the training of extractors that can then subsequently be applied directly to low-resource languages. This shared common semantic space also provides much richer representations for words than monolingual embedding due to the lack of monolingual data in low-resource languages.

Previous applications have focused on flat, sequence-level (word or phrase) representations that are not adequate for event extraction. These have, in effect, neglected the value of linguistic signals that are available in gold standard structured annotations (such as ACE and Entity, Relation, and Event [ERE] data sets) or that could be derived from linguistic analyses (such as syntactic and semantic parsed data sets). In contrast, we develop a novel multilingual, multimedia common semantic representation that incorporates structure-level and sequence-level information. In so doing, we treat the end-to-end event extraction in an IE pipeline as an information network construction problem over unstructured input texts. In the constructed information network, the extracted entity mentions and event triggers are network nodes and the extracted relations and event-argument links are network edges labeled with their relation and argument roles, respectively. An information network can be considered as a special form of semantic network (Simmons, 1963;

Geldenhuys et al., 1999; Do et al., 2017), where each node and edge belongs to one of a set of predefined types. Recent work on multilingual, multimedia common space construction makes use of linear mappings or canonical correlation analysis to transfer features or models across languages or data modalities. Unlike that work, our major innovation is to convert unstructured data into structured representations, as derived from universal semantic parses and enhanced with distributional information, to capture individual entities as well as the relations and events involving those entities, so that we can then share the resulting structured representations across multiple languages and data modalities. The structured representations can compress wide contexts in text and capture semantic relations between image regions for better disambiguation.

8.3.1 Multidomain Common Space Construction

For the first example of building a common space, consider the various linguistic resources available to rapidly move an event extraction system developed from known domains (e.g., *military action*) to new domains (e.g., *rescue*). Our approach is a novel and highly scalable, zero-shot grounding framework that makes use of a common structured space, as illustrated in Figure 8.2, for classifying event types and event arguments.

At training time, the common space is constructed with vector outputs of a shared CNN whose input is embeddings derived from two sets of sentences in the known (i.e, old) domain (here, *Attack*) and from the typed event structures of an event ontology. As a result of training, the CNN, shown spanning the middle of the figure, outputs vectors as derived from processing of ontology elements (e.g., such as *Military Action/Actor*) and semantically analyzed linguistic expressions (parsed fragments). These vectors collectively populate the same common space, shown in the upper left box of the figure. Note that with this method of construction, all event types and argument roles that form the event structures in the ontology are now incorporated in the common space, even though many of these typed structures have not been seen before in the training sentences. It will be the common space representation of these unseen typed structures that will provide for the next phase of our approach, zero-shot grounding (as shown in Figure 8.1), that results in cross-domain transfer, to extract events from sentences in a new, target domain (such as *Rescue*). We now defer until Section 8.4 further discussion of that phase, so that we can introduce two more examples of the share phase where we construct different common structured spaces.

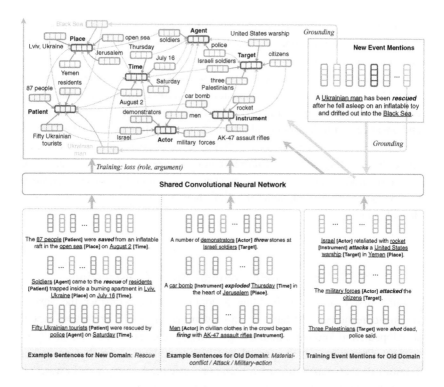

Figure 8.2 Multidomain common space construction and zero-shot transfer learning.

8.3.2 Multilingual Common Space Construction

Our next objective is to extend the common space beyond monolingual data to include representations from multiple languages for subsequent cross-lingual transfer learning of an event extractor from one language to new language. Support for this extension comes from recent research (Lin et al., 2017) that has found relational facts to be typically expressed by identifiable patterns *within* languages and demonstrated that the consistency in patterns observed *across* languages can be used to improve relation extraction. As shown in Figure 8.3, even for sentences in different languages with different meanings that include quite distinct events and entity mentions, we can see that the sentences' parsed structures can share similar language-universal symbolic features, such as common labeled dependency paths and part-of-speech (POS) tags, as well as distributional features from multilingual embeddings that are readily available for many languages. In particular, for these given parsed

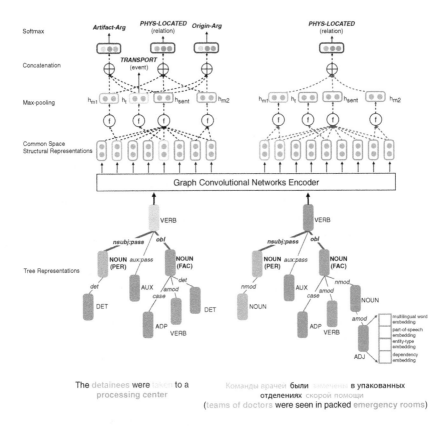

Figure 8.3 Multilingual common semantic space and cross-lingual structure transfer.

sentences with passivized verbs in both languages, the subjects (phrases and nodes colored pink) are both noun arguments of type PER (person) and the oblique objects (phrases and nodes colored blue) are both noun arguments of type FAC (facility).

Our approach to constructing a multilingual structured common space (shown as output layer above bar for encoder that spans the middle of Figure 8.3) consists of three steps: (1) Convert each sentence in any language into a language-universal tree structure based on universal dependency parsing. (2) For each node in the tree structure, create a representation from the concatenation of embeddings corresponding to the node's word, its language-universal POS tag, its dependency role within the sentence parse, and its entity type, so that all sentence nodes, independent of their language, can be encoded for uniform input at the next step (see lower right-hand side of figure for four levels of token-specific embeddings). (3) Adopt GCNs (Kipf and Welling, 2017) to generate contextualized node representations for the common space by leveraging information from each node's neighbors, as derived from the dependency parsing tree.

The graph representation that is obtained from dependency parsing of a sentence with N tokens, in (1), is converted into an $N \times N$ adjacency matrix A, with added self-connections at each node to capture information about the current node itself, in (2). In the matrix, $A_{i,j} = 1$ denotes the presence of a directed edge from node i to node j in the dependency tree. At the kth layer of convolution in the GCN, in (3), the hidden representation is derived from the representations of its neighbors at the $(k - 1)$th layer. The final hidden representation of each node after the kth layer is the encoding of each word $h_i^{(k)}$ in our language-universal common space and incorporates information about its neighbors up to k hops away in the dependency tree.

In contrast to the common space construction from a high-resource domain in a single language (Section 8.3.1), where event structures become available for grounding extractions in a low-resource domain, here the construction of a multilingual common space from high-resource languages makes available structures for training extractors with one or more high-resource languages. The resulting extractors are then applied, in a direct transfer, to a low-resource language.

8.3.3 Multimedia Common Space Construction

We now consider the construction of a third type of common space to bridge the representation of events originating in different resource modalities. By thinking of the content of an image or a video as a foreign language, we further extend our approach to constructing a multimedia structured common space from both text and visual sources.

On the text side, we select Abstract Meaning Representations (AMRs) for their semantic structures that capture whole sentence meanings in rooted, directed, labeled, and (predominantly) acyclic graph structures (Banarescu et al., 2013). AMRs have been developed in conjunction with multilayer linguistic analyses such as PropBank frames, noncore semantic roles, coreference, named entity annotation, modality, and negation and include 150 fine-grained semantic roles.

On the vision side, we work with a representation similar to AMR graphs that can encode the semantic structure of the image. Inspired by research on situation recognition (Yatskar et al., 2016), we represent an image using a context node that stands in for the event, along with one or more entity nodes that stand in for key arguments of the event, forming what we refer to as a *Situation Graph*. In order to identify candidate arguments for events in images, we seek to extract entities to fill argument roles. In computer vision, the task most similar to entity extraction is *object detection*. We apply a multi-layer perception (MLP) approach to detect visual objects of types defined in OpenImages (Kuznetsova et al., 2018). However, state-of-the-art object detection methods only cover a limited set of object types. Many objects in a scene in an image that may be salient to a human viewer, such as *stone* and *stretcher*, are not included in the ontologies developed in the computer vision research community. Moreover, when there are too many object instances to be detected in an image (e.g., a big crowd of protesters), the GCN representation tends to lose focus.

To address these issues, we construct a role-driven attention graph for images, where each argument node is derived based on the attention heatmap for each role. This way, the edges of AMR graphs (from text) and situation graphs (from images) both indicate semantic roles of the entities identified respectively within text and image events. The similarity between these two graph structures of verbal and visual information enables us to exploit structure-level alignment and learn a common embedding space where events, entities, and semantic roles can be represented, independent of the modality they come from.

Figure 8.4 illustrates the steps in the multimedia common space construction. Starting on the left side of the figures, because the image content is relevant to the sentence content and we can see that the protesters and bus appear in both modalities, we want the embedded nodes for these entities that correspond to each other cross-modally to be close to each other in the common space. More specifically, first, the embedding of the event node from the image, denoted by *throwing*, should be close to the embedding of the corresponding event node from the text *attack*. Then, second, the embedding of the visual entity node, denoted by *man*, should be close to the embedding of the text entity node from the text *protesters*. Furthermore, there should be available external relational knowledge that can be input to the common space to ensure that the embedding of the node representing the visual entity *car* is close to that for the text entity *bus*.

Because the visual *throwing* can be a component activity of the event *attack* mentioned in the text, we would also expect their embeddings to be close to each other within the constructed common space. Given this proximity, this image would be assigned to the sentence and the node *attack* from the text would be classified as a *Conflict.Attack* event type. In completing the representation of the event in the common space, the entity nodes *man* from

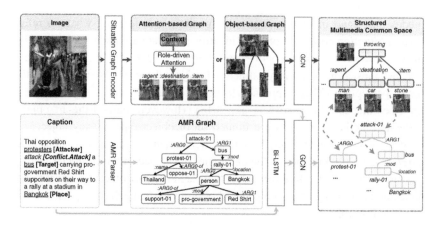

Figure 8.4 Multimedia structured common space construction.

the image and *protesters* from the text would both be classified as *agent* roles of *Attack* event, and the visual and text entity nodes, respectively *car* and *bus*, would both be classified for that event as the *target* role. More interesting, the entity node *Bangkok* from the text that is recognized as a place, even though it does not correspond to any node in the image, would be classified as the *place* role of the *Attack* event. Similarly, the entity node *stone* from the image would be classified as the *instrument* role for the event, even though there is no corresponding text mention of that entity and no other mention fills that role in text.

As shown in Figure 8.4, the cross-media common representation encoder is a two-branch representation network, with each branch encoding one modality. We first construct a graph for each modality independently and apply a GCN to encode the structured information of each graph. We then align them based on the image–caption pairs collected from 17 years of Voice of America news articles.

This approach to constructing a multimedia common space builds on the complementary strengths of modality-specific methods in identifying content that would not otherwise be available to extractors built in the next transfer phase, by way of mutual enhancement. In this way, the textual descriptions of events and arguments that are not typically photographed or not readily visualized can contribute their event structures and roles to the common space and the images of events and objects so typical of their setting that they are not described in text can contribute the entities associated with events of that type to the common space.

8.4 Transfer: From High- to Low-Resource Setting

Once we have constructed the common semantic space for the selected settings and built network models for our high-resource settings, we can apply various transfer learning strategies to new, previously unseen data, depending on the amount of available resources in each of the low-resource settings. The preprocessing methods to parse the input data need to be customized for the target setting. In cross-lingual transfer we choose dependency parsing instead of AMR parsing to convert sentences into graphs because the former is available for 76 languages, whereas the latter is only available for English and Chinese. In contrast, in both cross-domain transfer and cross-media transfer we use AMR for English because it is the richest symbolic semantic representation to date.

Cross-domain Transfer: In the cross-domain setting, we apply zero-shot transfer learning (Frome et al., 2013; Norouzi et al., 2013; Socher et al., 2013), which has been very successful in visual object classification, to text event extraction. The basic idea of zero-shot learning is to make use of separate, preexisting classifiers to build a semantic, cross-concept space that enables the accommodation of new types with no (zero) additional training examples.

We define a similarity metric on the space predicated on these features and map (*ground*) each event argument candidate to the closest argument role in this space. Consider now again Figure 8.2. Among the three roles of the *rescue* event in the new domain, the argument candidate *(Ukrainian man)* is closer to the embedding representation of the correct role, *patient*, than it is to the event's other roles, *agent* or *time*. Any training data available for a new role can use these instances to train the CNN and the metric. The crucial advantage is that we only have to train it once because this metric is *independent of event types and domains*, supporting event role transfer from old domains (e.g., *military action*) to new ones (e.g., *rescue*) with no additional annotation.

Cross-lingual Transfer: For our cross-lingual setting, we adopt a more straightforward *direct transfer* approach. Using the shared multilingual semantic space, we train event argument extractors with high-resource language training data, and then for transfer we apply the resulting extractors to texts of low-resource languages that do not have any relation or event argument annotations.

We adopt GCNs (Kipf and Welling, 2017; Marcheggiani and Titov, 2017) to encode graph structures over the input data, applying graph convolution operations to generate contextualized word vectors as representations in a latent space. In contrast to other encoders such a Tree-LSTM (Tai et al., 2015), GCNs can cover more complete contextual information from dependency parses because for each word it captures all dependency parse tree neighbors of the word, rather than just the child nodes of the word. Using this shared encoder, we treat the event argument role labeling task as mapping from the latent space to event type and argument role, respectively.

Cross-media Transfer: In the cross-media setting, some amount of manual annotations exists for both texts and images. We merge the training data from all data modalities to train the event extractor and argument role labeling component. Using the common representations across modalities as input (described earlier), we train the event classifier and argument role classifier separately.

In the test phase, our method takes a multimedia document with sentences $S = \{s_1, s_2, \dots,\}$ and images $M = \{m_1, m_2, \dots,\}$ as input. We first generate the structured common embedding for each sentence and each image, and then compute their pairwise similarities. We pair each sentence s with its closest image m and aggregate the features of each word of s with the aligned representation from m by weighted averaging. We use the aggregated multimedia features to classify each word into an event type and to classify each text-based entity into a role with multi-modal classifiers. Similarly, for each image m we find the closest sentence s, compute the aggregated multimodal features, and feed them into the shared classifiers to predict visual event and argument roles. Finally, we merge the cross-media events of the same event type if the similarity $\langle s, m \rangle$ is higher than a threshold. Figure 8.5 illustrates the cross-media joint inference procedure.

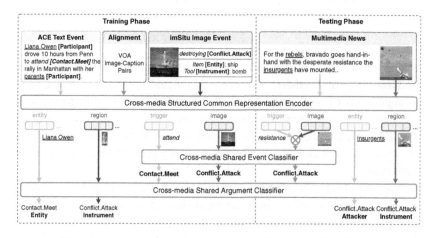

Figure 8.5 Joint inference based on multimedia structured common representations.

8.5 Transfer Learning Performance

In our preliminary English monolingual event extraction experiments, (Huang et al., 2018), without using any annotations in new domains, our zero-shot learning approach achieves performance comparable to that of a state-of-the-art LSTM model, trained on 3,000 fully annotated sentences for the new domains. Extensive experiments on cross-lingual relation and event transfer among English, Chinese, and Arabic demonstrate that our approach achieves performance comparable to that of state-of-the-art supervised models trained on up to 3,000 manually annotated mentions, which cost human annotators about one year to prepare. The event argument role labeling model transferred from English to Chinese achieves performance similar to that of the model trained from Chinese. We thus find that language-universal symbolic and distributional representations are complementary for cross-lingual structure transfer (Subburathinam et al., 2019). Compared to unimodal state-of-the-art methods, our cross-media transfer learning approach achieves 4.0% and 9.8% absolute F-score gains on text event argument role labeling and visual event extraction, respectively. Compared to state-of-the-art multimedia unstructured representations, we achieve 8.3% and 5.0% absolute F-score gains on multimedia event extraction and argument role labeling, respectively. By utilizing images, we extract 21.4% more event mentions than traditional text-only methods.

8.6 Remaining Challenges

As the most exciting and complex task of IE since it was proposed at the Message Understanding Conference (MUC; Grishman and Sundheim, 1996), event extraction remains a major challenge. The goal of this section is to lay out the current status and potential challenges of this task and suggest possible future research directions.

8.6.1 Triggers and Arguments in the Long Tail

One of the remaining challenges in labeling event triggers is the infamous *long tail* problem: many event triggers in the test data rarely appear beforehand in the training data. Most triggers are verbs or nouns, but some adverbs, multiword expressions, and informal metaphors may also function as triggers. Table 8.1 shows some challenging examples. Potential solutions include significantly expanding trigger candidate lists using linguistic resources such

Table 8.1. *Examples of missed rare event triggers and arguments*

Event Type	Event Trigger and Context
Movement.Transport	His men **back** to their compound.
Conflict.Attack	A suicide bomber **detonated** explosives at the entrance to a crowded ...
Movement.Transport	Medical teams **carting** away dozens of wounded victims.
Conflict.Attack	This morning in Michigan, a second straight night and into this morning, hundreds of people have been **rioting** in Benton Harbor.
Election_Person	We've seen in the past in Bosnia for example, you held elections and all of the old ethnic **thugs** get into power because they have organization and they have money and they stop the process of genuine building of democracy.
Sue_Crime	A source tells US Enron is considering suing its own investment bankers for **giving it bad financial advice**.
Employment_End-Position	Today I was **let go** from my job after working there for 4 1/2 years.
Life_Injure	Three boung boys, ages 2, 5 and 10 survived and are in **critical** condition after spending 18 hours in the cold.

as VerbNet (Kipper et al., 2008), and applying joint entity and word embeddings (Pan et al., 2019) for better semantic matching.

8.6.2 Ambiguous Argument-Dependent Trigger Words

A challenge at the other end of the distribution arises with frequent support verbs. They typically have multiple senses and are used to indicate various event types in the training data. As a result, they are often mistakenly extracted as triggers when used as abstract words in other contexts. Table 8.2 shows some error examples. Addressing these errors requires us to incorporate the full range of their semantics with associated arguments and contexts. For example, the support verb "get" may indicate a *Transfer.Ownership* event ("Ellison to spend $10.3 billion to **get** his company") or a *Movement.Transport* event ("Airlines are **getting** flyers to destinations on time more often") as a function of the verb's direct object, what is being gotten (W.-T. Chen et al., 2015).

Table 8.2. *Examples of spurious event triggers*

Incorrect Event Type	Event Trigger and Context
Contact.Correspondence	The memorial will take nine months to build. Victims of the regime have been **calling** for reparations for the suffering and loss caused by the Khmer Rouge, including memorials and mental health centers throughout the country.
Life.Die	I miss him to **death**.
Movement.Transport	Stewart has found the road to fortune wherever she has **traveled**.
Movement.Transport	I want to **take** this opportunity to stand behind the Mimi and proclaim my solidarity.
Movement.Transport	He's **left** a lot on the table.
Employment.End-Position	And it's hard to win back that sort of brand equity that she's **lost**.
Conflict.Attack	Still **hurts** me to read this.
Movement.Transport	We happen to be at a very nice spot by the beach where this is a chance for people to **get** away from CNN coverage, everything, and kind of relax.
Movement.Transport	He bought the machinery, **moved** to a new factory, rehired some of the old workers and started heritage programs.

8.6.3 Syntactic Structures

Deep neural models using lexical embedding features have achieved impressive gains on event extraction. However, most of these models are still sensitive to dependency parsing errors and sometimes are biased by embedding features. For example, consider the following sentence: "This supposition is strongly supported by the fact that on April 25, seven days before the **fire**, the **Ukrainian security service**, the SBU, caught a group of Putinite terrorists led by an operative from Crimea attempting to set fire to an Odessa bank using Molotov cocktails." Here the phrase "Ukrainian security service" is mistakenly identified as the *target* of *Conflict.Attack*, as triggered by "fire," because the phrase and the trigger appear close to each other in the sentence. Similarly, consider another sentence: "The EU foreign ministers **met** hours after U.S. President **George W. Bush** gave Saddam 48 hours to leave Iraq or face invasion." Here our model fails to identify the proper multiclausal syntactic structure of the sentence and so mistakenly identifies "George W. Bush" as the *entity* of the meeting event, rather than as the argument of the subordinating clause.

8.6.4 Localization of Visual Triggers and Arguments

The narrative flow of unstructured text allows event extraction systems to identify trigger and argument boundaries of each event from text. Unfortunately, this is not usually the case for images. It is often unclear which region in an image can be said to correspond to the equivalent of an event trigger indicating the image's event type. For example, for an image that shows two people shaking hands during a meeting, it is not clear whether we should label two hands, two faces, or the meeting table as the trigger. Similarly, not all arguments can be precisely localized. The task of object detection in computer vision research suffers from the limited number of object types. An attention-based method is not able to precisely localize the objects for each argument, because there is no supervision on attention extraction during training. Multiple entity arguments often share similar attentions in the same image. When one argument targets too many instances, attention heatmaps tend to lose focus and cover the whole image.

8.6.5 Reasoning with Cross-Event Knowledge

Most current IE methods based on neural networks are limited to sentence-level understanding because they classify single instances with sequence labeling. Progress in multimedia event extraction has helped automate some parts of event understanding, but current automated event understanding is overly simplistic; it is local, sequential, and flat. Real events are hierarchical and probabilistic. Understanding them requires knowledge in the form of a repository of abstracted event schemas (complex event templates), scenario models, understanding the progress of time, using background knowledge, and performing global inference.

Table 8.3 provides some remaining error examples from current approaches. In our ongoing work, we are developing approaches to inducing an event schema repository that can be used to automatically discover and verify semantic and structural constraints over extracted events. In Li et al. (2011) we encode interdependency among facts as global constraints in an integer linear

Table 8.3. *Error examples that require cross-event knowledge reasoning to address*

The Italian ship was captured by Palestinian terrorists back in 1985 and some may remember the story of Leon Klinghover, he was in a chair and the terrorists shot him and pushed him over the side of the ship into the Mediterranean where he obviously died.

Schema temporal composition: *capture*, *attack*, and *die* events happen on the same boat; they share the same year.

Inferred extraction results: *time* of *die* event = 1985

Turkish Armed Forces have taken over the administration. They will reinstate constitutional order, human rights and freedom.

Event interpretation and prediction: Armed forces are unlikely to enforce human rights and freedom in a generic coup schema, unless one is aware of the history of Turkish coups since the 1960s and the role of the army as the protector of Turkey's democracy. Each time afterward, the military has returned the country to democracy.

Inferred results: *Armed forces* can be predicted to be the *instrument* of *protecting democracy* given background knowledge, deviating from a generic schema.

Then police say the baby's mother pulled out a kitchen knife and on the 911 tape you can hear Williams tape say "go ahead kill me."

Scenario model: In the kitchen environment, *knife* is more likely to be a Die-Instrument argument than in other scenarios.

Fifteen people were killed and more than 30 wounded Wednesday as a suicide bomber blew himself up on a student bus in the northern town of Haifa.

Scenario model: A suicide bomber is both the attacker and the target of an attack event.

---

programming framework to effectively remove extraction errors. Our systems should now further compare extracted event arguments against background knowledge (e. g., entity profiles, event temporal attributes, schemas, and evolving patterns), as extracted from historical data. For example, if we can build a list of instruments employed by policemen when they are the attackers in protest events, our system can reason that, for an instance where a woman protester suffered an eye injury, she was not attacked by a Hong Kong policeman because the instrument used for the attack was a slingshot, not an item on the established list. Similarly, when the system has background knowledge of the size of a particular park, then when protestors demonstrate there, the relevant event schema may establish an upper bound on the number of protesters who may populate that location.

8.7 Conclusions and Future Research Directions

In this chapter we provide an overview of our recent research on open-domain event extraction from multimedia multilingual sources. We introduce a new cross-domain, cross-lingual, and cross-media structure transfer framework to enable event extraction in new target settings without additional event training data. Moreover, we identify several remaining challenges and possible future research directions. When complex events unfold in an emergent and dynamic manner, the multimedia multilingual digital data from traditional news media and social media often convey conflicting information. To understand the many facets of such complex, dynamic situations, we also need to develop cross-media cross-document event coreference resolution methods for information verification and disinformation detection. Event coreference resolution is a very complex and challenging task itself (Araki et al., 2014). The order of the events depends on local (discourse) cues as well as global understanding of the events unfolding. Cross-media consistency detection and reasoning is often a key to disambiguation. Compared to images, disinformation detection from text at the single-asset knowledge element level can be more challenging, especially when the text is written by a generally trustworthy source. For example, CNN published a news article titled "Police use petrol bombs and water cannons against Hong Kong protesters," but an original video revealed that protesters threw bombs at the police. CNN has apologized for its "erroneous" reporting since. Cross-media consistency detection and trustworthy assessment should be added into the research paradigm of events and the results should be used as feedback to enhance event extraction. Finally, once the quality of event extraction reaches a satisfactory level, we can also leverage Knowledge Base–to-text generation techniques (Wang et al., 2018) to describe event-centric knowledge bases and construct event timelines or even history books.

References

Ahn, David. 2006. The Stages of Event Extraction. Pages 1–8 of: *Proceedings of the Workshop on Annotating and Reasoning about Time and Events.* Association for Computational Linguistics.

Araki, Jun, Hovy, Eduard, and Mitamura, Teruko. 2014. Evaluation for Partial Event Coreference. In: *Proceedings of the Second Workshop on EVENTS: Definition, Detection, Coreference, and Representation.* Association for Computational Linguistics.

Banarescu, Laura, Bonial, Claire, Cai, Shu, et al. 2013. Abstract Meaning Representation for Sembanking. Pages 178–186 of: *Proceedings of the 7th Linguistic Annotation Workshop and Interoperability with Discourse*. Association for Computational Linguistics.

Chen, Wei-Te, Bonial, Claire, and Palmer, Martha. 2015. English Light Verb Construction Identification Using Lexical Knowledge. In: *Proceedings of the AAAI-15*. AAAI Press.

Chen, Yubo, Xu, Liheng, Liu, Kang, Zeng, Daojian, and Zhao, Jun. 2015. Event Extraction via Dynamic Multi-pooling Convolutional Neural Networks. In: *Proceedings of the 53rd Annual Meeting of the Association for Computational Linguistics and the 7th International Joint Conference on Natural Language Processing: Volume 1. Long Papers*. Association for Computational Linguistics.

Chen, Yubo, Yang, Hang, Liu, Kang, Zhao, Jun, and Jia, Yantao. 2018. Collective Event Detection via a Hierarchical and Bias Tagging Networks with Gated Multi-level Attention Mechanisms. In: *Proceedings of the 2018 Conference on Empirical Methods in Natural Language Processing*. Association for Computational Linguistics.

Do, Quynh Ngoc Thi, Bethard, Steven, and Moens, Marie-Francine. 2017. Improving Implicit Semantic Role Labeling by Predicting Semantic Frame Arguments. Pages 90–99 of: Kondrak, Greg, and Watanabe, Taro (eds.), *Proceedings of the Eighth International Joint Conference on Natural Language Processing*.

Doddington, George, Mitchell, Alexis, Przybocki, Mark, et al. 2004. The Automatic Content Extraction (ACE) Program – Tasks, Data, and Evaluation. Pages 837–840 of: *Proceedings of the Fourth International Conference on Language Resources and Evaluation (LREC'04)*. Lisbon: European Language Resources Association.

Frome, A., Corrado, G., Shlens, J., Bengio, S., Dean, J., and Mikolov, T. 2013. DeViSE: A Deep Visual–Semantic Embedding Model. Pages 2121–2129 of: Burges, C. J. C., Bottou, L., Welling, M., Ghahramani, Z., and K. Q. Weinberger (eds.), *NIPS'13: Proceedings of the 26th International Conference on Neural Information Processing Systems*. Vol. 2.

Geldenhuys, Aletta E., Rooyen, van Hendrik O., and Stetter, Franz. 1999. Some Approaches to Knowledge Representation. In: *Knowledge Representation and Relation Nets*. The Kluwer International Series in Engineering and Computer Science, Vol. 506. Boston: Springer.

Grishman, R., and Sundheim, B. 1996. Message Understanding Conference-6: A Brief History. Pages 466–471 of: *COLING '96: Proceedings of the 16th conference on Computational Linguistics*. Vol. 1.

Grishman, Ralph, Westbrook, David, and Meyers, Adam. 2005. NYU's English ACE 2005 System Description. In: *Proceedings of Automatic Content Extraction 2005 (ACE) Evaluation Workshop*, Gaithersburg, MD: NIST.

Harris, Zellig S. 1954. Distributional Structure. *Word*, **10**(23), 146–162.

Hong, Yu, Zhou, Wenxuan, Zhang Jingli, Jingli, Zhou, Guodong, and Zhu, Qiaoming. 2018. Self-regulation: Employing a Generative Adversarial Network to Improve Event Detection. Pages 515–526 of: Gurevych, Iryna, and Miyao, Yusuke (eds.), *Proceedings of the 56th Annual Meeting of the Association for Computational Linguistics: Volume 1. Long Papers*. Association for Computational Linguistics.

Huang, Lifu, Ji, Heng, Cho, Kyunghyun, et al. 2018. Zero-Shot Transfer Learning for Event Extraction. Pages 2160–2170 of: Gurevych, Iryna and Miyao, Yusuke (eds.), *Proceedings of the 56th Annual Meeting of the Association for Computational Linguistics: Volume 1. Long Papers.*

Huang, Ruihong, and Riloff, Ellen. 2012. Bootstrapped Training of Event Extraction Classifiers. Pages 286-295 of: Daelemans, Walter (ed.), *Proceedings of the 13th Conference of the European Chapter of the Association for Computational Linguistics.* Association for Computational Linguistics.

Ji, Heng, and Grishman, Ralph. 2008. Refining Event Extraction through Cross-document Inference. Pages 254–262 of: Moore, Johanna D., Teufel, Simone, Allan, James, and Furui, Sadaoki (eds.), *Proceedings of ACL-08: HLT.*

Kipf, Thomas N., and Welling, Max. 2017. Semi-supervised Classification with Graph Convolutional Networks. In: *5th International Conference on Learning Representations, ICLR 2017.*

Kipper, Karin, Korhonen, Anna, Ryant, Neville, and Palmer, Martha. 2008. A Large-Scale Classification of English Verbs. *Language Resources and Evaluation Journal,* **42**(1), 21–40.

Kuznetsova, Alina, Rom, Hassan, Alldrin, Neil, et al. 2018. The Open Images Dataset v4: Unified Image Classification, Object Detection, and Visual Relationship Detection at Scale. *arXiv preprint arXiv:1811.00982.*

Li, Qi, Anzaroot, Sam, Lin, Wen-Pin, Li, Xiang, and Ji, Heng. 2011. Joint Inference for Cross-document Information Extraction. Pages 2225–2228 of: Macdonald, Craig, Ounis, Iadh, and Ruthven, Ian (eds.), *Proceedings of the 20th ACM Conference on Information and Knowledge Management.* ACM.

Li, Qi, Ji, Heng, and Huang, Liang. 2013. Joint Event Extraction via Structured Prediction with Global Features. Pages 73–82 of: Schuetze, Hinrich, Fung, Pascale, Poesio, Massimo (eds.), *Proceedings of the 51st Annual Meeting of the Association for Computational Linguistics: Volume 1: Long Papers.* Association for Computational Linguistics.

Li, Qi, Ji, Heng, Yu, Hong, and Li, Sujian. 2014. Constructing Information Networks Using One Single Model. Pages 1846–1851 of: Mischitti, Alessandro, Pang, Bo, and Daelemans, Walter (eds.), *Proceedings of the 2014 Conference on Empirical Methods in Natural Language Processing (EMNLP).* Association for Computational Linguistics.

Liao, Shasha, and Grishman, Ralph. 2011. Acquiring Topic Features to Improve Event Extraction: In Pre-selected and Balanced Collections. Pages 9–16 of: Mitkov, Ruslan, and Angelova, Galia (eds.), *Proceedings of the International Conference Recent Advances in Natural Language Processing 2011.* Association for Computational Linguistics.

Lin, Yankai, Liu, Zhiyuan, and Sun, Maosong. 2017. Neural Relation Extraction with Multi-lingual Attention. Pages 34–43 of: Barzilay, Regina, and Kan, Min-Yen (eds.), *Proceedings of the 55th Annual Meeting of the Association for Computational Linguistics: Volume 1. Long Papers.* Association for Computational Linguistics.

Liu, Xiao, Luo, Zhunchen, and Huang, Heyan. 2018. Jointly Multiple Events Extraction via Attention-Based Graph Information Aggregation. Pages 1247–1256 of: Riloff,

Ellen, Chiang, David, Hockenmaier, Julia, and Tsujii, Jun'ichi (eds.), *Proceedings of EMNLP 2018*. Association for Computational Linguistics.

Marcheggiani, Diego, and Titov, Ivan. 2017. Encoding Sentences with Graph Convolutional Networks for Semantic Role Labeling. Pages 1506–1515 of: Palmer, Martha, Hwa, Rebecca, and Riedel, Sebastian (eds.), *Proceedings of the 2017 Conference on Empirical Methods in Natural Language Processing*. Association for Computational Linguistics.

Nguyen, Thien Huu, Cho, Kyunghyun, and Grishman, Ralph. 2016. Joint Event Extraction via Recurrent Neural Networks. Pages 300–309 of: Knight, Kevin, Nenkova, Ani, and Rambow, Owen (eds.), *Proceedings of the 2016 Conference of the North American Chapter of the Association for Computational Linguistics: Human Language Technologies*. Association for Computational Linguistics.

Nguyen, Thien Huu, and Grishman, Ralph. 2015. Event Detection and Domain Adaptation with Convolutional Neural Networks. Pages 365–371 of: Zong, Chengqing, and Strube, Michael (eds.), *Proceedings of the 53rd Annual Meeting of the Association for Computational Linguistics and the 7th International Joint Conference on Natural Language Processing: Volume 2. Short Papers*. Association for Computational Linguistics.

Nguyen, Thien Huu, and Grishman, Ralph. 2016. Modeling Skip-grams for Event Detection with Convolutional Neural Networks. Pages 886–891 of: Su, Jian, Duh, Kevin, and Carreras, Xavier (eds.), *Proceedings of the 2016 Conference on Empirical Methods in Natural Language Processing*. Association for Computational Linguistics.

Nguyen, Thien Huu, and Grishman, Ralph. 2018. Graph Convolutional Networks with Argument-Aware Pooling for Event Detection. Pages 5900–5907 of: McIlraith, Sheila A., and Weinberger, Kilian Q. (eds.), *Proceedings of the Thirty-Second AAAI Conference on Artificial Intelligence (AAAI-18)*. AAAI Press.

Norouzi, M., Mikolov, T., Bengio, S., et al. 2013. Zero-Shot learning by Convex Combination of Semantic Embeddings. *arXiv preprint arXiv:1312.5650*.

Pan, Xiaoman, Gowda, Thamme, Ji, Heng, May, Jonathan, and Miller, Scott. 2019. Cross-lingual Joint Entity and Word Embedding to Improve Entity Linking and Parallel Sentence Mining. Pages 56–66 of: Cherry, Colin, Durrett, Greg, Foster, George (eds.), *Proceedings of the 2nd Workshop on Deep Learning Approaches for Low-Resource NLP (DeepLo 2019)*. Association for Computational Linguistics.

Poon, Hoifung, and Vanderwende, Lucy. 2010. Joint Inference for Knowledge Extraction from Biomedical Literature. Pages 813–821 of: Kaplan, Ron, Burstein, Jill, Harper, Mary, and Penn, Gerald (eds.), *Human Language Technologies: The 2010 Annual Conference of the North American Chapter of the Association for Computational Linguistics*. Association for Computational Linguistics.

Riedel, Sebastian, Chun, Hong-Woo, Takagi, Toshihisa, and Tsujii, Jun'ichi. 2009. A Markov Logic Approach to Bio-molecular Event Extraction. Pages 41–49 of: *BioNLP '09: Proceedings of the Workshop on Current Trends in Biomedical Natural Language Processing: Shared Task*.

Simmons, Robert F. 1963. Synthetic Language Behavior. *Data Processing Management*, **5**(12), 11–18.

Socher, R., Ganjoo, M., Manning, C., and Ng, A. 2013. Zero-Shot Learning through Cross-modal Transfer. Pages 935–943 of: Burges, C. J. C., Bottou, L., Welling, M., Chahramani, Z, and Weinberger, K. Q. (eds.), *NIPS'13: Proceedings of the 26th International Conference on Neural Information Processing Systems*. Vol. 1. Red Hook, NY: Curran Associates.

Subburathinam, Ananya, Lu, Di, Ji, Heng, et al. 2019. Cross-lingual Structure Transfer for Relation and Event Extraction. Pages 313–325 of: Inui, Kentaro, Jiang, Jing, Ng, Vincent, and Wan, Xiaojun (eds.), *Proceedings of the 2019 Conference on Empirical Methods in Natural Language Processing and 9th International Joint Conference on Natural Language Processing (EMNLP-IJCNLP2019)*. Association for Computational Linguistics.

Tai, Kai Sheng, Socher, Richard, and Manning, Christopher D. 2015. Improved Semantic Representations from Tree-Structured Long Short-term Memory Networks. *arXiv preprint arXiv:1503.00075*.

Venugopal, Deepak, Chen, Chen, Gogate, Vibhav, and Ng, Vincent. 2014. Relieving the Computational Bottleneck: Joint Inference for Event Extraction with High-Dimensional Features. Pages 831–843 of: Moschitti, Alessandro, Pang, Bo, and Daelemans, Walter (eds.), *Proceedings of the 2014 Conference on Empirical Methods in Natural Language Processing (EMNLP)*. Association for Computational Linguistics.

Wang, Qingyun, Pan, Xiaoman, Huang, Lifu, et al. 2018. Describing a Knowledge Base. Pages 10–21 of: Krahmer, Emiel, Gatt, Albert, and Goudbeek, Martijn (eds.), *Proceedings of the 11th International Conference on Natural Language Generation*. Association for Computational Linguistics.

Yang, Bishan, and Mitchell, Tom. 2016. Joint Extraction of Events and Entities within a Document Context. Pages 289–299 of: Knight, Kevin, Nenkova, Ani, and Rambow, Owen (eds.), *Proceedings of the 2016 Conference of the North American Chapter of the ACL: Human Language Technologies*. Association for Computational Linguistics.

Yatskar, Mark, Zettlemoyer, Luke, and Farhadi, Ali. 2016. Situation Recognition: Visual Semantic Role Labeling for Image Understanding. Pages 5534–5542 of: *Proceedings of the IEEE Conference on Computer Vision and Pattern Recognition*.

9

Reading Certainty across Sources

Benjamin Miller

Abstract. Witness testimony provides the first draft of history and requires a kind of reading connecting descriptions of events from many perspectives and sources. This chapter examines one critical step in that connective process, namely, how to assess a speaker's certainty about the events they describe. By surveying a group of approximately 300 readers and their approximately 28,000 decisions about speaker certainty, this chapter explores how readers may think about factual and counterfactual statements and how they interpret the certainty with which a witness makes their statements. Ultimately, this chapter argues that readers of collections of witness testimony were more likely to agree about event descriptions when those providing the description were certain and that readers' abilities to accept gradations of certainty were better when a witness described factual, rather than counterfactual or negated events. These findings lead to a suggestion for how researchers in natural language processing could better model the question of speaker certainty, at least when dealing with the kind of narrative nonfiction one finds in witness testimony.

9.1 Introduction

Understanding and researching the impact of human rights violations, environmental disasters, and other types of collective trauma rely on reading large collections of witness statements and connecting the stories therein. These stories and the events they describe are evocative because of both the individual events they relate and their potential connections as they enrich, substantiate, or contradict the stories of others. Reading across witness statements and other sources is an essential task, one that requires making many small judgments about features like the relevance and reliability of sources (Martin, 2017).

Though that kind of connective reading could be supported by computational approaches, these types of sources, namely, witness statements, present a few challenges. First, they often indicate space, time, and entities indirectly more so than absolutely. Additionally, they do so with a fragmented syntactic structure and highly referential semantics. These features make them resistant to techniques reliant on named entity or temporal recognition. For example, often, such as in testimonies provided by first responders to the World Trade Center attacks of September 11, 2001, a witness either does not know where or when something specifically happened or they do not have the language with which to talk about it. In "World Trade Center Task Force Interview No. 9110335," an EMT says, "That's when we noticed a whole bunch of police cars responding somewhere" ("The September 11 Records", 2005). "We immediately jumped back into the vehicle," the same EMT says, "back into my car, and we get to the station"; at no point in that interview does the EMT indicate the specific name of the station she means. Although she relates the event with *certainty*, a critical term for this study, the geography of the event is poorly specified.

However difficult these stories are to read, these same witness testimonies from traumatic events such as environmental disasters, industrial accidents, social injustice, and attacks of terror provide the material with which the first draft of history is written. In the aftermath of these events, statements from witnesses often provide the public with their first glimpse into what happened. At later stages of individual and collective processing of traumatic events, long after the events they describe are concluded, these statements can serve to anchor collective understanding. By anchoring collective understanding, they work to limit people's ability to dissimulate and misuse events for political or personal gain, while providing emblematic voices that help communities process and survive these assaults.

Speaker certainty is one critical predicate for understanding the events that comprise these stories. Certainty, also known as veridicality, is the extent to which the speaker is certain about the statement they put forward. Many questions about the computational reading of event language is conditioned on whether or not it might be something an algorithm can be trained to identify, in addition to whether that perspective is meaningful relative to understanding the witness, their statement, and the event to which they offer testimony. A second critical predicate in relation to this material's role as an anchor of collective memory is the speaker's statement's facticity, or whether an event is being described or negated. Combined, these two measures provide a first step in ascertaining whether the description of an event in one witness testimony can be legitimately connected to an event description from another testimony. It can also provide a sense for how witnesses narrate and think about the events they observed or survived. Scholars of trauma and witnessing such as

Caruth (2016) and Herman (2015) describe how the linguistic features of a witness's testimony, such as the degree of specificity of their references and their degree of certainty, indicates aspects of their cognitive and mental state. In combination with observations of how readers interpret these stories of events, this sense can help us understand how readers approach this kind of difficult historical material.

To explore this idea, a large study was conducted that posed two related questions. First, how are certainty and uncertainty indicated in the language of witness statements? Second, how do readers interpret those statements? This study builds on the work in the area of using natural language processing (NLP) to quantify a speaker's certainty about their statements (Hyland, 2005; Saurí and Pustejovsky, 2009; De Marneffe et al., 2012; Wan and Zhang, 2014; Lee et al., 2015; Stanovsky et al., 2017). Prior work specifically on witness testimony is limited, with examples focusing on emotions (Truong et al., 2014), information extraction (Divitaa et al., 2018), collocations (Nugumanova and Bessmertny, 2013), cross-document coreference (Miller et al., 2013), narrative segmentation (Miller et al., 2015), domain-specific problems (Gibbons, 2014), social media (Soni et al., 2014), and news (Wan and Zhang, 2014), but, to my knowledge, none on the messier domain of witness statements and veridicality. These studies undertook a variety of approaches.

Some, like Soni et al. (2014) and Hahn and Engelmann (2014), pursued rule-based approaches that focused on quantifying usage of hedges, modals, and modifiers. What is valuable about these two studies is their focus on linguistic markers of certainty and uncertainty and their shared argument that interpretive discrepancies may emerge from "the interpretative hardness of the linguistic items in question" (Hahn and Engelmann, 2014). Others, like Wan and Zhang (2014), began with the annotated corpus from Saurí and Pustejovsky (2009) but then proceeded to build a classifier relying on their own enriched annotated data developed with a simplified five-point schema ranging from *Very Certain* to *Very Uncertain*. Though their distribution of scores is interesting, with only 1.3% of their 1,000 examples falling into the *Very Uncertain* category, they only used two raters per item, and their schema may oversimplify a critical aspect of veridicality. Namely, it ignores whether the event being described is being posited, and so took place, or negated, and so did not take place. As I will argue below, that difference seems to have an impact on the degree of certainty a speaker communicates. Along with the first finding of this chapter, a proposal for a new schema for the annotation of veridicality, that recognition of a kind of interpretive difference when considering posited versus negated events forms the second key finding of this chapter.

An additional challenge to those looking to adopt a computational approach to reading across witness statements is that they are often in nonstandard English or a mixture of languages. This polyphony makes them resistant to syntactical and semantic approaches, such as one reliant on quantifying uses of hedges, such as *maybe*, and modals, such as *could be*. In one testimony to the South African Truth and Reconciliation Commission, the witness says about her unlawful detainment, "When I was about to – to give a response to one of the questions, the other one said I am *spoggerig* – they kept on interrogating me for hours on end" (SABC, 1996). And, because they are often stories of traumatic, or at least challenging, events, their grammatical and narrative composition can reflect the psychologically difficult moments of their creation.

Scale presents an additional challenge. Collections such as the one resulting from the South African Truth and Reconciliation Commission contain thousands of testimonies, the above-referenced World Trade Center Task Force interviews are comprised of approximately 17,000 question and answer pairs, and government repositories like the Guatemalan National Police Historical Archive contain many millions of witness statements. Combined, these various challenges make the understanding of event language in real-world documents a meaningful but difficult research domain in computational linguistics. Nevertheless, the scale of these collections and the very close reading required to read across documents necessitate a computational approach. The effort put forward by various truth and reconciliation processes indicates that these materials serve vitally important functions for people and communities.

To assess the viability of current approaches to veridicality and facticity in the domain of witness testimony, I undertook a multistep process of (1) corpus building that drew on many different collections of real witness statements, (2) event detection and annotation, (3) cloud labor-based veridicality annotation, (4) preliminary categorization and interpretation by simple interrater reliability, (5) a more robust categorization by k-means clustering of mean ratings per item, and, finally, (6) a comparative interpretation of the results.

As a result of this research on 27,800 ratings of 2,490 witness descriptions of events, I propose two findings: first, a revision of an existing classification schema for veridicality and, second, a conceptual finding about how readers process descriptions of events differently when the events are about facts or negations of facts.[1]

---

[1] Project data are available at https://github.com/bjmiller16/witness-veridicality

Table 9.1. *Veridicality categories*

Positive or nonnegated

1	Certain+	According to the speaker, it is certainly the case that
2	Probable+	According to the speaker, it is possibly the case that
3	Possible+	According to the speaker, it is possibly the case that

Negative or negated

4	Certain–	According to the speaker, it is certainly not the case that
5	Probable–	According to the speaker, it is probably not the case that
6	Possible–	According to the speaker, it is possibly not the case that

Underspecified

7	Certain but underspecified	The speaker knows but does not fully communicate whether or not it is the case that
8	Uncertain	The speaker does not know or does not commit to whether or not it is the case that

Error

9	Error	There is something wrong with the sentence

The first finding is that the nine-element annotation schema put forward by Saurí and Pustejovsky (2009, 2012) does not describe this evidence. That schema, based on the work of Horn (1989), offers two types of polarity: facts and counterfacts. Each polarity has three degrees of certainty. Additionally, there are two more categories for partially or fully underspecified statements. The schema is further described in Table 9.1. Though theoretically sound, it presents a perspective on speaker certainty implying that statements, witnesses, and readers possess equal and opposite gradations for factual and counterfactual statements. Based on the evidence of the annotated witness statements, I argue that witnesses, and their annotators, have a greater sensitivity to gradations of certainty of facts, or positive evidence, than they do to certainty of counterfacts, or negative evidence. The second finding is that annotators, and the statements they read, are more sure of their ratings of facts than they are of uncertain statements or of counterfacts.

These observations suggest that an unbalanced categorization of veridicality and broader categories for more uncertain and counterfactual events would be more reflective of how events are presented by witnesses to traumatic events.

These findings suggest that NLP and computational social sciences should process assessments of veridicality with more allowances for counterfactual or uncertain statements and more gradations of certainty and positive evidence. To that end, I propose a modification to Saurí and Pustejovsky's schema. This new nine-element classification schema does away with one gradation of certainty for counterfacts, adds one additional gradation of certainty for facts, and revises the underspecified categories as certain unknowns and uncertain unknowns. This new schema better reflects the evidence from this study and potentially better describes how readers process information about events in witness testimony.

9.2 Background

The problem addressed here involves the linguistic concept of event certainty or veridicality. This concept arises from the observation that besides communicating propositional information, such as who did what to whom, language users routinely communicate other information about their propositions such as their attitudes toward the propositional information (Hyland, 2005). In particular, though every description of an event contains some combination of propositional information, specifying actors, acts, time, and location, language users make use of various linguistic mechanisms that allow them to commit more or less strongly to the information they present in their utterances.

For example, Hyland (2005) distinguishes between hedges and boosters. Speakers and writers use hedges to communicate that they are not fully certain about a proposition. Hedges are commonly communicated through features like modal verbs (e.g., *might* and *may*) or adverbs (e.g., *perhaps* and *possibly*). In contrast, boosters allow the speaker to more fully commit to being certain about a proposition. Commonly, boosters are adverbs such as "definitely." These examples, however, are far from exhaustive. Prior research (Saurí and Pustejovsky, 2009; De Marneffe et al., 2012) suggests that a large inventory of linguistic features is necessary to even begin approaching a comprehensive description of how language users communicate veridicality. Stanovsky et al. (2017) go further to suggest that this type of dictionary approach is of limited generalizability and a phraseological approach would be of more value.

More specifically for the purpose of making quantitative generalizations about the contents of corpora, veridicality presents an issue for projects attempting to use NLP, a common research tool in the computational social sciences. For example, our own research attempts to derive summative analyses of human rights violation events by automatically processing the testimony of many eyewitnesses stored in digitized corpora. One potential threat to the validity of these analyses is that tools for named event recognition identify potentially relevant elements in discourse without regard for whether the speaker is positing a fact or counterfact about an event. Thus, such tools may not make any distinction between the events represented by the verb "kill" in Examples 9.1 and 9.2, even though for work on witness statements the two need to be distinguished.

He definitely did kill that person.   (9.1)

He definitely did **not** *kill that person.*   (9.2)

Annotation of the corpora would need to indicate that 9.1 is a report of a human rights violation event, whereas 9.2 is not. Automatically distinguishing between these two requires an NLP tool that is able to make judgments about facticity. Past research has already been undertaken on the general form of this problem by Saurí and Pustejovsky (2009), De Marneffe et al. (2012), and Stanovsky et al. (2017), but the text types used in the first two were constrained to newspaper articles, a well-structured, standardized genre. The third looked to develop a more generalizable method for assessing factuality by moving away from a balanced eight-category approach for assessing factuality to a single numeric value. Unfortunately, that singular value, though easier to calculate, conflates the multidimensionality presented by the problem of veridicality; namely, that it is a measure of both certainty and facticity. These data, transcribed oral interviews, differ greatly in composition from newspaper articles and serve to highlight a potential shortcoming in the initial nine-category schemas used by these projects, namely, that schema are symmetrical, offering the same kinds of choices for readers about statements describing events and statements describing the negation of an event. Though elegant, it is possible that a reader does not have the same ability to discriminate about concrete statements as they do about more ambiguous ones or about statements of facts versus statements about counterfacts. Therefore, to help better understand how people think about speaker certainty in writing about events, this work extends and refines prior research by testing already established computational approaches in a new context in ways that highlight the shortcomings of prior schemas.

9.3 Methods

Following the example of Saurí and Pustejovsky (2009) and De Marneffe et al. (2012), a questionnaire was created to gather judgments of veridicality from Amazon Mechanical Turk users. mTurk is a cloud-labor platform that connects workers with information processing tasks. For this task, first, sentences were extracted from different corpora of interviews from different contexts: the South African Truth and Reconciliation Commission, the Cambodian Khmer Rouge Tribunal, interviews with survivors of the Holocaust, statements from survivors of the Rwandan genocide, and interviews with survivors of ethnic cleansing in the former Yugoslavia. One goal of this study was to use real-world data, rather than simulated data. Though it can be argued that simulated data would allow for a stronger statement to be made about the quantitative findings and sources of variation, it would not reflect how witnesses use language or how readers grapple with the complex problem of understanding witness testimony.

Readers' attention was focused on the events described by each statement. Using EVITA (Saurí et al., 2005), events in each sentence were tagged. The author chose to use EVITA, as opposed to a more contemporary event tagger, because the tool was sufficient for generating candidate event sentences. Only sentences containing *OCCURRENCE* or *STATE* event tags were retained as candidates for the questionnaire. An *OCCURRENCE* tag implied that the event was a specific action that took place over a defined period of time. A *STATE* event describes an ongoing condition, rather than an action. A random sample of sentences containing about 800 events was taken from each of the five corpora, leading to a total of approximately 4,000 events.

Second, sentences were preprocessed so that each event in a multi-event sentence was identified and a different iteration of the sentence was created to highlight (through bolding) the individual event. In this manner, a sentence that contained two events like Example 9.3 would be rendered as two items in our questionnaire: Examples 9.4 and 9.5.

> *He ran up the street and jumped on the train.* (9.3)

> *He **ran** up the street and jumped on the train.* (9.4)

> *He ran up the street and **jumped** on the train.* (9.5)

As previously stated, a total of 2,490 items similar to Examples 9.4 and 9.5 were contained in our overall bank of items for our questionnaires.

Third, a series of different versions of the questionnaire were created that first trained mTurk users in how to make judgments about certainty in the sentences and then asked them to place items like Examples 9.4 and 9.5 above in one of nine categories presented in Table 9.1. A total of 227 unique raters participated in the study, providing a total of 27,800 individual event ratings. On average, each rater accounted for 0.44% of the total by providing 122.5 ratings with a standard deviation of 193.3. Each rater was provided with a slate of 55 survey items to categorize, of which 5 were training and norming items, 49 were unknown items to rate, and 1 was a known answer question instructing raters to select a particular option. Informal estimates suggested that a rater fluent in English could comfortably complete 5 items per minute. In all, 556 surveys were completed, of which 56 were rejected for failing to correctly answer the known question item. For each accepted set of ratings, raters were paid six dollars (in 2014). Each survey was limited to 10 accepted assignments, and raters could not work on the same survey twice. For each survey, raters were provided with a description of the task, a consent form, brief descriptions of each of the categories identical to those provided in 9.1, and instructions to rate how certain each speaker is about the key event bolded in each sentence item.

Once the rating results were returned, cleaned, and concatenated with their sentences, the categories were replaced with numeric values. Drawing on the work of Stanovsky et al. (2017) and Saurí and Pustejovsky (2012), values divisible by three were selected for the x-dimension of fact-to-counterfact, or facticity, and the y-dimension of certainty. A *certain+* rating received a value of (30; 30), reflecting maximal facticity and maximal certainty. A *certain–* rating received a value of (−30; 30). Examples of *uncertain* received a rating of (0; −30). Item means were calculated based on these values and the resulting data clustered using these two means. The number of clusters was increased until the graph of clustered to unclustered items revealed an "elbow" shape (Kodinariya and Makwana, 2013). One of the oldest methods for determining the correct number of clusters, k, the elbow method relates the potential number of clusters to sum of squares distances from the data points to the cluster centers. As one increases the number of possible clusters, the sum of squares decreases toward zero. Often there is a value of k at which the value of the sum of squares slows its rate of decrease. That change shows up as an "elbow" in the graph. This visual cue indicates that increasing the number of clusters beyond a certain number barely improves the clusters' description of the data.

9.4 Results

Table 9.2 shows the results of using a simple standard of majority agreement for interrater reliability where 6 out of 10 raters selected the same rating

Table 9.2. *Simple majority interrater reliability agreement results*

Certain+	1083
Probable+	370
Possible+	21
Certain−	18
Probable−	5
Possible−	0
Certain but underspecified	0
Uncertain	0
Error	0

Table 9.3. *K-means clustering results*

Cluster	Within SS	Variance	SD	Nomenclature	Certainty	Counter/ Fact	No. of Items
6	4,596.2	71.8	8.5	Certain Fact	27.6	26.6	483
3	7,625.9	119.2	10.9	Probable Fact	22.9	20.2	581
5	5,062.1	79.1	8.9	Likely Fact	16.6	15.6	451
7	4,798.2	75.0	8.7	Possible Fact	10.9	10.0	336
8	3,843.4	60.1	7.7	Certain Unknown	21.9	5.1	117
2	4,106.8	64.2	8.0	NA/Other	2.6	4.6	173
1	3,846.9	60.1	7.8	Uncertain Unknown	−9.7	−0.9	64
9	5,068.0	79.2	8.9	Possible Counterfact	9.5	−7.9	113
4	8,555.1	133.7	11.6	Certain Counterfact	23.4	−16.5	172

category from the eight-bin classification schema. In this schema, "+" denotes a positing of an event as fact and "−" denotes a negation of an event as a counterfact. Using this majority threshold, only 60.1% of results, or 1,497 out of 2,490 items, were categorized. Of those, 72.3% were in the same category, *Certain+*, and 98.5% were in the three categories of fact, *Certain*, *Probable*, or *Possible*. Additionally, of the counterfact or uncertain categories, only *Certain−* and *Probable−* contained any items at all.

Instead of discarding items that prompted disagreement among raters, I propose incorporating those results in the model using the central tendencies of each rated item. Figure 9.1 presents a visualization of the results from Table 9.3 that were based on taking the average and standard deviation of the valid ratings for each item. It yields a different, more complete picture than Table 9.2. Of principal interest is that the items are more evenly distributed

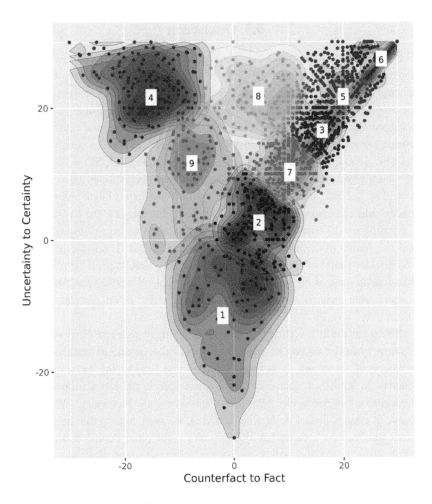

Figure 9.1 Clusters of veridicality.

across the categories and that items that prompted disagreement among raters can still be categorized. Most critical, these aggregate ratings show that in order to describe a reader's perception of veridicality, an additional category of certainty is required for facts and one fewer for counterfacts; that both counterfactual and uncertain categories are well populated with items; and that cluster variance is not directly associated to the number of items per cluster. The fitness of the clustering model as a ratio of the Between sum of squares (SS) /Within SS values is 91.9%.

9.5 Discussion

The simple explanation that the relatively lower number of observations of uncertain or counterfactual statements resulted in a less refined categorization schema is arguable, except for four points. First, the variance within each of the proposed categories does not correlate with the number of observations per category. Rather, the highest variation occurs within the second most certain category, *Probable Fact* (SD = 10.9), and the lowest variation occurs within the *Certain* and *Uncertain Unknown* categories (SD = 7.7, SD = 7.8), each of which possess among the smallest number of observations (n = 64 and n = 117). Second, it ignores the higher cognitive demands negations place on readers and evaluators (Marsh, 1986), demands that increase the likelihood of generating results with higher dispersion. Third, the language of the witnesses and the literature on modality such as Hacquard (2011) indicate that there is a broader range of articulations for uncertainty than there is for certainty. And fourth, there is no apparent reason why speakers would have a balanced observational scale of either fact versus counterfact or of certainty versus uncertainty.

Based on these assertions, I find it more likely that the observation of asymmetry in the coding of witnesses' veridicality is due to features of the language of testimony. It is these features that lead to the categorizations featured in Table 9.4. Consider the first example in the table, a quote from the testimony of Alexander Ehrmann, a survivor of the Holocaust. "We didn't know, of course, at that point what it meant, we were hoping that he is being sent to uh, maybe a camp for elderly peo … for older people and uh, he's going to be treated according to his age" (Ehrmann and Bolkosky, 1983). Readers' evaluations of the the certainty with which the witness spoke are arrayed to the right of the sentences, indicating the number of ratings per category. This statement, in terms of its syntactic and semantic style, is typical of witness testimony. It indicates the complex stances adopted by witnesses and demonstrates some of the challenges this material presents to readers and computational approaches for the assessment of veridicality. Ehrmann speaks both of himself and of a collective "we." He hedges, self-corrects, and speaks of beliefs while communicating the underlying conflict of an evolving, difficult, contemporary understanding and a collective past hope. Readers responded to this complexity – this challenge – by evaluating the sentence as belonging to any of six different veridicality categories. The approach taken by this study suggests that the collective understanding of this sentence best describes it as communicating an *Uncertain Unknown*.

Table 9.4. *Recategorized "lost" sentences*

Sentence ID	Sentence	Cluster No.	Cluster Name	Certain−	Certain+	Possible−	Possible+	Certain but underspecified	Probable−	Probable+	Uncertain	NA/Error
704	We didn't know, of course, at that point what it meant, we were hoping that he is being sent to uh, maybe a camp for elderly peo…for older people and uh, he's going to be treated according to his age.	1	Uncertain Unknown	1	1	1	4			2	1	
2306	The medics who drew the blood, there were the two, as far as I know clearly.	5	Likely Fact	5		2				3		
809	But you know that uh, I'm sure you know that it has come into somebody's mind, you know, we have Neo-Nazi organizations.	7	Possible Fact		1	1	1	1	1	5	2	

The approach taken by this study provides for categorization of 2,317 items out of 2,490 (93%), versus a simple majority interrater reliability (IRR) approach that only categorized 1,497 out of 2,490 (60.1%). Additionally, this study's approach recognizes that the variation in rater assessments is actually indicative of their responses to an item's own uncertainty and the psychological difficulty posed by these event sentences, rather than a failure to accurately classify those items.

9.6 Conclusion

The ultimate goal of this work is to better understand a fundamental aspect of narration – a speaker's belief in their own statements. That belief, for a reader, is most obviously encoded in the use of hedges, modals, and attitude markers. Though one goal for work like this would be a tool that can assign a classification with regards to interpreted speaker veridicality of events in the domain of witness testimony, an equally significant finding has to do with the distribution of results. Noting that the preponderance of results tended toward descriptions of events, rather than of nonevents, and that annotators showed far greater agreement in examples seen to be more certain suggests something about how people perceive testimonial writing; namely, that we are possibly more attuned to reading about events, rather than about negations of events, and that readers may be more precise in their agreement about more certain events and nonevents than they are about more uncertain events and nonevents. In developing training data to support that goal, it was discovered that simple IRR did not adequately describe how raters were evaluating contextual examples.

To better capture the relative certainty and facticity implied by those ratings, an alternative to simple majority agreement was implemented. Instead, the means of all valid ratings were calculated and then plotted where the x-axis denoted a continuum from counterfact, or event-negation, to fact, or event, and the y-axis denoted certainty. Those plotted results were clustered using a number of clusters determined by the elbow method, wherein the number of clusters is increased until an elbow appears in the graph. Based on these clusters, a new nine-element schema for the evaluation of veridicality that better reflects how readers interpreted real-world testiomny was proposed. That schema draws upon the study's evidence and suggests that (1) readers and witnesses have a greater sensitivity to gradations of fact than they do to gradations of counterfacts and (2) readers and witnesses exhibit more variation and less surety in their evaluation of uncertain statements. What these two aspects of reader cognition mean for the writing of history has yet to be explored.

Acknowledgments This research was supported in part by the Minerva Research Initiative, U.S. Department of Defense. The author thanks the reviewers for their careful, detailed, knowledgeable, and extremely helpful feedback and Kristopher Kyle, Shakthidhar Gopavaram, and Jennifer Olive, the graduate research assistants who helped collect the initial survey data. Lastly, I want to thank my wife, Elora; she is my most supportive and critical reviewer.

References

Caruth, Cathy. 2016. *Unclaimed Experience: Trauma, Narrative, and History*. Johns Hopkins University Press.

De Marneffe, Marie-Catherine, Manning, Christopher D., and Potts, Christopher. 2012. Did It Happen? The Pragmatic Complexity of Veridicality Assessment. *Computational Linguistics*, **38**(2), 301–333.

Divitaa, Guy, Brignonea, Emily, Carter, Marjorie E., et al. 2018. Extracting Sexual Trauma Mentions from Electronic Medical Notes Using Natural Language Processing. Pages 351–355 of: Gundlapalli, A. V., Jaulent, M.-C., and Zhao, D. (eds.), *MEDINFO 2017: Precision Healthcare through Informatics: Proceedings of the 16th World Congress on Medical and Health Informatics*, Vol. 245. Amsterdam: IOS Press.

Ehrmann, Alexander, and Bolkosky, Sidney M. 1983. *Alexander Ehrmann, First Impressions of Auschwitz*. University of Michigan–Dearborn [Television Services].

Gibbons, John Peter. 2014. *Language and the Law*. Routledge.

Hacquard, Valentine. 2011. *Modality. Semantics: An International Handbook of Natural Language Meaning*, Maienborn, Claudia, von Heusinger, Klaus, and Portner, Paul (eds.).

Hahn, Udo, and Engelmann, Christine. 2014. Grounding Epistemic Modality in Speakers' Judgments. Pages 654–667 of: Pham, Duc-Nghia, and Park, Seong-Bae (eds.), *Pacific Rim International Conference on Artificial Intelligence*. Springer.

Herman, Judith L. 2015. *Trauma and Recovery: The Aftermath of Violence From Domestic Abuse to Political Terror*. London: Hachette.

Horn, Laurence R. 1989. *A Natural History of Negation*. University of Chicago Press.

Hyland, Ken. 2005. Stance and Engagement: A Model of Interaction in Academic Discourse. *Discourse Studies*, **7**(2), 173–192.

Kodinariya, Trupti M., and Makwana, Prashant R. 2013. Review on Determining Number of Cluster in K-Means Clustering. *International Journal*, **1**(6), 90–95.

Lee, Kenton, Artzi, Yoav, Choi, Yejin, and Zettlemoyer, Luke. 2015. Event Detection and Factuality Assessment with Non-expert Supervision. Pages 1643–1648 of: Lluís Màrquez, Chris Callison-Burch, and Jian Su (eds.), *Proceedings of the 2015 Conference on Empirical Methods in Natural Language Processing*.

Marsh, Herbert W. 1986. Negative Item Bias in Ratings Scales for Preadolescent Children: A Cognitive-Developmental Phenomenon. *Developmental Psychology*, **22**(1), 37–49.

Martin, Nora. 2017. Journalism, the Pressures of Verification and Notions of Post-truth in Civil Society. *Cosmopolitan Civil Societies: An Interdisciplinary Journal*, **9**(2), 41–56.

Miller, Ben, Shrestha, Ayush, Derby, Jason, et al. 2013. Digging into Human Rights Violations: Data Modelling and Collective Memory. Pages 37–45 of: Lin, Tsau Young, Raghavan, Vijay, and Wah, Benjamin (eds.), *2013 IEEE International Conference on Big Data*. IEEE.

Miller, Ben, Olive, Jennifer, Gopavaram, Shakthidhar, and Shrestha, Ayush. 2015. Cross-document Non-fiction Narrative Alignment. Pages 56–61 of: Caselli,

Tommaso, van Erp, Marieke, Minard, Anne-Lyse, et al. (eds.), *Proceedings of the First Workshop on Computing News Storylines.*

Nugumanova, Aliya, and Bessmertny, Igor. 2013. Applying the Latent Semantic Analysis to the Issue of Automatic Extraction of Collocations from the Domain Texts. Pages 92–101 of: Klinov, Pavel, and Mouromtsev, Dmitry (eds.), *International Conference on Knowledge Engineering and the Semantic Web.* Springer.

Saurí, Roser, and Pustejovsky, James. 2009. FactBank: A Corpus Annotated with Event Factuality. *Language Resources and Evaluation,* **43**(3), 227–268.

Saurí, Roser, and Pustejovsky, James. 2012. Are You Sure That This Happened? Assessing the Factuality Degree of Events in Text. *Computational Linguistics,* **38**(2), 261–299.

Saurí, Roser, Knippen, Robert, Verhagen, Marc, and Pustejovsky, James. 2005. Evita: A Robust Event Recognizer for QA Systems. Pages 700–707 of: Mooney, Raymond J. (ed.), *Proceedings of the conference on Human Language Technology and Empirical Methods in Natural Language Processing.* Association for Computational Linguistics.

The Sept 11 Records. 2005. *The New York Times,* November 30. https://archive .nytimes.com/www.nytimes.com/indexes/2005/11/30/nyregion/nyregionspecial3/ index.html

Soni, Sandeep, Mitra, Tanushree, Gilbert, Eric, and Eisenstein, Jacob. 2014. Modeling Factuality Judgments in Social Media Text. Pages 415–420 of: Toutanova, Kristina, and Wu, Hua (eds.), *Proceedings of the 52nd Annual Meeting of the Association for Computational Linguistics: Volume 2. Short Papers.*

The South African Broadcasting Corporation. 1996 (Jun). Human Rights Violation Hearings, Case Number CT/00530.

Stanovsky, Gabriel, Eckle-Kohler, Judith, Puzikov, Yevgeniy, Dagan, Ido, and Gurevych, Iryna. 2017. Integrating Deep Linguistic Features in Factuality Prediction over Unified Datasets. Pages 352–357 of: Barzilay, Regina, and Kan, Min-Yen (eds.), *Proceedings of the 55th Annual Meeting of the Association for Computational Linguistics: Volume 2. Short Papers.*

Truong, Khiet P., Westerhof, Gerben J., Lamers, Sanne M.A., and de Jong, Franciska. 2014. Towards Modeling Expressed Emotions in Oral History Interviews: Using Verbal and Nonverbal Signals to Track Personal Narratives. *Literary and Linguistic Computing,* **29**(4), 621–636.

Wan, Xiaojun, and Zhang, Jianmin. 2014. CTSUM: Extracting More Certain Summaries for News Articles. Pages 787–796 of: Geva, Shlomo, Trotman, Andrew, Bruza, Peter, Clarke, Charles L. A., and Järvelin, Kal (eds.), *Proceedings of the 37th International ACM SIGIR Conference on Research & Development in Information Retrieval.*

10

Narrative Homogeneity and Heterogeneity in Document Categories

Dan Simonson and Anthony R. Davis

Abstract. In this chapter, we present techniques for examining the distributional properties of narrative schemas (Chambers and Jurafsky, 2009) in the news, particularly in a subset of the New York Times (NYT) Corpus (Sandhaus, 2008), to see how well they capture the events and stories presented there. In one technique, the narrative argument salience through entities annotated (NASTEA) task, we use the event participants indicated by narrative schemas to replicate salient entity annotations from the NYT Corpus. In another technique, we measure narrative schema stability by generating schemas with various permutations of input documents. Both of these techniques show differences between homogeneous and heterogeneous document categories, where homogeneous categories being those written from templates such as Weddings and Obituaries. Homogeneous categories tend to perform better on the NASTEA task using fewer schemas and exhibit more stability, whereas heterogeneous categories require more schemas applied on average to peak in performance at the NASTEA task and exhibit less stability. This suggests that narrative schemas succeed at detecting and modeling the repetitive nature of template-written text, whereas more sophisticated models are required to understand and interpret the complex novelty found in heterogeneous categories.

10.1 Introduction: Narrative Schemas and Their Evaluations

Two core components of the storyline of a narrative are the events of the story and the participants in those events. One technique that captures these two aspects of the storylines of a corpus is *narrative schemas* (Mooney and DeJong, 1985; Chambers and Jurafsky, 2009; Balasubramanian et al., 2013), generalizations over narratives that reflect common patterns of events and their participants. Narrative schemas complement other approaches to

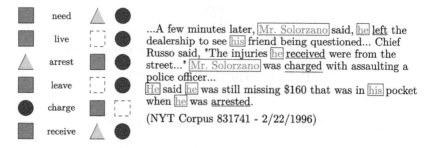

Figure 10.1 An example of a narrative schema with an associated text. The schema is represented by rows representing each event and its associated slots. Each column of symbols represents a particular slot, either SUBJ, OBJ, or PREP, which participated in that event. Each symbol represents a chain of mentions of a particular entity in different slots around those events. For example, the square here represents a person, student, or "self" type. Dashed squares in the schema indicate singleton chains not linked to any other slot in the schema. In the prose, underlines indicate events that occur in the schema; rectangles indicate the chain of mentions that correlated with the square in the schema.

the automated analysis of topical and narrative information in documents. Unlike template-filling techniques, they do not require a defined set of human-crafted templates; instead, template-like structures are induced. Unlike topic models, they generate representations in which event types and participant types are organized into relational structures, specifying shared participants between events. Unlike automatic summarization, they generalize over similar but distinct narratives to reveal their underlying common elements.

Figure 10.1 features an illustration of a narrative schema generated in this study, with an example of a document that contains events described by the schema. The schema correctly predicts that, in the given text, a particular individual should leave somewhere, be arrested, be charged with something, and receive something. However, it makes some inaccurate predictions as well – for example, that whatever arrested the individual should also be received by the individual. Because a schema is generated from many thousands of documents, it makes generalizations that are not guaranteed to be represented in every text.

Fundamentally, this chapter reviews efforts to evaluate narrative schemas. Determining whether a narrative schema is "correct" is not a well-defined task; yet, we do not want to abandon evaluation entirely. Rather, we chose two tasks to assess properties that reflect intuitions of what a good schema might be. The first is the *narrative argument salience through entities annotated* or *NASTEA* task (Section 10.4), where entities are retrieved using narrative schemas. The intuition behind this is that a "good" narrative schema should include elements that involve prominent participants in narrative. The second is a *stability procedure* (Section 10.5), which measures the stability of a set of schemas by ablating and cross-validating a set of documents to see how consistent the schemas themselves are. A "good" set of narrative schemas should be resilient to small perturbations in the source corpora. These properties of narrative schemas demonstrate the existence of two types of document categories: *homogeneous* and *heterogeneous*. *Homogeneous* categories are categories of documents with a consistent set of storylines with relatively fixed events and participant slots, albeit with new participant identities. They are often written from templates, such as *Obituaries* and *Weddings and Engagements*, whereas *heterogeneous* categories often describe new combinations of events or circumstances, or what is typically thought of as "news." The evidence for this distinction seems to be robust across both measurements of properties. Given their difference from one another in terms of what they measure and how they measure it, the two provide convergent evidence for such a distinction between document categories.

10.2 Background

Narrative schemas originate as an interpretation of Schank and Abelson's (1977) "scripts" – a conception of cognition and episodic memory where abstractions of repeated sequences of events are learned as abstractions of the events themselves. Attempts were made to learn these scripts during the prestatistical era of natural language processing (NLP), such as Mooney and DeJong's (1985) work generating schemas from individual documents.

Chambers and Jurafsky (2008, 2009) reintroduced the idea of scripts to the NLP literature. They used advances in parsing and coreference to aggregate statistics on the relationships between event verbs through shared, coreferring arguments, selected through their relationships to the verb, as either a SUBJ, OBJ, or PREP. Through these relations, they count pairs of event-dependency pairs. Though space does not allow a full overview, the formula for *sim* expresses a core intuition of their technique. $\langle e, d \rangle$ and $\langle e', d' \rangle$ are tuples of events and dependencies, respectively, and a is an argument type based on the most frequent noun phase type in each coreference chain:

$$sim(\langle e,d \rangle, \langle e',d' \rangle, a) = pmi(\langle e,d \rangle, \langle e',d' \rangle) + \lambda \log freq(\langle e,d \rangle, \langle e',d' \rangle, a)$$
$$(10.1)$$

pmi is the pointwise mutual information,[1] *freq* is the frequency that both tuples and the argument type *a* appeared together, and λ is a weighting parameter, which balances the influence between the simple "generic" coreferent sharing expressed in the *pmi* with the more precise yet sparse typed coreferent sharing contained in the log *freq* term.

Balasubramanian et al. (2013) followed up Chambers and Jurafsky (2009) with additional architectural improvements to schema generation. Additionally, they conducted the first manual evaluation of schemas, both of their own and of Chambers and Jurafsky's (2009) schemas, showing broadly that, to some extent under human evaluation, a portion of unsupervised schemas reflect some sort of reality for layman annotators.

For Chambers and Jurafsky's (2008) evaluation, they introduced the *cloze task* as a metric for understanding performance of their system. However, the cloze task does not measure schemas directly. A substantial body of work has been produced to further performance on the cloze task. Much of this work optimizes performance solely on the cloze task and does not generate schemas (Pichotta and Mooney, 2014, 2016). Some work critical of the cloze task has either presented new versions of the cloze task more focused on narrative (Mostafazadeh et al., 2016) or more fundamental tasks (Bisk et al., 2019) or looked at the problem of script induction as one of language modeling (Rudinger, Demberg et al., 2015; Rudinger, Rastogi et al., 2015).

10.3 Data and Schema Generation

The data for both of these experiments comes from the New York Times (NYT) Corpus (Sandhaus, 2008), a corpus containing 1.8 million articles from the (NYT) from January 1987 to June 2007. Each document in the corpus itself is tagged with document categories and entity annotations. The document categories were selected to represent a broad range of topics with similar frequencies (Table 10.1). The schemas used in this study are induced from this set of documents – minus a holdout set of 10% of the documents – and the document categories used in this study refer to this set.

Once the documents of these categories were extracted, they were preprocessed using Stanford CoreNLP (de Marneffe et al., 2006; Lee et al., 2013; Manning et al., 2014).[2] Dependency parsing and coreference resolution are

[1] For our purposes, $pmi(a,b) = p(a,b)/(p(a) \times p(b))$.
[2] Version 3.4.1.

Table 10.1. *Counts of document categories selected from the* online producer *tag for use in this study*

online producer category	Counts
Law and Legislation	52,110
Weddings and Engagements	51,195
Crime and Criminals	50,981
Education and Schools	50,818
United States Armament and Defense	50,642
Computers and the Internet	49,413
Labor	46,321
Obituaries	36,360

Note: Frequencies vary but were chosen to be around the same order of magnitude and to represent different sorts of topics.

effectively the first step of schema generation. Documents where parsing or coreference failed to complete[3] were removed from processing as well.

For schema generation, we use Chambers and Jurafsky's (2009) original generation technique with some modifications. The model employed here is conditioned by document category; separate sets of schemas are trained on each document category instead of all documents. Furthermore, though Chambers and Jurafsky's (2009) schema germination technique has no intrinsic limit, we cut off generation for each category at 800 schemas. This was the limit it was practical to evaluate within the two proposed frameworks.

Additionally, there are a few small changes at some of the post-score steps in the procedure. The score value from Chambers and Jurafsky (2009) does not explicitly describe how the various slots from an event newly added to a schema should be connected into forming chains within that schema. This occurs in a separate step – after it is decided that an event should be added to a schema, each individual slot from the candidate event is scored against the existing chains in the schema. The highest scoring chain for each slot has the slot added as a link in that chain; if the score is not high enough, the slot starts a new singleton chain in the schema. Also, an event may be added to multiple schemas if the score is high enough.

Lastly, we genericize some types – similar to Balasubramanian et al. (2013) – but not in all circumstances; instead, we do so only in the event that there is no common noun available to learn from, first checking the Stanford

---

[3] 14,239 documents, or 0.7% of the 1.8 million total documents.

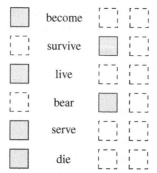

Figure 10.2 A relatively simple schema from the *Obituaries* document category. The squares indicate a chain that is strongly represented by the generic type PERSON but with many other lionizing human types: scholar, hero, advocate, philosopher, etc. The dashed squares represent slots attested in the data but not connected during schema generation.

Named Entity Recognition (NER) (Finkel et al., 2005) output for alternatives and, then guessing a type based on pronouns in a given chain. Finally, if nothing else is found, it aborts to a fallback type. Figures 10.1 and 10.2 depict schemas generated by this procedure.

10.4 Evidence through NASTEA Task

Ideally, a model of narrative should be able to extract the same entities that humans think are important with respect to a certain story. Because the NYT Corpus has entity annotations, the NASTEA task attempts to do exactly that: use narrative schemas to extract a set of annotated salient entities from a document. We use as a gold standard those contained in the NYT Corpus. Ideally, if a set of narrative schemas is a sufficient model of narrative, the participants a schema captures should match those marked as salient by NYT library scientists.

It is worth noting that our objective is not to achieve state-of-the-art performance on entity extraction. Rather, our goal is to use entity extraction as a proxy for schema quality. NASTEA provides a local measure of schema success, seeing whether in instances of particular documents it can successfully identify salient entities.

The most complicated component of this is the identifcation of the presence of a schema in a document, which is not trivial to determine. We explain our technique for doing so in Section 10.4.1, followed with a few of the particulars about how NASTEA was done here (Section 10.4.2), and ending this section with the results of the task (Section 10.4.3).

10.4.1 The Presence of a Schema in a Document

Determining whether or not a word or n-gram appears in a document is a relatively simple task, but identifying whether a narrative schema is present or not is neither trivial nor categorical. The NASTEA task relies on some sort of notion of *presence* to determine what schemas should be applied to which documents.

In the following sections, we deploy a measure of *presence* that reflects the *canonicality* of a document – that is, how closely a document matches a schema. This measure uses the events of a schema as a proxy for its content – excluding the arguments from the measure. We explicitly exclude coreference information from the measure because coreference is error prone; though we trust it *en masse* for generalizing over many documents, we do not trust it on a document-to-document basis.

Measuring the presence $p_{S,D}$ of a schema S in a document D begins with $V_{S,D}$, the set of verbs in D that represent events in S:

$$V_{S,D} = \{v_i : v_i \in D \wedge v_i \in S_e\}, \quad (10.2)$$

where $v_i \in D$ is true when an instance of verb v_i is inside document D. S_e is the set of events in a schema, each represented by a verb. The same verb type can appear multiple times in the set, because each instance is uniquely indexed. As with the schemas, the set of verbs does not include nominalizations. A sentence can have multiple verbs, and all relevant verbs are included in $V_{S,D}$.

There are two ways to consider the distribution of verbs within a document, both of which contribute to defining presence: *density* and *dispersion*, illustrated in Figure 10.3. Density ρ is defined as

$$\rho_{S,D} = \frac{|V_{S,D}|}{|D|}. \quad (10.3)$$

$\rho_{S,D}$ measures the fraction of sentences in document $|D|$ that contain verbs $V_{S,D}$ representing the events in schema S. If this factor is high, then the document as a whole is very close to being only the series of events expressed in the schema S.

Though a high density value is a strong indicator of presence, some cases where the density is not as high may still be interesting. If a set of relevant verbs is close together, this indicates some expression of the schema, whereas

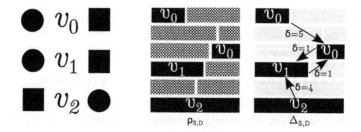

Figure 10.3 An illustration of how a document looks through the two components
of schema presence. In other words, it is how the document D looks through
density $\rho_{S,D}$ and dispersion $\Delta_{S,D}$ for a hypothetical schema S. In D, a rectangular
block represents each sentence. v_i in that each rectangular block indicates an
instance of the verb corresponding to the v_i event in S.

a disperse set of verbs is less likely to be an expression of the events listed in
the schema. This we call Δ, defined as

$$\Delta_{S,D} = \frac{1}{|V_{S,D}|} \sum_{v_i \in V_{S,D}} \min_{v_j \in V_{S,D}-\{v_i\}} \delta(v_i, v_j), \tag{10.4}$$

where $\delta(v_i, v_j)$ indicates the distance in sentences between two verbs v_i and v_j.
The minimization seeks to find the nearest v_j to v_i in $V_{S,D}$, which is computed
for every v_i contained in $V_{S,D}$.

The presence measure should be higher for those documents in which
the elements of a schema are both dense (throughout the document) and not
disperse. We define *canonical presence p* as

$$p_{S,D} = \frac{\rho_{S,D}}{\Delta_{S,D}}. \tag{10.5}$$

This defines the extent to which a schema is present in a document – more
specifically, the degree to which a document itself comes close to being an
exemplar of the schema.

10.4.2 Evaluating Schemas at the Document Level with NASTEA

Once schemas have been ranked for presence, the best match must be applied
to the matching document in some way. We use the verb/dependency pairs
found in that document that are also present in a schema to extract entities of

importance. From each pair, any NP governed through the indicated dependency is extracted in whole. Only NPs containing proper nouns (`/NNP.*/`) are retained, because common nouns are not indicated in the NYT metadata. Additionally, we exclude any schemas containing only one event from the NASTEA task.

The entities extracted are compared with the entities indicated in the NYT metadata. Each person, organization, or location from the metadata is tokenized with NLTK (Bird et al., 2009) and normalized for capitalization. Punctuation tokens are removed. Each entity extracted from the data is considered equal to the metadata entity if a fraction of the tokens r are equal between the two. This r value is set at 0.2, which is quite low but justifiable, because any overlap between the open-class proper noun components likely indicates a match expressed differently from the normalized representation in the metadata: for example, an extraction of "Mr. Clinton" should match "William Jefferson Clinton" in the metadata. A higher threshold would have excluded these sorts of matches, which are typical of the writing style of the NYT but differ in their metadata. A manual inspection of this low r value showed a meta-accuracy of around 98% (Simonson, 2017, p. 112).

The fraction of entities from the metadata captured represents the *recall* and the fraction of entities extracted that are actually found in the metadata indicates *precision*. NASTEA scores are reported as the F1 score of both of these values. In evaluation, only schemas generated with documents from a specific category were applied to that category. Documents that were members of multiple categories (about 9% of the held-out documents) were removed from the hold-out data to remove any possible penalties due to categorical overlap.

10.4.3 Results

Figure 10.4 illustrates results for the NASTEA task. Most categories follow a general trend of performing poorly with the highest-presence guess alone. As more schemas are applied, the system is better able to retrieve annotated entities on most categories, with F1 scores leveling off around 40%. These values remain more or less stable *ad infinitum* with a few minor variations in value as n continues to increase.

However, two categories are exceptions to this trend: *Weddings and Engagements* and *Obituaries*. These two categories, instead of producing concave down curves, produce curves that are concave up, indicating peak perfor-

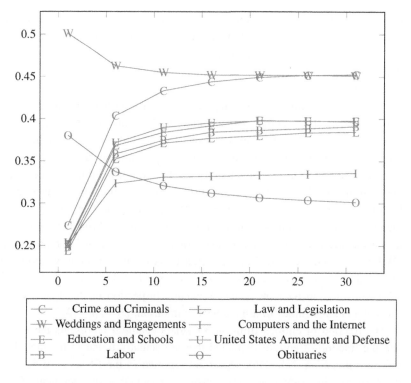

Figure 10.4 Plot of test-by-test performance on the NASTEA task for each topic. The *x*-axis indicates number of top-*n* present schemas applied. The *y*-axis indicates F1 score (i.e., N_n).

mance when only one schema is applied (at N_1) and decreasing performance as more schemas are applied.

This exceptional N_1 performance necessitates closer inspection. Because NASTEA is applying schemas to documents, those schemas can be retained and counted, allowing for illustration of the variety of different schemas that seem to best fit a particular document, what we will refer to as *narrative homogeneity*. Figure 10.5 takes a subset of the N_1 results and illustrates the totals of counts for schemas that were applied in each N_1 case. Categories that performed well on N_1 were also more homogenous at N_1, choosing a single schema as most present more often than their more heterogeneous counterparts.

In the next section, this distinction arises from a very different sort of experiment, one that does not use annotated entities at all.

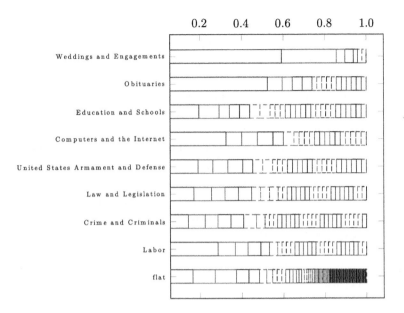

Figure 10.5 Plot of N_1 document categorical narrative homogeneity. A representation of the variety of schemas with the highest presence in documents in each category ($n = 1$ for the NASTEA task) in a subset of 324 of the holdout documents; "flat" represents a set of schemas generated without categorical distinctions and applied to all documents in the corpus. Fewer slices represent a smaller fraction of schemas being most present. A larger slice indicates that the single schema it represents had the highest presence for more documents.

10.5 Evidence through Schema Stability

The NASTEA task provides one angle to examine narrative schemas, through the correlation between what human annotators thought were central to a narrative and what the extracted schemas presented as central. This has limitations. It requires human annotations to evaluate schemas, as well as recorrelating output of the system with documents to examine them.

An alternative is to examine schemas against one another. Ideally, a set of schemas should be consistent, even given perturbations of the input data; in other words, a few missing documents should not significantly alter the resulting schemas. These result in a more global measure than NASTEA provided: the inputs as a whole are modified, and the outputs as a whole are scored collectively for their intrinsic stability.

Though there are things to be learned from different schema germination techniques, we will not be examining those differences here.[4] Instead, we will be focused on how the stability further reifies the homogeneous/heterogeneous distinction exhibited by the NASTEA task.

The stability evaluation procedure alternates two stages: an ablation step and a cross-validation step. At each ablation step, 10% of the starting set of documents is removed – not 10% of the previous ablation – on a category-by-category basis. Then 10-fold cross-validation partitions the set of documents; the 9/10ths of documents in each fold are used to generate 10 sets of schemas for each category at that ablation. These splits are not preserved across ablations. Though these procedures involve removing portions of the original corpus, the most intuitive way to interpret the intent is in reverse – that is, to think of some sort of search and retrieval procedure yielding slightly different results (cross-validation step) at each step in a larger data collection effort (ablation step). This results in 100 sets of schemas generated for each document category.

10.5.1 Fuzzy Jaccard Coefficient and the Jaccard Reciprocal Fraction

The described stability ablation procedure still needs a technique for comparing the hundreds of thousands of schemas across sets of them. Evaluating the similarity between two sets of schemas is not so straightforward, particularly when a measure that awards partial credit for partial matches would return the most intuitive results. Essentially, we would like to determine, for each schema in one set, how similar its best match is in the other.

To give an intuitive but also set-theoretically informed measure of the similarity between sets of schemas, we report values for the schema stability in terms of the *Jaccard Reciprocal Fraction* or JRF:

$$JRF(S,T) = \frac{4}{J_{J_e}^{-1}(S,T) + 3},\qquad (10.6)$$

where S and T are sets of schemas, and $J_{J_e}^{-1}$ is the reciprocal of the *Fuzzy Jaccard measure* (J_{J_e}):

---

[4] For a comparison between different germinator types, see Simonson and Davis (2018).

$$J_{J_e}(S,T) = \frac{|S \cap_{J_e} T|}{|S| + |T| - |S \cap_{J_e} T|},$$ (10.7)

where S and T are sets of schemas and $|S \cap_{J_e} T|$ is a fuzzy measure of the cardinality of the intersection of two sets, where

$$|S \cap_{J_e} T| = \sum_{\tau \in T} \max_{\sigma \in S} J_e(\sigma, \tau),$$ (10.8)

where σ and τ are sets of events contained in a single schema in S and T and $J_e(\sigma, \tau)$ is the Jaccard coefficient between the two sets. The full derivation for these is detailed in Simonson and Davis (2018). Most important, the JRF gives approximately the typical fraction of shared events between schemas in two sets of schemas, regardless of the size of schemas in each set. As the fuzzy Jaccard value approaches 1, so does the JRF; as the fuzzy Jaccard value approaches 0, the denominator approaches infinity, and thus the JRF approaches 0.

10.5.2 Results

For each individual pair of sets of schemas within an ablation, we compute fuzzy Jaccard scores, their means, and their standard deviations, transformed into JRF form.[5] Average values are shown in Figure 10.6.

Note that increasing ablation number refers to a decreasing number of documents; in other words, ablation 8 refers to 8/10ths of the documents having been *removed*. In total, the experiments generated 2,698,865 schemas, cut down to 640,000: 800 per category, across 8 categories, 10 cross-validations, and 10 ablations. These are not unique because the goal was to generate schemas as similar to one another as possible.

In Figure 10.6, the document categories found to be homogeneous – Weddings and Obituaries – are notably more stable than the categories shown to rely on fewer schemas to identify participants in Section 10.4. The difference is larger for Weddings and Engagements than for Obituaries; the gap between Obituaries and the other categories is small at ablation 0 but increases as fewer documents are used.

---

[5] The full table of values is available at https://schemas.thedansimonson.com/

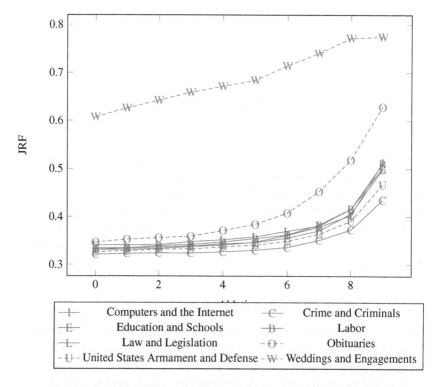

Figure 10.6 Stability in each ablation in each document category. Ablation is on the *x*-axis; Jaccard Reciprocal Fraction (e.g., events typically shared) is on the *y*-axis.

10.6 Discussion

A homogeneous category is one with a consistent set of storylines – the identities of the participants may change but the events and the roles stay the same. We can see clear evidence for homogeneity in the *Weddings and Engagements* and *Obituaries* categories of the (NYT), distinct from the other, more heterogeneous categories examined. The NASTEA task shows that, for the homogeneous categories, the participants in those narratives can be identified with a handful of schemas; for heterogeneous narratives, it requires far more schemas to identify the participants. The stability procedure shows that the schemas derived from a homogeneous document category remain more consistent when derived from a different subset of documents. Both of these results are clear evidence of consistent storylines – of homogeneity – among the Weddings and Obituaries categories.

The strength of this result is reinforced by the very different nature of the tasks used here, examining properties of narrative schemas from very different angles. Whereas the NASTEA task looks at participants in a narrative, the stability procedure compares events across schemas. The NASTEA task uses human annotations to accomplish its objective, whereas the stability procedure requires none. The NASTEA task is very localized, gathering participants from a specific narrative to score; the stability procedure is global, examining properties of schemas as a whole set of sets. Nevertheless, in both cases, we see evidence of the same phenomena: heterogeneous and homogeneous document categories. The stability procedure does this most intuitively. Schemas derived from a homogenous document category should be more stable under perturbations of its data, and this is what is seen quite consistently across the board. The NASTEA task requires more interpretation but also shows a clear distinction between the two types of categories. In the categories that are more homogeneous, a single schema does most of the work of the entity retrieval, as shown in Figure 10.5.

The homogeneous document categories are written from templates, so in some respects it is not surprising that a template extractor should exhibit different properties on the categories written from templates. However, a quantitative procedure for identifying this is valuable, especially when trying to leverage or understand properties of new kinds of data, such as the variety of genres found in the GUM corpus (Zeldes, 2017). The NASTEA task showed that this can be ascertained from broadly labeled data about participants in a narrative; the stability procedure used here shows the same distinction without any labeled data.

10.7 Conclusions

We showed two experimental results that both confirm that some document categories are homogeneous, whereas others are heterogeneous, based on how well narrative schemas can be used to extract entities in the NASTEA task and how consistent the schemas are that they produce under perturbations of the data. Both of these tasks shared a corpus and a schema generation technique in common but showed consistently the separation between the types of document categories despite coming at the problem from very different angles.

This distinction has implications not just for analyzing storylines but for problems beyond them as well. For example, when working on the problem of event extraction, the variety of events extracted is contingent on the type of data under analysis. A homogeneous category will have a predictable and tightly constrained set of events, whereas the events extracted from a heterogeneous document category are far more variable. Similarly, if a system is reasoning about storylines, such as Qin et al.'s (2019) work on counterfactuals, homogenous categories' storylines should have a more constrained search space than hetergeneous categories.

Toward a broader understanding of storylines and narrative, Caselli and Vossen (2016) critiqued narrative schemas as a model of narrative for the lack of causality in them. Causality is a core part of narrative understanding, yet schemas do not point toward causality in any particular direction between events. When we set out on this work, we hoped that narrative schemas could be used to analyze narrative structure more broadly, possibly employed as a sort of "tokens of narrative" model. Though schemas might provide a primitive example of a structured model of narrative knowledge, they remain incomplete. We further augment Caselli and Vossen's (2016) critique: many types of narrative are flexible, but discrete schemas are rigid. That said, the existence of some stable schemas, even in heterogeneous categories, may help highlight the components of text that exist in more calcified forms. Further, in certain genres, the determination of homogeneity maybe prove helpful in their analysis. The results here indicate that a complete model of storylines will require both.

References

Balasubramanian, Niranjan, Solderland, Stephen, Mausam, and Etzioni, Oren. 2013. Generating Coherent Event Schemas at Scale. Pages 1721–1731 of: *Proceedings of the Conference on Empirical Methods in Natural Language Processing (EMNLP)*. Association for Computational Linguistics.

Bird, S., Loper, E., and Klein, E. 2009. *Natural Language Processing with Python*. Cambridge: O'Reilly Media.

Bisk, Yonatan, Buys, Jan, Pichotta, Karl, and Choi, Yejin. 2019. Benchmarking Hierarchical Script Knowledge. Pages 4077–4085 of: *Proceedings of the 2019 Conference of the North American Chapter of the Association for Computational Linguistics: Human Language Technologies, Volume 1 (Long and Short Papers)*. Minneapolis, MN: Association for Computational Linguistics.

Caselli, Tommaso, and Vossen, Piek. 2016. The Storyline Annotation and Representation Scheme (StaR): A Proposal. Pages 67–72 of: *Proceedings of the 2nd Workshop on Computing News Storylines (CNS 2016)*. Austin, TX: Association for Computational Linguistics.

Chambers, Nathanael, and Jurafsky, Dan. 2008. Unsupervised Learning of Narrative Event Chains. Pages 789–797 of: *Proceedings of the Conference of the Association for Computational Linguistics (ACL)*. Association for Computational Linguistics.

Chambers, Nathanael, and Jurafsky, Dan. 2009. Unsupervised Learning of Narrative Schemas and Their Participants. Pages 602–610 of: *Proceedings of the Joint Conference of the 47th Annual Meeting of the ACL and the 4th International Joint Conference on Natural Language Processing of the AFNLP: Volume 2*. Association for Computational Linguistics.

de Marneffe, M., MacCartney, B., and Manning, C. D. 2006. Generating Typed Dependency Parses from Phrase Structure Parses. In: *Proceedings of the Language Resources and Evaluation Conference of the European Language Resources Association (LREC)*. Association for Computational Linguistics.

Finkel, J. R., Grenager, T., and Manning, C. 2005. Incorporating Non-local Information into Information Extraction Systems by Gibbs Sampling. Pages 363–370 of: *Proceedings of the 43rd Annual Meeting on Association for Computational Linguistics*. Association for Computational Linguistics.

Lee, H., Chang, A., Peirsman, Y., et al. 2013. Deterministic Coreference Resolution Based on Entity-centric, Precision-Ranked Rules. *Computational Linguistics*, **39**(4), 885–916.

Manning, Christopher D., Surdeanu, Mihai, Bauer, John, et al. 2014. The Stanford CoreNLP Natural Language Processing Toolkit. Pages 55–60 of: *Proceedings of the 52nd Annual Meeting of the Association for Computational Linguistics: System Demonstrations*.

Mooney, Raymond, and DeJong, Gerald. 1985. Learning Schemata for Natural Language Processing. Pages 681–687 of: *Proceedings of the 9th International Joint Conference on Artificial Intelligence (IJCAI)*.

Mostafazadeh, Nasrin, Grealish, Alyson, Chambers, Nathanael, Allen, James, and Vanderwende, Lucy. 2016. CaTeRS: Causal and Temporal Relation Scheme for Semantic Annotation of Event Structures. Pages 51–61 of: *Proceedings of the Fourth Workshop on Events*. San Diego: Association for Computational Linguistics.

Pichotta, Karl, and Mooney, Raymond. 2014. Statistical Script Learning with Multi-argument Events. Pages 220–229 of: *Proceedings of the 14th Conference of the European Chapter of the Association for Computational Linguistics*.

Pichotta, Karl, and Mooney, Raymond J. 2016. Using Sentence-Level LSTM Language Models for Script Inference. Pages 279–289 of: *Proceedings of the 54th Annual Meeting of the Association for Computational Linguistics: Volume 1. Long Papers*. Berlin: Association for Computational Linguistics.

Qin, Lianhui, Bosselut, Antoine, Holtzman, Ari, et al. 2019. Counterfactual Story Reasoning and Generation. Pages 5043–5053 of: *Proceedings of the 2019 Conference on Empirical Methods in Natural Language Processing and the 9th International Joint Conference on Natural Language Processing (EMNLP-IJCNLP)*. Hong Kong: Association for Computational Linguistics.

Rudinger, Rachel, Demberg, Vera, Modi, Ashutosh, Van Durme, Benjamin, and Pinkal, Manfred. 2015. Learning to Predict Script Events from Domain-Specific Text. Page 205 of: *Lexical and Computational Semantics (* SEM 2015)*.

Rudinger, Rachel, Rastogi, Pushpendre, Ferraro, Francis, and Van Durme, Benjamin. 2015. Script Induction as Language Modeling. In: *Proceedings of the 2015 Conference on Empirical Methods in Natural Language Processing (EMNLP-15)*.

Sandhaus, Evan. 2008. *The New York Times Annotated Corpus LDC2008T19*.

Schank, Roger, and Abelson, Robert. 1977. *Scripts, Plans, Goals and Understanding: An Inquiry into Human Knowledge Structures*. NJ: London: Lawrence Erlbaum.

Simonson, Dan. 2017. *Investigations of the Properties of Narrative Schemas*. Ph.D. Thesis, Georgetown University.

Simonson, Dan, and Davis, Anthony. 2018. Narrative Schema Stability in News Text. In: *Proceedings of COLING 2018*. Santa Fe, NM: Association for Computational Linguistics.

Zeldes, Amir. 2017. The GUM Corpus: Creating Multilayer Resources in the Classroom. *Language Resources and Evaluation*, **51**(3), 581–612.

11

Exploring Machine Learning Techniques for Linking Event Templates

Jakub Piskorski, Fredi Šarić, Vanni Zavarella, and Martin Atkinson

Abstract. Traditional event detection systems typically extract structured information on events by matching predefined event templates through slot filling. Automatically linking of related event templates extracted from different documents over a longer period of time is of paramount importance for analysts to facilitate situational monitoring and manage the information overload and other long-term data aggregation tasks. This chapter reports on exploring the usability of various machine learning techniques, textual, and metadata features to train classifiers for automatically linking related event templates from online news. In particular, we focus on linking security-related events, including natural and man-made disasters, social and political unrest, military actions and crimes. With the best models trained on moderate-size corpus (ca. 22,000 event pairs) that use solely textual features, one could achieve an F1 score of 93.6%. This figure is further improved to 96.7% by inclusion of event metadata features, mainly thanks to the strong discriminatory power of automatically extracted geographical information related to events.

11.1 Introduction

With the rapid proliferation of large digital archives of textual information on what happens in the world, a need has risen recently to apply effective techniques that go beyond the classification and retrieval of text documents in response to profiled queries. Systems already exist that automatically distill structured information on events from free texts; e.g., with the goal of monitoring disease outbreaks (Yangarber et al., 2008), crisis situations (King and Lowe, 2003), and other security-related events from online news.

Classical event extraction engines typically extract knowledge by locally matching predefined event templates in text documents, by filling template slots with detected entities. However, when not coupled with modules for event

221

coreference detection, these systems tend to suffer of the event duplication problem, consisting of extracting several mentions referring to the same occurring event. That makes their output misleading for both real-time situation monitoring and long-term data aggregation and analysis.

Though event coreference is a semantically well-defined relationship (Mitamura et al., 2015), additional, more fuzzy types of links typically occur between events and potentially contribute to the information overload of the user of an event extraction engine. Capturing such kinds of relationships may be crucial in order to further compress the information and increase the validity of event data.

Imagine a scenario where, given a large set of news reports about a major terrorist attack event, an event extraction engine returns a number of event templates like the ones shown in Figure 11.1. As can be noticed from title and text of the source articles, templates a and b describe the same main fact (the attack itself), c provides updates on some police operations following it, d tells about some public reactions to the event, and e is about an official claiming of the attack by one terrorist organization. Recognizing a and b as duplicate reporting of the same event would help mitigate the information redundancy in the system. At the same time, though c, d, and e should be regarded as semantically distinct events from a, extracting them as independent templates would result in a loss of information. That loss could prevent a user from obtaining a complete picture of the ongoing situation. On the contrary, we envision a user-centered process, where an end-user fed with an initial event template is allowed to explore additional event templates, by calling an on-the-fly computation of related events.

In this context, we explore the possibility of merging a number of distinct event–event relationships (Caselli and Vossen, 2017) into a more general, user-centered definition of event linking and experiment on training statistical classifiers for automatically detecting those links based on textual and nontextual contents of event templates.

The motivation behind our work is fourfold. Firstly, we are interested in elaboration of techniques for linking event information in existing event data sets, such as the one presented in Atkinson et al. (2017), in order to improve their usability by the analysts. Therefore, we have exploited this corpus to carry out the presented work. Secondly, because the event extraction engine underlying the corpus presented in Atkinson et al. (2017) is multilingual, we focus on exploring linguistically lightweight event similarity metrics. Thirdly, we are interested in exploring how inclusion of automatically extracted event metadata (e.g., location) impacts the performance of the trained event linking models. Finally, our aim is to provide a publicly available data set resembling

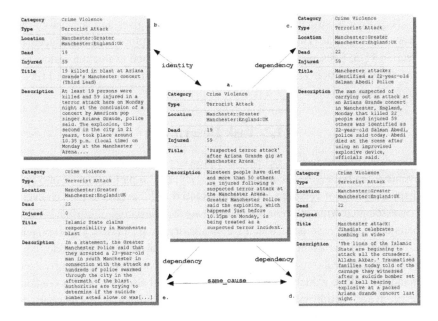

Figure 11.1 Event templates extracted from news reports following the 2017 Manchester terrorist attack, and the different relations linking them to the initial event report in a.

a real-world scenario where end-users are primarily interested in having access to all relevant event information rather than being provided with fine-grained labeling of event relations (e.g., temporal and causal).

Event linking has been modeled as the task of matching monolingual clusters of news articles, describing the same event, across languages. For example, Rupnik et al. (2016) used a number of techniques, including canonical correlation analysis, exploiting comparable corpora such as Wikipedia.

Work similar to ours was performed in the context of the event co-reference resolution task, which consists of clustering of event mentions that refer to the same event (Bejan and Harabagiu, 2010; Cybulska and Vossen, 2014). We diverge from both task formulations in that our underlying representation of events is richer than local event mentions, including metadata and text slots from clusters of articles. Guo et al. (2013) proposed a task of linking tweets with news articles to enable other natural language processing (NLP) tools to better understand Twitter feeds. Related work to event linking was also reported in Nothman et al. (2012), Krause et al. (2016), and Vossen et al. (2016).

The article is structured as follows. Section 11.2 gives an overview of the event linking task. The event similarity metrics explored are introduced in Section 11.3. Subsequently, the experimental setup and evaluation results are presented in Section 11.4. Finally, we end with conclusions in Section 11.5.

11.2 Task Description

The event linking task is defined as follows: given an event e and a set of events $E = \{e_1, \ldots, e_n\}$, compute $E^* = \{E^R, E^U\}$ a partition of E into two disjoint subsets of **related** (E^R) and **unrelated** (E^U) events to e. Each event e is associated with an event template $Temp(e)$ consisting of attribute–value pairs describing e, some of which are mandatory – e.g., TYPE, CATEGORY, and LOCATION of the event – while others are optional and event-specific, e.g., PERPETRATOR, WEAPONS_USED. An event template contains three string-valued mandatory slots, namely, TITLE, DESCRIPTION, and SNIPPET, which contain, respectively, the title and the first two sentences from the body of a news article on the event[1] and some text snippet that triggered the extraction of the event.[2]

Figure 11.1 shows a simplified version of a target event template (a) and a number of additional templates (b through e), all belonging to the subset of events related to a.

The semantics of the **related** relationship in our context is defined in a rather broad manner. An event $e' \in E$ is considered to be related to e if the corresponding event templates $Temp(e)$ and $Temp(e')$ refer to (a) the same event (identity); (b) reporting about different aspects of the same ongoing situation/focal event (cooccurrence); (c) two events, where one event occurrence is temporally following and is induced by that of the other event (dependency) with an explicit mention of the prior event; e.g., a trial following a man-made disaster; and (d) two distinct events that were triggered by the same event (same cause).

Due to the application scenario sketched in Section 11.1, the event linking task is modeled here as a classification task applied over a set of events E that does not coincide with the whole search space of events gathered over time but is rather a subset thereof retrieved as some function of the target event e (e.g., events within the same time window as e). This differentiates our approach from clustering methods that attempt to build a partition of the entire event search space based on some relatedness criteria.

---

[1] The centroid article of the cluster of articles from which the event template was extracted
[2] Please refer to Atkinson et al. (2017) for more details.

11.3 Event Similarity Metrics

In our experiments, we explore two types of event similarity metrics. Text-based event similarity metrics compute similarity based on the content of the textual slots in the event templates (e.g., TITLE, DESCRIPTION, etc; see Section 11.2), whereas meta-data-based event similarity metrics compare information contained in the slots that were automatically computed, such as event type and location. The specific metrics of both types are described in Sections 11.3.1 and 11.3.2.

11.3.1 Text-Based Metrics

To determine semantic similarity of text-based event slots, we exploit a wide range of similarity measures, including string similarity metrics, measures that exploit knowledge bases (e.g., WORDNET, BABELNET), and corpus-based similarity metrics, among others. Because our working definition of event linking emphasizes that events should be recognizable even in different languages, we did not explore measures not easily portable across languages; e.g., ones relying on syntactic parsing (Šarić et al., 2012). The remainder of this section briefly introduces the text-based metrics.

First, we use two string distance metrics, namely, **Levenshtein Distance (LT)**, an edit distance metric given by the minimum number of character-level operations needed to transform one string into another (Levenshtein, 1966), and **Longest Common Substrings (LCS)**, which recursively finds and removes the longest common sub-string in the two texts compared (Navarro, 2001). Next, we use **Word Ngram Overlap (WNO)**, which measures the fraction of common word ngrams in both texts, and **Weighted Word Overlap (WWO)**, which measures the overlap of words between the two texts, where words bearing more content are assigned higher weight (Šarić et al., 2012). The formal definitions of LCS, WNO, and WWO are presented in Figure 11.2.

The second pool of event similarity measures exploits various knowledge bases and includes (a) **Named-Entity Overlap (NEO)**, which computes similarity of the named entities found in both texts; (b) **Hypernym Overlap (HO)**, which computes an overlap of the set of hypernyms associated with named entities and concepts found in the texts being compared; and (c) **WordNet Similarity Word Overlap (WSWO)**, a metric that exploits semantic similarity of word pairs computed using WORDNET.[3] The respective formal definitions of NEO, HO and WSWO are provided in Figure 11.3.

---

[3] We deployed the WS4j library for this purpose: https://github.com/Sciss/ws4j

$$LCS(T_1, T_2) = \begin{cases} 0 \text{ if } |lcs(T_1, T_2)| < 3, \\ \frac{|lcs(T_1, T_2)|}{max(|T_1|, |T_2|)} + LCS(T_{1-lcs(T_1, T_2)}, T_{2-lcs(T_1, T_2)}), \end{cases}$$

where $lcs(T_1, T_2)$ denotes the first longest common substring in T_1 and T_2, and T_{i-p} denotes a text obtained by removing from T_i the first occurrence of p in T_i,

$$WNO(T_1, T_2) = \frac{2 \cdot |Ngrams(T_1) \cap Ngrams(T_2)|}{|Ngrams(T_1)| + |Ngrams(T_2)|},$$

where $Ngrams(T_i)$ denotes the set of consecutive ngrams in T_i,

$$WWO(T_1, T_2) = \frac{2 \cdot WoCov(T_1, T_2) \cdot WoCov(T_2, T_1)}{WoCov(T_1, T_2) + WoCov(T_2, T_1)},$$

where $WoCov(T_1, T_2)$ denotes *Weighted Word Coverage* of T_2 in T_1 and is defined as

$$WoCovC(T_1, T_2) = \frac{\sum_{w \in Words(T_1) \cap Words(T_2)} InfoContent(w)}{\sum_{x \in Words(T_2)} InfoContent(x)},$$

where $InfoContent(w) = \ln \sum_{x \in C} frequency(x)/frequency(w)$ (with C and $frequency(x)$ being the set of words in the corpus and the frequency of x in C, respectively[4]) and $Words(T_i)$ denotes the set of words occurring in T_i.

Figure 11.2 Longest Common Substrings (LCS), Word Ngram Overlap (WNO), and Weighted Word Overlap (WW) similarity metrics.

As regards recognizing names in order to compute NEO, a combination of three lexico-semantic resources is used in the respective order on the unconsumed part of the text: (a) JRC Variant Names database (ca. 4 million entries; Ehrmann et al., 2017), (b) a collection of multiword named entities from BABELNET (Navigli and Ponzetto, 2012; ca. 6.8 million entries) that have been semi-automatically derived using the method described in Chesney et al. (2017), and (c) toponyms (only populated places) from the GeoNames[5] gazetteer (ca. 1.4 million entries). Additionally, heuristics are used to join adjacent named entities (NEs). The aforementioned lexical resources cover a wide range of languages and the metric as such can be directly used on texts in other noninflected languages.

To retrieve the hypernyms in the context of computing HO measure, we use version 3.6 of BABELNET (Navigli and Ponzetto, 2012).[6]

---

[4] The event corpus introduced in Atkinson et al. (2017) was used for this purpose.
[5] www.geonames.org/
[6] We used BabelNet API method which returns all hypernyms for a given synset (depth one).

$$NEO(T_1, T_2) = \frac{2 \cdot NeCo(T_1, T_2) \cdot NeCo(T_2, T_1)}{NeCo(T_1, T_2) + NeCo(T_2, T_1)},$$

where *Named-Entity Coverage (NeCo)* of T_1 in T_2 is defined as follows:

$$NeCo(T_1, T_2) = \frac{1}{|N(T_1)|} \cdot \sum_{n \in N(T_1)} max_{m \in N(T_2)} sim(n, m),$$

where $N(T_i)$ is the set of named entities in T_i and $sim(n, m)$ denotes the similarity score of n and m.[7]

$$HO(T, S) = \frac{2 \cdot HypCov(T, S) \cdot HypCov(S, T)}{HypCov(T, S) + HypCov(S, T)},$$

where $HypCov(T, S)$ denotes *Hypernym Coverage* of T in S, defined as

$$HypCov(T, S) = \frac{1}{|T^*|} \cdot \sum_{t \in T^*} \max_{s \in S^*} hypSim(t, s),$$

where T^* and S^* denote the set of potentially overlapping text fragments in T and S, respectively, which can be associated either with a named entity or a concept in a knowledge base. Furthermore, $hypSim(t, s)$ denotes the hypernym similarity between t and s and is computed as follows:

$$hypSim(t, s) = \begin{cases} 1, & t = s \\ x, & \alpha + \beta \cdot \frac{|hyp(t) \cap hyp(s)|}{|hyp(t) \cup hyp(s)|}, \\ 0, & hyp(t) \cap hyp(s) = \emptyset \end{cases}$$

where $hyp(s)$ denotes the set of hypernyms for s and α and β have been set to 0.2 and 0.5, respectively, based on empirical observations.

$$WSWO(T, S) = \frac{2 \cdot WnCov(T, S) \cdot WnCov(S, T)}{WnCov(T, S) + WnCov(S, T)},$$

where *WordNet Coverage (WnCov)* of T_1 in T_2 is defined as follows:

$$WnCov(T_1, T_2) = \frac{1}{|Words(T_1)|} \cdot \sum_{w_1 \in Words(T_1)} \max_{w_2 \in Words(T_2)} sim(w_1, w_2),$$

where $sim(w_1, w_2)$ denotes WordNet-based semantic similarity measure between w_1 and w_2.

Figure 11.3 Named Entity Overlap (NEO), Hypernym Overlap (HO), and Word-Net Similarity Word Overlap (WSWO) metrics.

Regarding computing WSWO we exploited various WORDNET-based semantic similarity measures between pair of words, including, inter alia: **Path**,[8] **WP** presented in Wu and Palmer (1994), **Lesk** (Banerjee and Pedersen,

---

[7] To compute $sim(n, m)$, we used a weighted version of the LCS metric called *Weighted Longest Common Substrings* introduced in Piskorski et al. (2009).

[8] Counting the length of the path in "is-a" Verb and Noun hierarchy.

$$ANO(T_1, T_2) = \frac{2 \cdot |Num(T_1) \cap Num(T_2)|}{|Num(T_1)| + |Num(T_2)|},$$

where $Num(T_i)$ denote the set of numerical expressions found in T_i,

$$RNO(T_1, T_2) = \frac{2 \cdot |NumClos(T_1) \cap NumClos(T_2)|}{|NumClos(T_1)| + |NumClos(T_2)|},$$

where $NumClos(T_1, T_2)$ denotes *Numerical Closeness* between T_1 and T_2 and is defined as follows:

$$NumClos(T_1, T_2) = \frac{1}{|Num(T_1)|} \cdot \sum_{t \in T_1} \max_{s \in T_2} closeness(t, s),$$

where $closeness(t, s)$ is defined as follows:

$$closeness(t, s) = \begin{cases} 1 - \log_2(1 + \frac{|t-s|}{\max(t,s)}), & type(t) = type(s) \\ 0, & type(t) \neq type(s). \end{cases}$$

Figure 11.4 Absolute (ANO) and Relative Numerical Overlap (RNO) similarity metrics.

2002), and **HirstStOnge, LeacockChodorow, Resnik, JiangConrath,** and **Lin** (Budanitsky and Hirst, 2001).

Because an overlap of numerical information contained in texts might constitute an indication of relatedness thereof, we also compute metrics that compute an overlap of the set of numerical expressions found in the texts being compared. Though reported features for computing "similarity" of sets of numerical expressions do not differentiate between the specific types of such expressions (Socher et al., 2011), we do exploit numerical expression–type information. To be more precise, all recognized numerical expressions are classified into one of the following categories: currency (e.g., *200mln$*), percentage, measurement (*one million kilograms*), age (e.g., *20-year-old*), number (e.g., *20 thousand*), whereas numbers being part of temporal references (e.g., *1 May 2017*) are discarded. We computed two numerical overlap measures, namely, **Absolute Numerical Overlap (ANO)** and **Relative Numerical Overlap (RNO)**, whose definitions are presented in Figure 11.4.

Finally, we also use **Cosine of Text Vectors (CTV)**, defined as $CTV(T_1, T_2) = Cosine(Doc2Vec(T_1), Doc2Vec(T_2))$, where $Doc2Vec(T_i) = \frac{1}{|T_i|} \sum_{w \in T_i} embedding(w)$ (Le and Mikolov, 2014) is computed using GloVe (Pennington et al., 2014) word embeddings.

Text Preprocessing

Before applying most of the metrics, we deploy preprocessing of the text, which mainly boils down to (a) lowercasing it, (b) normalizing whitespaces, (c) removing constructs such as URLs, etc. For WNO, WSWO, and WWO, some initial/final token characters are stripped (e.g., brackets), and to compute WSWO, WWO, and CVT we remove stop words using a list of ca. 250 English word forms. In the case of NEO and HO the texts are not downcased because this might deteriorate NE recognition performance, which relies on orthographic features. To compute ANO and RNO, no preprocessing is carried out because nonalphanumeric characters often constitute part of numerical expressions.

11.3.2 Metadata-Based Metrics

For metadata information we define four metrics that exploit event location, category, and type information. Because the reported quality of extraction of event-type specific slots (e.g., number of injured, perpetrators, etc.) is not very high, we decided not to exploit such information in the experiments.

Location Administrative Similarity (LAS) computes the administrative distance between locations. It is a modification of the WUP metric presented in Wu and Palmer (1994) and aims to reflect how close two locations are with respect to an administrative hierarchy of geographical references. Let T_{GEO} denote the four-level (Country, Region, Province, and Populated Place) administrative hierarchy in the GeoNames gazetteer,[9] let $lcs(x, y)$ denote the lowest common subsumer for nodes x and y in T_{GEO}, and let $Loc(e)$ denote the node in T_{GEO} that corresponds to the location of the event e. LSA is then defined as follows:

$$LSA(e_1, e_2) = \frac{2 \cdot \omega(lcs(Loc(e_1), Loc(e_2)))}{\omega(Loc(e_1)) + \omega(Loc(e_1))}, \qquad (11.1)$$

where $\omega(v) = \sum_{i=0}^{depth(v)} \delta/2^i$ is a weighted depth of a node v in T_{GEO}, with δ empirically set to 10. The intuition behind LSA is to apply a higher weight to path segments closer to the root of T_{GEO}; e.g., distance paths at the Country level are penalized more than paths at the level of Province.

---

[9] www.geonames.org

Location Geographical Similarity (LGS) computes geographical distance between two event locations:

$$LSG(e_1, e_2) = (\ln(dist(coord(e_1), coord(e_2)) + e))^{-1}, \qquad (11.2)$$

where $coord(e)$ denotes the coordinates of the location of the event e as found in the GEONAMES gazetteer, and $dist(p_1, p_2)$ denotes the physical distance in kilometers between points p_1 and p_2.

Event Category Similarity (ECS) and **Event Type Similarity (ETS)** are two metrics that exploit the event category and type information. Let $cat(e)$ and $type(e)$ denote event category and type, respectively. The metrics are then defined as follows:

$$ECS(e_1, e_2) = Prob(REL(e_1, e_2)|(cat(e_1), cat(e_2))) \qquad (11.3)$$

$$ETS(e_1, e_2) = Prob(REL(e_1, e_2)|(type(e_1), type(e_2))), \qquad (11.4)$$

where $REL(e_1, e_2)$ denotes events e_1 and e_2 being related. The respective probabilities for category and type pairs were computed using the GOLD data set (see Section 11.4.1). In case a certain combination of types (categories) was not observed the respective probability was set to zero, whereas in case of type/category equality the respective probability was set to 1.

11.4 Experiments

11.4.1 Data Set

We built a GOLD corpus consisting of event template pairs taken from the event data set described in Atkinson et al. (2017) and labeled as either related or unrelated. First, we attempted to create balanced groups of event templates, where initial groups were built by extracting events (not less than five) around keys consisting of a category, location (country), and a time slot (e.g., time window of ± 2 days) in 2017. All such initial groups G were subsequently amended with a set of max. $|G|/6$ most similar events from the same time window and another set of max. $|G|/6$ most similar events from 2017 but outside of the original time window. The events were selected through computing cosine similarity with the centroid template in G.[10] Finally, G was amended by adding $|G|/3$ of randomly selected events (disjoint from the

---

[10] Vector representations of event templates and thus centroid templates of groups are derived by computing Doc2Vec on joined DESCRIPTION, TITLE and SNIPPET textual slots and converting each word with GloVe word embeddings (Pennington et al., 2014)

TITLE: *Militants attack police party in Srinagar*
DESCRIPTION: *Two cops were injured tonight when militants attacked a police party in the Hyderpora area of the city here, police said. Unidentified militants fired upon a night police party near the branch in Hyderpora tonight, resulting in injuries to two policemen, a police official said.*

TITLE: *Civilian gunned down by militants in J-K's Pulwama, 3rd death this week*
DESCRIPTION: *This was the third civilian killed in firing incidents this week. Earlier, one civilian was killed in Srinagar's Rangreth area as security personnel allegedly opened fire to disperse stone-pelters, while another died during an encounter in Arwani village in Bijbehara area.*

Figure 11.5 An example of two events perpetrated by the same group as part of the same armed conflict.

previous groups) from the same time window, regardless of location, category, and similarity.

This original sampling method had some limitations, namely: (a) a significantly unbalanced distribution of the event types, (b) a relatively low number of unique event templates, and (c) a limited range of unique locations of the events. In order to alleviate the aforementioned shortcomings, we repeated the event grouping mechanism described above after selecting groups for a wider range of locations, including event templates that do not have any location information extracted.[11] Moreover, we only annotated a smaller fraction of potential event pair combinations for each event group, to increase the number of unique events. Finally, an additional set of event template pairs with relatively high lexical similarity was sampled and a fraction thereof tagged as unrelated was added to the new corpus in order to increase the fraction of nonobvious event pairs.

All event pairs in each group were computed and subsequently labeled by four annotators, by taking into account only the textual and metadata information available in the templates. The average pairwise κ score for interannotator agreement on a sample of around 13,400 event pairs was over 0.85. Questionable cases were typically due to event granularity issues. For example, the two events in Figure 11.5 were arguably perpetrated by the same armed group as part of a same armed conflict on the same day and in the larger area. Whether the two killing incidents should be considered as different consequences of the same larger event, and thus only related, or be considered as distinct events is an open question. We used pairs with at least two nonconflicting judgments to build the GOLD data set.

Detailed statistics of the corpus are provided in Table 11.1.

---

[11] This resulted in principle due to a failure of event extraction system to detect locations, i.e., the event location was not covered in the underlying linguistic resource or the location information was considered by the system as other type of named entity.

Table 11.1. GOLD *data set statistics*

#REL	#UN	#EVT	#CRI	#CIV	#MM	#NAT	#MIL
13051	9587	4214	38.2%	16.2%	16.9%	11.1%	17.6%

The first two columns (REL and UN) provide the number of related (unrelated) event pairs, the third (EVT) provides the total number of unique events, and the others provide the percentage of events falling into crisis-violence (CRI), civic-political action (CIV), man-made disasters (MM), natural disasters (NAT), and military actions (MIL).

11.4.2 Discriminative Power of the Metrics

In order to have a preliminary insight into the discriminative power of the various event similarity metrics, we exploit an objective measure of *absolute Distance* (*absDistance*). Let for some event similarity metric histogram h, $\{u_h\}$, and $\{r_h\}$ denote the sequences of heights of the bars for unrelated and related event pairs, respectively, for all considered bins $i \in I$. *absDistance* is then defined as follows:

$$absDistance(h) = \sum_{i \in I} |u_i^h - r_i^h|/200. \qquad (11.5)$$

This metric computes the fraction of the area under the histogram curves being compared that corresponds to the symmetric difference between them, where the area under each histogram has 100 units. The higher values of *absDistance* indicate better discriminative power of a metric being considered.

We have considered five different modes as regards computation of the features corresponding to the text-based event similarity metrics, namely: (a) only text from the event DESCRIPTION and SNIPPET slots (see Section 11.2) from the event template is used (D); (b) only event TITLE slot is used (T); (c) in addition to (a), the TITLE slot is exploited as well (D+T); (d) similarity score for the TITLE, DESCRIPTION/SNIPPET slot is computed separately and an average thereof is returned (AVG(D,T)); and (e) similarity score for the TITLE, and DESCRIPTION/SNIPPET slot is computed separately and the maximum thereof is returned (MAX(D,T)).

Figure 11.6 provides a comparison of the discriminative power computed using *absDistance* on GOLD data set for all event similarity metrics and four aforementioned modes in which text-based metrics are calculated. One can observe high potential of some of the metadata metrics, namely, LSG (close to 90% of the area under the curve [AUC]) and ETS (close to 40% of the AUC), whereas NEO and WWO (both of which can be computed efficiently) lead

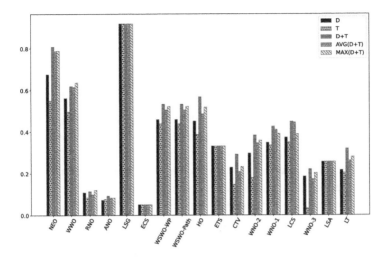

Figure 11.6 Discriminative power of the event similarity metrics. The different versions of WNO depending on the n-gram type are denoted with WNO-i.

the ranking of text-based metrics, followed by metrics exploiting WORDNET, BABELNET, which also have relatively high discriminatory power (in the range of 45% – 80% of the AUC). In particular, HO discriminative power is very similar to the WORDNET-based distance metrics, which is due to the fact that BABELNET encompasses WORDNET resources. Interestingly, the surface-level LCS metric exhibits much higher discriminative power vis-a-vis CTV. Numerical overlap features seems to be least attractive in this comparison, most likely due to the fact that a large fraction of event template pairs tagged as related do not refer to same events but rather to different events linked through the same cause or being in some other type of dependency and thus more likely reporting on different numerical values. Nevertheless, we hypothesize that exploitation of numerical overlap metrics might come in handy in case of natural and man-made disaster events, which unfortunately constitute only a small fraction of all events in our corpora.

11.4.3 Experimental Setup

Experiments were carried out using five different machine learning (ML) models, namely: support vector machine (SVM), stochastic gradient descent classifier (regularized linear model learned), decision tree, random forest, and AdaBoost classifier. All models were implemented using scikit learn library (Pedregosa et al., 2011). Each model was trained using a full set of event similarity metrics as features[12] and on a subset of features obtained using feature selection with *SelectFromModel* base estimator being random forest. All models consistently exhibited better performance when using all features vis-a-vis a subset of features obtained through feature selection. All models were trained and evaluated on the same training–test split (80:20) in order to ensure the comparability of the models. In order to tune the hyperparameters of the models, we performed grid search over hyperparameter space for each model and evaluated it using fivefold cross-validation using only the training data. The performance metrics of best performing models were further evaluated on held-out test set and used for model comparison.

Noteworthy, in case of missing features – i.e., whenever an event metric could not be computed (e.g., due to missing elements such as named entities or numerical expressions to be compared) – we set the respective values to the mean in the corresponding feature distribution assuming that lack of elements to compare should be scored higher than zero overlap (e.g., different named entities in both texts).

Finally, we carried out the evaluation in two setups, one with text-based features only and a second one with both textual and metadata features.

11.4.4 Results

The performance of the models on the GOLD data set is shown in Table 11.2. The observed results indicate that the task is well modeled by the different classification paradigms, with random forest being in general the top scoring model across all settings. We trained additional models using the random forest paradigm using subsets of the text-based features set by excluding in each run a single feature in order to explore how the exclusion of each feature impacts the performance. The resulting significance order of the features matched to a larger extent the discriminative power ranking depicted in Figure 11.6; i.e., NEO and WWO topped the rankings and ANO and RNO ranked lowest.

As expected (see Section 11.4.2), adding metadata features (in particular, given the discriminatory power of LSG) on top of the text-based features significantly boosts the performance, raising the upper bound from 93.6% to as much as 96.7%. Nevertheless, this is a remarkable finding considering that the metadata features (i.e., the slots LOCATION, TYPE, and CATEGORY)

---

[12] For the WSWO metric family we finally considered only WSWO-Path and WSWO-WP variants based on some empirical observations that revealed that the other variant returns very similar scores.

Table 11.2. *Performance on the* GOLD *data set (F1 scores)*

ML Paradigm	Text and Metadata features				
	D	T	D + T	AVG(D,T)	MAX(D,T)
SVM	95.29%	94.76%	96.02%	95.87%	95.55%
SDG	95.25%	94.73%	95.85%	96.01%	94.73%
RANDOM FOREST	**96.34%**	**96.24%**	**96.62%**	**96.70%**	**96.48%**
DECISION TREE	95.12%	94.28%	95.34%	95.82%	95.93%
ADABOOST	95.21%	94.92%	95.47%	95.64%	95.17%
ML Paradigm	Text-based features				
	D	T	D + T	AVG(D,T)	MAX(D,T)
SVM	84.55%	75.20%	92.29%	89.27%	90.23%
SDG	84.44%	76.61%	91.77%	89.76%	90.31%
RANDOM FOREST	**87.54%**	**82.16%**	**93.60%**	**91.59%**	**91.53%**
DECISION TREE	83.66%	77.50%	91.94%	90.25%	90.59%
ADABOOST	85.02%	78.38%	92.49%	90.69%	90.80%

are automatically generated by an event extraction engine and their extraction is more error prone vis-a-vis the computation of similarity metrics on the textual slots. One needs to emphasize in this context that the surprisingly high discriminative power of the LSG metric that contributed to the overall performance might have been due to the way in which the evaluation corpora were built (see Section 11.4.1); i.e., the discriminative power of the LSG metric might be lower when applied on an event corpus with a higher number of distinct (unrelated) events of the same type that happened in the same location.

Moreover, D + T mode seems to be the best choice overall as regards the various modes for computing text-based features and is statistically different with $p < 0.05$ compared to other modes on the GOLD data set with only textual features. Exploiting only title information (T mode) when using text-based features resulted in a respectable F1 score of 82.2%.

A rudimentary error analysis on the output of the GOLD data set–trained random forest classifier with metadata features and D+T option revealed that most of the false negatives consisted of event pairs referring to different, related aspects of the same target event, like in the article titles in Figure 11.7 (top). This was expected because the text pairs have little lexical overlapping and (more) background knowledge (e.g., access to full news articles) is required in

TITLE: *"Concert bomber targeted children"*
DESCRIPTION: *British Prime Minister Theresa May said police know the identity of the bomber, who died in the blast late Monday, and believed he acted alone. [...]*

TITLE: *Miley Cyrus "more cautious" after terror attack at Ariana Grande's gig*
DESCRIPTION: *Miley Cyrus says the terror attack at Ariana Grande's concert has made her "more cautious". A bomb was detonated after Ariana's gig. [...]*

TITLE: *Ex-Qaeda affiliate leaders among 25 dead in Syria strike*
DESCRIPTION: *An air strike in Syria on Tuesday killed at least 25 members of former Al-Qaeda affiliate Fateh al-Sham Front including senior figures, a monitor said. Unidentified aircraft hit one of the group's most important bases in Syria, in the northwestern province of Idlib. [...]*

TITLE: *Syrian air strikes kill at least six civilians*
DESCRIPTION: *ALEPPO - Syrian government air strikes killed at least six civilians, including four children, in Aleppo province on Thursday, despite a fragile two-week-old truce, a monitor said. In neighbouring Idlib province, at least 22 jihadists were killed in air strikes over the past 24 hours. [...]*

Figure 11.7 A sample false negative (top) and false positive (bottom) event pair.

order to draw a relatedness link. On the other hand, the models struggled to set apart individual incidents (see Figure 11.7, bottom) belonging to a larger event context, which typically share lexical profile, LOCATION, and TYPE slots. Among all false classifications 60% were false negatives and 40% were false positives.

11.5 Conclusions

This chapter reported on experiments of testing ML methods using a wide range of textual and metadata features to train classifiers for linking related event templates that have been automatically extracted from online news. Though exploiting solely textual features resulted in a 93.6% F1 score evaluated on a 22,000 event-pair corpus, adding metadata features allowed to improve it up to 96.7% on the same corpora, mainly thanks to exploitation of an event similarity metric that computes geographical distance between events with high discriminatory power.

Future research envisaged encompasses (a) adaptation and evaluation of the approach on event data in other languages; (b) consideration of additional lightweight features (e.g., exploitation of country/region size assuming that events occurring in larger countries are less likely to be related, utilization of the structure of the URLs to the related sources that might hint at reporting over time on some bigger events/stories over certain period of time); (c) based on the work carried out, elaboration of additional event similarity metrics to train models for cross-lingual event linking (Rupnik et al., 2016; Al-Badrashiny et al., 2017); and (d) introducing an additional subclassification of the related class. As a matter of fact, we carried out an initial attempt to subclassify a sample of 150 event pairs (e_1, e_2) labeled as related into one of the four subclasses: IDENTITY (reporting on the same event), SAME_CAUSE (e_1 and e_2 were triggered by the same event; e.g., arrests/investigations and visit of a political leader, both following a terrorist attack), e_1 UPDATES_OR_DEPENDS_ON e_2 and the symmetric case (terrorist attack followed by an introduction of an emergency situation). However, the bilateral κ scores between the three annotators involved ranged from 0.45 to 0.63, which indicates the complexity of the task.

The event linking data set GOLD used for carrying out the reported study, which includes both labeled event pairs and the full set of the event templates from which the event pairs were selected, is available at: http://piskorski.waw .pl/resources/eventLinking/GoldNew.zip.

References

Al-Badrashiny, Mohamed, Bolton, Jason, Chaganty, Arun Tejasvi, et al. (eds.). 2017. *Proceedings of the 2017 Text Analysis Conference, TAC 2017, Gaithersburg, Maryland, USA, November 13–14, 2017.* NIST.

Atkinson, Martin, Piskorski, Jakub, Tanev, Hristo, and Zavarella, Vanni. 2017. On the Creation of a Security-Related Event Corpus. Pages 59–65 of: Caselli, Tommaso, Miller, Ben, van Erp, Marieke, et al. (eds.), *Proceedings of the Events and Stories in the News Workshop 2017.* Vancouver: Association for Computational Linguistics.

Banerjee, Satanjeev, and Pedersen, Ted. 2002. An Adapted Lesk Algorithm for Word Sense Disambiguation Using WordNet. Pages 136–145 of: Gelbukh, Alexander F. (ed.), *Proceedings of the Third International Conference on Computational Linguistics and Intelligent Text Processing.* CICLing '02. Berlin: Springer.

Bejan, Cosmin Adrian, and Harabagiu, Sanda. 2010. Unsupervised Event Coreference Resolution with Rich Linguistic Features. Pages 1412-1422 of: Hajič, Jan, Carberry, Sandra, Clark, Stephen, and Nivre, Joakim (eds.), *Proceedings of the 48th Annual Meeting of the Association for Computational Linguistics.*

Budanitsky, Alexander, and Hirst, Graeme. 2001. Semantic Distance in WordNet: An Experimental, Application-Oriented Evaluation of Five Measures. In: *Proceedings of the Workshop on WORDNET and Other Lexical Resources, NAACL 2001.*

Caselli, Tommaso, and Vossen, Piek. 2017. The Event StoryLine Corpus: A New Benchmark for Causal and Temporal Relation Extraction. Pages 77–86 of: Caselli, Tommaso, Miller, Ben, van Erp, Marieke, et al. (eds.), *Proceedings of the Events and Stories in the News Workshop.* Vancouver: Association for Computational Linguistics.

Chesney, Sophie, Jacquet, Guillaume, Steinberger, Ralf, and Piskorski, Jakub. 2017. Multi-word Entity Classification in a Highly Multilingual Environment. Pages 11–20 of: Markantonatou, Stella, Ramisch, Carlos, Savary, Agata, and Vincze, Veronika (eds.), *MWE@EACL*. Association for Computational Linguistics.

Cybulska, A., and Vossen, P. 2014. Using a Sledgehammer to Crack a Nut? Lexical Diversity and Event Coreference Resolution. In: *Proceedings of the 9th Language Resources and Evaluation Conference (LREC2014)*.

Ehrmann, Maud, Jacquet, Guillaume, and Steinberger, Ralf. 2017. JRC-Names: Multilingual entity name variants and titles as Linked Data. *Semantic Web*, **8**(2), 283–295.

Guo, Weiwei, Li, Hao, Ji, Heng, and Diab, Mona. 2013. Linking Tweets to News: A Framework to Enrich Short Text Data in Social Media. Pages 239–249 of: Schuetze, Hinrich, Fung, Pascale, and Poesio, Massimo (eds.), *Proceedings of the 51st Annual Meeting of the Association for Computational Linguistics: Volume 1. Long Papers*. Sofia, Bulgaria: Association for Computational Linguistics.

King, Gary, and Lowe, Will. 2003. An Automated Information Extraction Tool For International Conflict Data with Performance as Good as Human Coders. *International Organization*, **57**, 617–642.

Krause, Sebastian, Xu, Feiyu, Uszkoreit, Hans, and Weissenborn, Dirk. 2016. Event Linking with Sentential Features from Convolutional Neural Networks. Pages 239–249 of: Riezler, Stefan, and Goldberg, Yoav (eds.), *Proceedings of the 20th SIGNLL Conference on Computational Natural Language Learning*. Berlin: Association for Computational Linguistics.

Le, Quoc, and Mikolov, Tomas. 2014. Distributed Representations of Sentences and Documents. Pages II–1188–II–1196 of: Xing, Eric P., and Jebara, Tony (eds.), *Proceedings of the 31st International Conference on International Conference on Machine Learning. Volume 32*. ICML'14. JMLR.org.

Levenshtein, V.I. 1966. Binary Codes Capable of Correcting Deletions, Insertions and Reversals. *Soviet Physics Doklady*, **10**, 707.

Mitamura, Teruko, Liu, Zhengzhong, and Hovy, Eduard H. 2015. Overview of TAC KBP 2015 Event Nugget Track. In: *TAC 2015*.

Mohamed Al-Badrashiny, Jason Bolton, Arun Tejasvi Chaganty Kevin Clark Craig Harman Lifu Huang Matthew Lamm Jinhao Lei Di Lu Xiaoman Pan Ashwin Paranjape Ellie Pavlick Haoruo Peng Peng Qi Pushpendre Rastogi Abigail See Kai Sun Max Thomas Chen-Tse Tsai Hao Wu Boliang Zhang Chris Callison-Burch Claire Cardie Heng Ji Christopher D. Manning Smaranda Muresan Owen Rambow Dan Roth Mark Sammons, and Durme, Benjamin Van (eds). 2017. *Proceedings of the 2017 Text Analysis Conference, TAC 2017, Gaithersburg, Maryland, USA, November 13-14, 2017*. NIST.

Navarro, Gonzalo. 2001. A Guided Tour to Approximate String Matching. *ACM Computing Surveys*, **33**(1), 31–88.

Navigli, Roberto, and Ponzetto, Simone Paolo. 2012. BabelNet: The Automatic Construction, Evaluation and Application of a Wide-coverage Multilingual Semantic Network. *Artificial Intelligence*, **193**, 217–250.

Nothman, Joel, Honnibal, Matthew, Hachey, Ben, and Curran, James R. 2012. Event Linking: Grounding Event Reference in a News Archive. Pages 228–232 of: Li,

Haizhou, Lin, Chin-Yew, Osborne, Miles, Lee, Gary Geunbae, and Park, Jong C. (eds.), *Proceedings of the 50th Annual Meeting of the Association for Computational Linguistics: Volume 2. Short Papers.* Jeju Island, Korea: Association for Computational Linguistics.

Pedregosa, F., Varoquaux, G., Gramfort, A., et al. 2011. Scikit-learn: Machine Learning in Python. *Journal of Machine Learning Research*, **12**, 2825–2830.

Pennington, Jeffrey, Socher, Richard, and Manning, Christopher D. 2014. Glove: Global Vectors for Word Representation. Pages 1532–1543 of: Moschitti, Alessandro, Pang, Bo, and Daelemans, Walter (eds.), *Proceedings of EMNLP 2014*, Vol. 14.

Piskorski, Jakub, Wieloch, Karol, and Sydow, Marcin. 2009. On Knowledge-Poor Methods for Person Name Matching and Lemmatization for Highly Inflectional Languages. *Information Retrieval*, **12**(3), 275–299.

Rupnik, Jan, Muhič, Andrej, Leban, Gregor, et al. 2016. News Across Languages – Cross-lingual Document Similarity and Event Tracking. *Journal of Artificial Intelligence Research*, **55**(1), 283–316.

Šarić, Frane, Glavaš, Goran, Karan, Mladen, Šnajder, Jan, and Bašić, Bojana Dalbelo. 2012. TakeLab: Systems for Measuring Semantic Text Similarity. Pages 441–448 of: Agirre, Eneko, Bos, Johan, Diab, Mona, et al. (eds.), *Proceedings of the 1st Joint Conference on Lexical and Computational Semantics: Volume 1. Proceedings of the Main Conference and the Shared Task, and Volume 2. Proceedings of the Sixth International Workshop on Semantic Evaluation.* SemEval '12. Stroudsburg, PA: Association for Computational Linguistics.

Socher, Richard, Huang, Eric H., Pennington, Jeffrey, Ng, Andrew Y., and Manning, Christopher D. 2011. Dynamic Pooling and Unfolding Recursive Autoencoders for Paraphrase Detection. Pages 801–809 of: *Proceedings of the 24th International Conference on Neural Information Processing Systems.* NIPS'11. Red Hook, NY: Curran Associates.

Vossen, Piek, Agerri, Rodrigo, Aldabe, Itziar, et al. 2016. NewsReader: Using knowledge resources in a Cross-lingual Reading Machine to Generate More Knowledge from Massive Streams of News. *Knowledge-Based Systems*, **110**, 60–85.

Wu, Zhibiao, and Palmer, Martha. 1994. Verbs Semantics and Lexical Selection. Pages 133–138 of: *Proceedings of the 32nd Annual Meeting on Association for Computational Linguistics.* ACL '94. Stroudsburg, PA: Association for Computational Linguistics.

Yangarber, Roman, Von Etter, Peter, and Steinberger, Ralf. 2008. Content Collection and Analysis in the Domain of Epidemiology. In: *Proceedings of DrMED 2008: International Workshop on Describing Medical Web Resources at MIE 2008: the 21st International Congress of the European Federation for Medical Informatics 2008.*

12

Semantic Storytelling

From Experiments and Prototypes to a Technical Solution

Georg Rehm, Karolina Zaczynska, Peter Bourgonje,
Malte Ostendorff, Julián Moreno-Schneider, Maria Berger,
Jens Rauenbusch, André Schmidt, Mikka Wild, Joachim Böttger,
Joachim Quantz, Jan Thomsen, and Rolf Fricke

Abstract. In the past we experimented with variations of an approach we call semantic storytelling, in which we use multiple text analytics components including named entity recognition and event detection. This chapter summarises some of our previous work with an emphasis on the detection of movement action events and describes the long-term semantic storytelling vision as well as the setup and approach of our future work towards a robust technical solution, which is primarily driven by three industry use cases. Ultimately, we plan to contribute an implemented approach for semantic storytelling that makes use of various analytics services and that can be deployed in a flexible way in various industrial production environments.

12.1 Introduction: Technologies for Content Curation

With the ever increasing amount of digital content, users face the challenge of coping with enormous quantities of information. This is especially true for digital content curators; i.e., analysts or knowledge workers such as journalists (Moreno-Schneider et al., 2017b), television producers (Rehm et al., 2018), designers (Rehm et al., 2017a), librarians (Neudecker and Rehm, 2016), and academics (Rehm et al., 2019a), among others. These, and other, professional profiles have in common that they monitor and process *incoming content* with the goal of producing *new content*. This involves various processes – for example, to scan, translate, skim, contextualise, sort, summarise, evaluate, validate, cross-reference and to assess content – often under extreme time pressure. In several research and innovation projects (Rehm et al., 2015, 2019a) and most recently in QURATOR (Rehm et al., 2020b), we have been developing technical approaches with the goal of supporting knowledge workers in their day-to-day jobs, curating large amounts of content with language and knowledge technologies more efficiently and more effectively. One of our focus areas is the identification and generation of storylines (see below). This includes both the (semi-)automatic creation of new content as well as helpful presentation and visualisation techniques that make use of the results of our semantic technologies. We call the approach semantic storytelling (Bourgonje et al., 2016b; Moreno-Schneider et al., 2016, 2017b; Rehm et al., 2017b, 2018, 2019b).

We focus on storytelling as a generic human technique to order a series of events in the world or, in a more abstract way, pieces of information, and find meaningful patterns in them (Bruner, 1991). By telling a story, we partially or fully relate events to a schematic structure – e.g., in terms of topic, locality or causal relationships – and construct explanatory models. Humans are able to dynamically adjust their narratives and tell their stories differently depending on who the listener is (Rishes et al., 2013), whereas this is still a challenging task for machines.

In recent years, storytelling has mostly been interpreted as a natural language generation (NLG) task (see, e.g., Fan et al., 2018, 2019), where the goal is actually to generate texts based on a headline or keywords, for example. We interpret the concept differently by concentrating on the *extraction* and *presentation* of stories and their individual parts, contained in incoming content streams; for example, document collections or social media feeds. The goal is to enable content curators to create new storylines based on the information extracted and presented by our technologies.

We see storylines as sets of building blocks that depending on their combination (temporal, geographical, causal etc.), can be assembled into a story in various ways. Our goal is the recognition of various atomic pieces of information (e.g., facts, propositions, entities, events) in multiple documents and the identification of semantic relations between these atomic pieces. Corresponding applications can be conceptualised, among others, as information systems (for the retrieval of existing content) or recommender systems (focusing upon the creation of new content).

The remainder of this chapter is structured as follows. First, Section 12.2 summarises our previous work on the topic, focusing on technical components and developments. Section 12.3 briefly presents our three current industry application scenarios from which we derive a set of requirements. These inform our most recent technical approach, which is especially geared towards robustness and flexibility as well as practical application in the three use cases (Section 12.4). Section 12.5 presents related work. Section 12.6 concludes the chapter.

12.2 Semantic Storytelling: Selected Components

Semantic storytelling can be conceptualised as the automatic or semi-automatic generation of different storylines based on information extracted from extensive document collections or social media streams and then processed, classified, annotated and visualised, typically in an interactive way. In the following, we describe selected preliminary approaches and experimental components, as well as their interactions, that we developed over the years working on the topic.

12.2.1 Text and Document Analytics and Linked Data

A set of text analytics services is the technological foundation of our semantic storytelling architecture (see, e.g., Bourgonje et al., 2016a,b; Moreno-Schneider et al., 2016; Rehm et al., 2018). These belong to the following three larger groups:

1. Services that analyse complete documents (or document collections) to provide document-level metadata: language identification, document structure analysis, text genre detection, topic detection
2. Services that extract, annotate and enrich specific parts of the incoming content: named entity recognition (including rudimentary co-reference resolution), named entity linking, time expression analysis, topic detection, event detection
3. Services that transform parts of the content or whole documents: single document summarisation, multidocument summarisation, automated translation

The services are in different stages of maturity. They are orchestrated using a workflow manager and additional platform-related tooling (Moreno-Schneider et al., 2020). Eventually, they will be made available through the European Language Grid (Rehm et al., 2020a).

Named entity recognition and linking as well as time expression analysis are performed to identify named entities of various types and classes (persons, locations, organisation etc.). Whenever possible, entities, topics etc. are anchored to external knowledge graphs (e.g., DBPedia, Wikidata, Geonames), which enables us to perform SPARQL queries to retrieve additional information for each item such as, e.g., Global Positioning System (GPS) coordinates for locations. The integration of the results of the time expression analysis allows reasoning over temporal expressions and anchoring entities and events to a timeline. We use topic detection to assign abstract topics to individual sentences, paragraphs, chapters and documents. Annotated topics constitute yet another layer of accessing and recombining the processed content. For the annotations themselves we use NLP Interchange Format (Hellmann et al., 2013), which allows the exploitation of the Semantic Web and Linked Data paradigm (including its vast set of formats, formalisms and tools) and Linked Open Data resources for storyline generation.

To be able to analyse a wide variety of incoming documents with the same setup, we distinguish between different classes or genres of documents; i.e., we experiment with different approaches for identifying document structures (Rehm et al., 2019b) and document genres (Rehm, 2007). An ontology to represent a heterogeneous set of document characteristics, essentially tying together all the different annotations mentioned above, is currently under development.

12.2.2 Detection of Movement Action Events

To describe one service and experiment in more detail, we implemented an event detection system based on Yang and Mitchell (2016) to pinpoint words or phrases in sentences that refer to events involving participants and locations affected by other events and spatiotemporal aspects. The module is trained on the ACE 2004 data (Doddington et al., 2004). This service can also perform event detection crosslingually by automatically translating non-English-language documents to English first and then detecting events in the translated documents.

The prototype described below enables putting together a story interactively based on semantically enriched content. As a first use case, we concentrated on the approximately. 2,800 letters exchanged between German architect Erich Mendelsohn and his wife, Luise, between 1910 and 1953. The collection contains 2,796 letters, written between 1910 and 1953, with a total of 1,002,742 words (359 words per letter on average) on more than 11,000 sheets of paper. Most are in German (2,481); the rest is written in English (312) and French (3).

Table 12.1. *Automatically extracted movement action events (MAEs)*

Letter Text	Extracted MAEs
Another train stopped [...] this would be the train with which Eric had to leave Cleveland.	Eric, Cleveland, [ ], [ ], [ ], train
because I have to leave on the 13th for Chicago.	I [*Erich*], Croton on Hudson, NY, Chicago, 13th Dec. 1945, [ ], [ ]
April 5th 48 Sweetheart – Here I am – just arrived in Palm Springs [...]	I [*Erich*], [ ], Palm Springs, [ ], 5th April 1948, [ ]
Germaine wants me to come up with her to Tahoe – she will be there for 2 weeks from July 15th [...]	Germaine, [ ], Tahoe, [ ], 15th July, [ ]
Thompsons are leaving for a week – [...] at the Beverly Hills on Thursday night!!	Thompsons, [ ], Beverly Hills, 8th July, [ ], [ ]

In the letters, the Mendelsohns discuss their private and professional lives, their relationship, meetings with friends and business partners, and also their travels. Bienert and de Wit (2014) provide transcriptions of the letters together with scans, photos and metadata.

We want to transform this set of interconnected *letters* into a *travelogue* that provides an engaging story to the reader and that also enables additional modes of access; e.g., through map-based or timeline-based visualisations. In this experiment we explore to what extent it is possible to automate the production of a travelogue from a collection of letters. We focused on a specific class of events, movement action events (MAEs). A complete description of the experiment can be found elsewhere (Rehm et al., 2017b); here we only present a few examples of extracted MAEs to demonstrate the functionality (Table 12.1). In the letters, MAEs are typically mentioned whenever the author is undertaking or about to undertake a trip from A to B using a specific mode of transport. An MAE consists of the six-tuple $MAE = <P, L_O, L_D, t_d, t_a, m>$, where P is a reference to the participant (E. or L. Mendelsohn), L_O and L_D are the origin and destination locations (named locations, GPS coordinates), t_d and t_a are the time of departure and arrival and m is the mode of transport. Each component is optional as long as the MAE contains a participant and a destination. We have been able to successfully retrace the various journeys of the Mendelsohns. Through additional modes of access to the content base (i.e., the letters themselves, photographs, sketches), by means of maps or timelines, the authoring environment (Section 12.2.3) provides suggestions – i.e., potential story paths – to the content curator who is using the tool for putting together a new story on the Mendelsohns' lives and journeys.

12.2.3 Storytelling Prototypes and User Interfaces

Following the general approach described above, we implemented a number of experimental prototypes and corresponding interactive user interfaces (UIs; Bourgonje et al., 2016b; Rehm et al., 2017b; Moreno-Schneider et al., 2016; Rehm et al., 2018). On top of the semantic analysis of document collections, we map the extracted information, whenever possible, to Linked Open Data (LOD), and visualise the result (Moreno-Schneider et al., 2017a; Rehm et al., 2017a). The UIs support content curators in the process of identifying interesting or surprising relationships between different concepts or entities mentioned in the processed documents. By providing feedback to the output of certain semantic services, content curators have some amount of control on the workflow. They are able to upload existing language resources to adapt individual services. For example, the Named Entity Recognition (NER) service allows users to supply dictionaries for entity linking and the event detection service allows users to supply lists of entities for the identification of agents for events.

The storytelling UIs involve the dynamic and interactive recomposition and visualisation of extracted information based on the information extracted from the text analytics services. This especially involves arranging content elements (documents, paragraphs, sentences, claims or events) on a dynamic timeline. The summarisation services are used to compress larger pieces of content into bites that can be easily digested, moved around on the screen and maybe expanded back into their original versions. We currently experiment with the algorithmic construction of storylines based on the recomposition of previously extracted information (for more details, see Section 12.4).

To complement the experiment in which we extracted movement action events (Section 12.2.2), an authoring environment was developed, and several screens of the UI are shown in Figure 12.1. It was a conscious design decision to move beyond the typical notion of a 'web page' that is broken up into different 'modules' using templates. The focus of this prototype is the development of engaging stories told through informative content. With this tool the content curator can interactively put together a story based on the semantically enriched content. In this example case we work with the letters exchanged between Erich and Luise Mendelsohn (see Section 12.2.2).

1. Create new story from a collection

2. Drag and drop content into the story

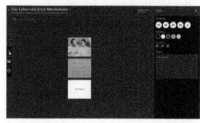

3. Arrange the story

4. Search additional content pieces

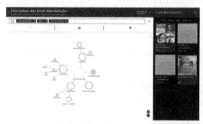

5. Examine relations between entities

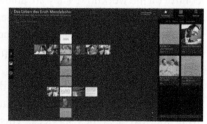

6. Final story, ready to be deployed

Figure 12.1 Semantic storytelling authoring environment.

12.3 Semantic Storytelling in Industry Use Cases

The emerging semantic storytelling technologies described in this chapter, especially in Section 12.4, are primarily developed for three of the industry partners in the QURATOR project (Rehm et al., 2020b). The goal is to integrate them as base technologies into the three use cases (UC1, UC2, UC3) and prototype applications. In the following subsections we describe these use cases, from which we derive a set of basic requirements that inform the final design of our technical approach.

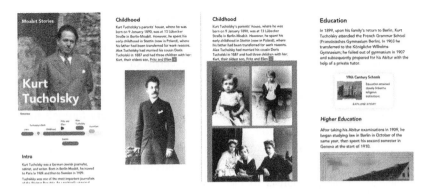

Figure 12.2 Example screens of the 'Explore the Neigbourhood!' concept.

12.3.1 Use Case: Explore the Neighbourhood!

The first use case, conceptualised by 3pc GmbH (http://3pc.de), enables urban explorers to discover a neighbourhood (UC1). The idea is to collect content from online sources, cultural heritage archives or publishing houses to identify relevant content that matches the current location. This enables the location-aware application to 'tell stories' about the neighbourhood. In the prototype we use Moabit, a multicultural Berlin district with a rich history and lively present. Our vision for the app is to present stories that have been generated (semi-)automatically according to their location, time, relevance for a certain user, location and budget.

The app presents curated interactive stories to a user who is located in Moabit or generates new ones. Figure 12.2 shows an example of the option to explore the life of Kurt Tucholsky, a German-Jewish journalist and writer, born in Moabit in 1890. The user can follow the linear story through Tucholsky's life, consuming texts, (historic) images, video and audio files and interactive elements. Stories are conceptualised as hypertexts, where users can dive deeper into certain aspects, expanding, shortening or bypassing topics. The app also reacts to data, such as weather, traffic, and, crucially, the current location. It has access to further information, such as opening times of points of interest. Augmenting these pieces of information through digitised archives enables stories with interactive paths and junctions that are better suited to the users' personal interests. Semantic storytelling is needed to support editors in their curation process and, eventually, to generate stories automatically.

12.3.2 Use Case: Smart Newsboard

The Smart Newsboard is a vision by Condat AG (http://condat.de) that uses semantic storytelling technologies for the production of new content based on articles on a specific topic (UC2). This involves various curation services, such as, e.g., (1) finding original sources (through targeted searches in RSS feeds or social media); (2) categorising these sources into clusters through topic detection or text classification; (3) applying text analytics and recognising and linking named entities to resources such as Wikidata. This allows the creation of knowledge graphs to identify connections between people and events, to enable journalists to take a deep dive. A crucial feature is the detection of temporal expressions, assigning them to facts or claims, whether they are absolute (e.g., *2019, October 3rd*) or relative (e.g., *last week, next Monday, after that*), that can be used to generate timelines. Other important services include fact checking to help journalists evaluate the trustworthiness of content and multidocument summarisation (Aksenov et al., 2020). Putting these services in practice, the outline of a news story can be generated together with related content. The main focus of storytelling in the Smart Newsboard is to generate a story outline in a linear and neutral way.

12.3.3 Use Case: Wikipedia Trails

This use case, devised by ART+COM AG (http://artcom.de), produces a visual map based on Wikipedia usage, with the aim of supporting knowledge workers and analysts in the process of acquiring, recording, and passing on knowledge (UC3; Figure 12.3). Inspired by Vannevar Bush's seminal essay

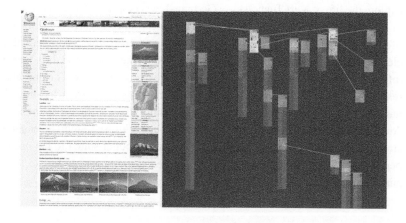

Figure 12.3 Example screen of the 'Wikipedia Trails' concept.

'As We May Think' (Bush, 1945), the tool records timestamped snapshots of Wikipedia pages while a user navigates through them. Positions in pages and clicked links are also recorded. The data are continually pieced together in a visualisation, yielding long, thumbnail-like representations of pages. These thumbnails are then placed in relation to each other using force-directed graph layout techniques. The approach allows for the gradual buildup of what we imagine Bush termed a 'trail': an integrated recording of how users navigate a knowledge space. The aim is a novel method that sits somewhere between existing perspectives for the preservation of knowledge acquisition that are either too broad (browser history) or too piecemeal (files, bookmarks, tabs) by visualising a map of the process itself.

12.3.4 Integrating Semantic Storytelling

From the three use cases, we can derive requirements for the methodology of the prototype development. Our goal is to design the approach in such a way that we can implement, based on the various experimental developments presented in Section 12.2, *one* robust and flexible technology solution that addresses the requirements of *all three* industry project partners at the same time.

UC1 needs storytelling support for the (semi-)automatic production of interactive stories. Either a human editor or an automated system is putting together stories that can be experienced by users of the mobile app. UC2 is similar to UC1. In both use cases, semantic storytelling functionalities are needed to suggest content relevant for the topic on which a journalist is currently writing a story. In contrast to UC1, in UC2 this needs to happen dynamically and in real time. The main purpose of UC3 is the dynamic visualisation of the browsing history of Wikipedia pages to support knowledge workers in desk research and knowledge acquisition tasks; i.e., storytelling technologies are meant to provide further insights into the semantic relationships between Wikipedia pages beyond the mere fact that hyperlinks exist between them.

Regarding the input, all three use cases need support for the processing of complete documents but also for addressing (including linking to) only parts of documents – i.e., individual paragraphs or sentences – to expose only key sentences to the user. The technology needs to be able to handle different text types, from historical cultural heritage documents and information made available by a municipality or city administrations (UC1) to RSS feeds and news articles (UC2) to web texts, e.g., Wikipedia pages (UC3). All three include multimedia elements, the processing of which is also needed. Furthermore, UC1 and UC2 have a demand for services such as summarisation and machine translation.

12.4 Towards a Flexible and Robust Technology Solution for Semantic Storytelling

We performed an analysis of the three use cases with the goal of identifying technical building blocks that can be shared by UC1, UC2 and UC3. The key insight of this analysis is that three simple yet technically ambitious processing steps, operating on two text segments, are needed to address the demands in the three use cases, in addition to the various tools and services mentioned previously (Section 12.2).

We can illustrate the functionality of these three technical building blocks with an example: a journalist is working on a story on a topic T. Our goal is to identify and to suggest new content that can be included in the emerging story. First, we need to identify whether, e.g., a certain tweet or text from an incoming RSS feed is *relevant* for T. Second, we need to determine the *importance* of the incoming tweet or article for the emerging story. Third, we identify the *semantic relation* between the incoming and the emerging article, which could be, among others, *background*, *cause*, *contrast* and *example*. The result of the third step can be also used in terms of visualisation; e.g., putting background information in the margins or recommending arguments in favour of or against a certain point of view; i.e., the approach should be able to extract and classify semantic relations between text segments (see Figure 12.4 and Rehm et al., 2019c, for more details).

Below, we describe the three steps (identification of a new or incoming text segment's *relevance* and *importance* as well as the *semantic or discourse relation* that holds between the new, incoming segment and topic T) that are at the core of our approach in more detail. Note that steps 1 and 2 as well as steps 2 and 3 overlap in terms of their corresponding scope. For example, when dealing with self-contained document collections in UC1, step 1 can be omitted because *relevance* may be an inherent property of a collection that includes content about a certain neighbourhood. Similarly, the type of relation that holds between two segments can also bear information on their relative importance, rendering the separation between steps 2 and 3 less strict.

Step 1: Determine the Relevance of a Segment for a Topic The approach starts with a topic T, instantiated through a text segment (e.g., a complete document, headline, summary, or a named entity), specified by a journalist who is writing a story on T. In order to identify content pieces relevant for T, we process – maybe even continuously – incoming news feeds, self-contained document collections, systematically compiled corpora or knowledge bases. For each piece of content processed, we need to decide whether its topic is relevant for T.

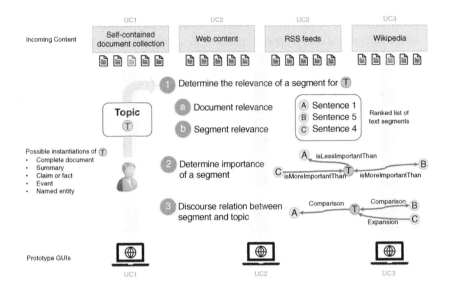

Figure 12.4 Architecture of the approach.

Relevance can be computed in various ways. We can employ text similarity measures, approaches from information retrieval or the overlap in terms of named entities contained in the segments. Crucially, the (accuracy of the) approach is dependent on the length of the segments. We currently concentrate on topic modeling (latent Dirichlet allocation [LDA], latent semantic analysis [LSA]). Without explicitly modeling topics, we can also perform pair-wise comparisons of document similarity (see, e.g., Salton and McGill, 1983; Pagliardini et al., 2018; Selivanov and Wang, 2016).

Step 2: Determine the Importance of a Segment If a document d is related to T, we can determine the importance of d (and its individual segments) with regard to T. Though this task is related to step 1, off-the-shelf approaches for determining the importance of a text segment with regard to a topic do not exist. Various cues can potentially be exploited, though. For example, with regard to UC2, an incoming news piece on T, published seconds ago, that includes the cue word 'BREAKING' in its title can surely be considered important. Determining the topical importance can also be framed as a question answering task, where T is the question. Transformer-based language models have achieved state-of-the-art results for question answering (Devlin et al., 2019), highlighting the relevance of these model architectures for storytelling.

We can also borrow from rhetorical structure theory (RST, Mann and Thompson, 1988). The construction of an RST tree involves various decisions with regard to the status of text segments including their discourse relation to other segments and also regarding their role as a *nucleus* (N, the important part of a relation) or as a *satellite* (S, the contributing part) in a specific discourse relation. Two segments are assigned either an S–N, N–S or N–N structure. This subtask can be done in isolation (Hernault et al., 2010; Soricut and Marcu, 2003) or combined with the relation classification task (Joty et al., 2015). Performed iteratively, this pair-wise classification can result in a set of most important segments regarding T. Due to low amounts of training data (Carlson et al., 2002), resulting in less robust classifiers, we follow Sporleder and Lapata (2005) in isolating the nuclearity assignment task.

Step 3: Determine the Discourse Relation between Two Segments The modeling of coherence relations in textual content is at the core of discourse processing and corresponding parsing frameworks. These analyse a text for, typically, intratextual but intersentential relations. Some of the frameworks also indicate, given two segments, which is the more important one. We borrow from discourse parsing, but there are several added challenges. Crucially, our system needs to be able to robustly process and compare short segments (typically, sentences or paragraphs) extracted from *different* texts for which we have ample evidence from step 1 that the two texts are relevant to each other. After having established the relevance and relative importance, we proceed with determining the discourse or semantic relation that exists between these individual segments from *different* texts. Our initial experiments are based on the Penn Discourse Tree Bank (PDTB). We adopt Penn Discourse Tree Bank's (PDTB) four top-level senses and achieve promising results (Rehm et al., 2019c). Once established between the two segments, the key idea is to make use of the discourse relation in visualisations and UIs recommendations, text generation approaches etc.

12.5 Related Work

In the following, we provide a brief overview of related work conducted in several areas including narratology, discourse theory, and applied work in computational linguistics and language technology.

Several approaches grounded in narratology address storytelling as a way of automatising the detection of instances of story grammars (Rumelhart, 1975), especially events, in texts. Vossen et al. (2021) present a data set for the detection of temporal and causal relations and use a plot structure (Bal, 1997) to order events found in narratives or, more generally, text documents, chronologically and logically. According to Bal (1997), narratives follow a plot structure that consists of ordered events, told by an agent or author and caused or experienced by actors. Yarlott and Finlayson (2016) use Propp's (1968) morphology of Russian hero tales for story detection and generation systems. In his book, first published in 1928, Propp analyzes the basic structural elements of Russian folk tales, which always occur in a fixed, consecutive order.

Yan et al. (2019) describe a system that learns 'functional story schemas' as sets of functional structures (e.g., character introduction, conflict setup, etc.) in social media narratives. They extract patterns of functional structures. Afterwards their formation in a story is analyzed across all stories to find schematic structures. In contrast, Gordon et al. (2011) use stories from blog articles to perform automated causal reasoning. Their statistical and information retrieval–focused experiments show that a simple co-occurrence measure among the words of an antecedent (cause, reason) and a consequent (result) in a corpus of personal stories can help to derive causal information.

Cucchiarelli et al. (2018) examine news recommendations and present a technique that, for a given event, suggests news articles not covered previously by a journalist's research work. They measure an event in relation to its media coverage and compare it to the potential reader's communicative patterns, according to Twitter and Wikipedia analyses. The method recommends topics of interest to the reader that are only poorly covered in published news but emerge as topics of interest in Twitter and Wikipedia. In contrast, Bois et al. (2017) recommend articles based on simple lexical similarity. They link news articles in the form of a graph and label links to inform users on the nature of the relation between two news pieces.

Ribeiro et al. (2017) cluster news articles based on identified event instances and word alignment. They attempt to form clusters of online articles that deal with a certain event type. Nie et al. (2019) use dependency parsing and discourse relations to determine sentence relations by learning corresponding vector representations. Yarlott et al. (2018) apply the theory of hierarchical discourse by Dijk (1988) to examine how paragraphs behave when used as discourse structure units in news articles. They describe the relations of paragraphs with regard to the events in an article. Learning the discourse structure of sections of news articles helps the authors to understand the importance and temporal order of story items.

12.6 Conclusions and Future Work

After laying the groundwork for the full implementation of semantic storytelling through various experiments in a number of areas, we are now approaching the last phase, in which we attempt to combine the different preliminary pieces described in Section 12.2, including various text analytics and semantic enrichment services that operate on documents, document collections or smaller segments of documents (Rehm et al., 2019b), with the emerging set of technologies described in Section 12.4. To this end, we identified the key common building blocks of three industry use cases for semantic storytelling technologies. Though step 1 can be implemented using one of several known approaches, steps 2 and 3 are much more challenging (Figure 12.4). Essentially, our approach is grounded in the assumption that different texts that deal with the *same* topic but that are from *different* authors and *different* sources can be interconnected in a meaningful way through discourse relations, which we attempt to extract automatically in order to expose the identified relations to the respective downstream application. It is exactly these semantic relations or discourse relations and their directionality that we want to expose to the respective user in the corresponding prototype. With regard to the authoring environment, such relations hold between two media assets (as seen in the screenshots shown in Figure 12.1), and we want to support content curators making use of these relations by exposing them explicitly and exploiting them in the construction of storylines in a semiautomatic or fully automatic way. Though our initial experiments are promising (Rehm et al., 2019c), they also show that additional research is needed before we can integrate these technologies into the respective prototypes. Data sets annotated for rhetorical structure, discourse structure or, closely related, event structure are still rather limited both in availability and in size.

Our future work will thus focus on expanding our setup significantly, especially with regard to the analysis and classification of discourse relations and more sophisticated processing of connectives. We will also integrate a more flexible approach with regard to the processing of single documents by concentrating on larger parts of a document including longer summaries and paraphrased variants to increase coverage and recall. Taking into account explicit ontological knowledge to identify semantic relations between texts will also be an important next step towards the completion of the envisaged semantic storytelling architecture (Rehm et al., 2019b).

Acknowledgments This work is funded by the German Federal Ministry of Education and Research (BMBF) through the project QURATOR (http:// qurator.ai, Unternehmen Region, Wachstumskern, grant no. 03WKDA1A).

References

Aksenov, Dmitrii, Moreno-Schneider, Julián, Bourgonje, Peter, Schwarzenberg, Robert, Hennig, Leonhard, and Rehm, Georg. 2020. Abstractive Text Summarization Based on Language Model Conditioning and Locality Modeling. Pages 6682–6691 of: Calzolari, Nicoletta, Báchet, Frédéric, Blache, Philippe, et al. (eds.), *Proceedings of the 12th Language Resources and Evaluation Conference (LREC 2020)*. Marseille, France: European Language Resources Association.

Bal, Mieke. 1997. *Narratology: Introduction to the Theory of Narrative*. University of Toronto Press.

Bienert, Andreas, and de Wit, Wim (eds.). 2014. *EMA – Erich Mendelsohn Archiv. Der Briefwechsel von Erich und Luise Mendelsohn 1910–1953*. Berlin: Staatliche Museen zu Berlin.

Bois, Rémi, Gravier, Guillaume, Jamet, Eric, Robert, Maxime, Morin, Emmanuel, Sébillot, Pascale, and Robert, Maxime. 2017. Language-Based Construction of Explorable News Graphs for Journalists. Pages 31–36 of: Popescu, Octavian, and Strapparava, Carlo (eds.), *Proceedings of the 2017 EMNLP Workshop on Natural Language Processing Meets Journalism*. Copenhagen: Association for Computational Linguistics.

Bourgonje, Peter, Moreno-Schneider, Julián, Rehm, Georg, and Sasaki, Felix. 2016a. Processing Document Collections to Automatically Extract Linked Data: Semantic Storytelling Technologies for Smart Curation Workflows. Pages 13–16 of: Gangemi, Aldo, and Gardent, Claire (eds.), *Proceedings of the 2nd International Workshop on Natural Language Generation and the Semantic Web (WebNLG 2016)*. Edinburgh: The Association for Computational Linguistics.

Bourgonje, Peter, Moreno-Schneider, Julián, Nehring, Jan, Rehm, Georg, Sasaki, Felix, and Srivastava, Ankit. 2016b. Towards a Platform for Curation Technologies: Enriching Text Collections with a Semantic-Web Layer. Pages 65–68 of: Sack, Harald, Rizzo, Giuseppe, Steinmetz, Nadine, Mladenic, Dunja, Auer, Sören, and Lange, Christoph (eds.), *The Semantic Web*. Lecture Notes in Computer Science, no. 9989. Springer.

Bruner, Jerome. 1991. The Narrative Construction of Reality. *Critical Inquiry*, **18**(1), 1–21.

Bush, Vannevar. 1945. As we may think. *The Atlantic*, **176**(1), 101–108.

Carlson, Lynn, Marcu, Daniel, and Okurowski, Mary Ellen. 2002. *RST Discourse Treebank*. Linguistic Data Consortium, Online. https://catalog.ldc.upenn.edu/LDC2002T07.

Cucchiarelli, Alessandro, Morbidoni, Christian, Stilo, Giovanni, and Velardi, Paola. 2018. What to Write and Why: A Recommender for News Media. Pages 1321–1330 of: Haddad, Hisham M., Wainwright, Roger L., and Chbeir, Richard (eds.), *Proceedings of the 33rd Annual ACM Symposium on Applied Computing*. ACM.

Dijk, Teun van. 1988. *News as Discourse*. Communication Series. Lawrence Erlbaum Associates.

Doddington, George, Mitchell, Alexis, Przybocki, Mark, Ramshaw, Lance, Strassel, Stephanie, and Weischedel, Ralph. 2004. The Automatic Content Extraction

(ACE) Program – Tasks, Data, and Evaluation. In: *Proceedings of the Fourth International Conference on Language Resources and Evaluation (LREC'04)*. Lisbon: European Language Resources Association.

Fan, Angela, Lewis, Mike, and Dauphin, Yann. 2018. Hierarchical Neural Story Generation. Pages 889–898 of: Gurevych, Iryna, and Miyao, Yusuke (eds.), *Proceedings of the 56th Annual Meeting of the Association for Computational Linguistics, Volume 1: Long Papers*. Association for Computational Linguistics.

Fan, Angela, Lewis, Mike, and Dauphin, Yann. 2019. *Strategies for Structuring Story Generation*. arXiv preprint arXiv:1902.01109.

Gordon, Andrew S., Bejan, Cosmin A., and Sagae, Kenji. 2011. Commonsense Causal Reasoning Using Millions of Personal Stories. In: Burgard, Wolfram, and Roth, Dan (eds.), *Proceedings of the Twenty-Fifth AAAI Conference on Artificial Intelligence*. AAAI Press.

Hellmann, Sebastian, Lehmann, Jens, Auer, Sören, and Brümmer, Martin. 2013. Integrating NLP Using Linked Data. Pages 98–113 of: Alani, Harith, Kagal, Lalana, Fokoue, Achille, Groth, et al. (eds), *Proceedings of the 12th International Semantic Web Conference*. 21–25 October. Springer.

Hernault, Hugo, Prendinger, Helmut, duVerle, David A., and Ishizuka, Mitsuru. 2010. HILDA: A Discourse Parser Using Support Vector Machine Classification. *Dialog & Discourse*, **1**(3), 1–33.

Joty, Shafiq, Carenini, Giuseppe, and Ng, Raymond T. 2015. CODRA: A Novel Discriminative Framework for Rhetorical Analysis. *Computational Linguistics*, **41**(3), 385–435.

Mann, William C., and Thompson, Sandra A. 1988. Rhetorical Structure Theory: Towards a Functional Theory of Text Organization. *Text-interdisciplinary Journal for the Study of Discourse*, **8**(3), 243–281.

Mikolov, Tomas, Chen, Kai, Corrado, Greg, and Dean, Jeffrey. 2013. Efficient Estimation of Word Representations in Vector Space. In: Bengio, Yoshua, and LeCun, Yann (eds.), *1st International Conference on Learning Representations*.

Moreno-Schneider, Julián, Bourgonje, Peter, Nehring, Jan, et al. 2016. Towards Semantic Story Telling with Digital Curation Technologies. In: Birnbaum, Larry, Popescu, Octavian, and Strapparava, Carlo (eds.), *Proceedings of Natural Language Processing Meets Journalism – IJCAI-16 Workshop (NLPMJ 2016)*.

Moreno-Schneider, Julián, Bourgonje, Peter, Kintzel, Florian, and Rehm, Georg. 2020. A Workflow Manager for Complex NLP and Content Curation Pipelines. Pages 73–80 of: Rehm, Georg, Bontcheva, Kalina, Choukri, Khalid, Hajic, Jan, Piperidis, Stelios, and Vasiljevs, Andrejs (eds.), *Proceedings of the 1st International Workshop on Language Technology Platforms (IWLTP 2020, co-located with LREC 2020)*. 16 May.

Moreno-Schneider, Julián, Bourgonje, Peter, and Rehm, Georg. 2017a. Towards User Interfaces for Semantic Storytelling. Pages 403–421 of: Yamamoto, Sakae (ed.), *Human Interface and the Management of Information: Information, Knowledge and Interaction Design, 19th International Conference, HCI International 2017 (Vancouver, Canada)*. Lecture Notes in Computer Science (LNCS), no. 10274, Part II. Cham, Switzerland: Springer.

Moreno-Schneider, Julián, Srivastava, Ankit, Bourgonje, Peter, Wabnitz, David, and Rehm, Georg. 2017b. Semantic Storytelling, Cross-Lingual Event Detection and

Other Semantic Services for a Newsroom Content Curation Dashboard. Pages 68–73 of: *Proceedings of the 2017 EMNLP Workshop: Natural Language Processing Meets Journalism.*

Neudecker, Clemens, and Rehm, Georg. 2016. Digitale Kuratierungstechnologien für Bibliotheken. *Zeitschrift für Bibliothekskultur 027.7*, **4**(2).

Nie, Allen, Bennett, Erin, and Goodman, Noah. 2019. DisSent: Learning Sentence Representations from Explicit Discourse Relations. Pages 4497–4510 of: *Proceedings of the 57th Annual Meeting of the Association for Computational Linguistics.*

Pagliardini, Matteo, Gupta, Prakhar, and Jaggi, Martin. 2018. Unsupervised Learning of Sentence Embeddings Using Compositional n-Gram Features. Pages 528–540 of: *Proceedings of the 2018 Conference of the North American Chapter of the Association for Computational Linguistics: Human Language Technologies.*

Propp, Vladimir Y. 1968. *Morphology of the Folktale.* University of Texas Press (Original publication date 1928).

Rehm, Georg. 2007. *Hypertextsorten: Definition – Struktur – Klassifikation.* PhD Thesis, Justus-Liebig-Universität Giessen.

Rehm, Georg, Berger, Maria, Elsholz, Ela, et al. 2020a. European Language Grid: An Overview. Pages 3359–3373 of: *Proceedings of the 12th Language Resources and Evaluation Conference (LREC 2020).* Marseille, France: European Language Resources Association.

Rehm, Georg, Bourgonje, Peter, Hegele, Stefanie, et al. 2020b. QURATOR: Innovative Technologies for Content and Data Curation. In: Paschke, Adrian, Neudecker, Clemens, Rehm, Georg, Qundus, Jamal Al, and Pintscher, Lydia (eds.), *Proceedings of QURATOR 2020 – The Conference for Intelligent Content Solutions.* January 2021.

Rehm, Georg, He, Jing, Moreno-Schneider, Julian, Nehring, Jan, and Quantz, Joachim. 2017a. Designing User Interfaces for Curation Technologies. Pages 388–406 of: Yamamoto, Sakae (ed.), *Human Interface and the Management of Information: Information, Knowledge and Interaction Design, 19th International Conference, HCI International 2017 (Vancouver, Canada). Lecture Notes in Computer Science (LNCS)*, no. 10273, Part I. Cham, Switzerland: Springer.

Rehm, Georg, Lee, Martin, Schneider, Julián Moreno, and Bourgonje, Peter. 2019a. Curation Technologies for a Cultural Heritage Archive: Analysing and Transforming a Heterogeneous Data Set into an Interactive Curation Workbench. Pages 117–122 of: Antonacopoulos, Apostolos, and Büchler, Marco (eds.), *DATeCH 2019: Proceedings of the 3rd International Conference on Digital Access to Textual Cultural Heritage.* 8–10 May.

Rehm, Georg, Moreno Schneider, Julián, Bourgonje, Peter, et al. 2017b. Event Detection and Semantic Storytelling: Generating a Travelogue from a large Collection of Personal Letters. Pages 42–51 of: Caselli, Tommaso, Miller, Ben, van Erp, Marieke, et al. (eds.), *Proceedings of the Events and Stories in the News Workshop.*

Rehm, Georg, Moreno Schneider, Julián, Bourgonje, Peter, et al. 2018. Different Types of Automated and Semi-Automated Semantic Storytelling: Curation Technologies for Different Sectors. Pages 232–247 of: Rehm, Georg, and Declerck, Thierry (eds.), *Language Technologies for the Challenges of the Digital Age: 27th International Conference, GSCL 2017, Berlin, Germany, 13–14 September, 2017. Lecture Notes in Artificial Intelligence (LNAI)*, no. 10713. Springer.

Rehm, Georg, and Sasaki, Felix. 2015. Digitale Kuratierungstechnologien – Verfahren für die eziente Verarbeitung, Erstellung und Verteilung qualitativ hochwertiger Medieninhalte. Pages 138–139 of: *Proceedings der Frühjahrstagung der Gesellschaft für Sprachtechnologie und Computerlinguistik (GSCL 2015).* 30 September–2 October.

Rehm, Georg, Zaczynska, Karolina, and Schneider, Julián Moreno. 2019b. Semantic Storytelling: Towards Identifying Storylines in Large Amounts of Text Content. Pages 63–70 of: Jorge, Alpio, Campos, Ricardo, Jatowt, Adam, and Bhatia, Sumit (eds.), *Proceedings of Text2Story – Second Workshop on Narrative Extraction From Texts co-located with 41th European Conference on Information Retrieval (ECIR 2019).* 14 April.

Rehm, Georg, Zaczynska, Karolina, Schneider, Julián Moreno, et al. 2020c. Towards Discourse Parsing-Inspired Semantic Storytelling. In: Paschke, Adrian, Neudecker, Clemens, Rehm, Georg, Qundus, Jamal Al, and Pintscher, Lydia (eds.), *Proceedings of Semantic Storytelling 269 QURATOR 2020 – The Conference for Intelligent Content Solutions.* 20–21 January.

Ribeiro, Swen, Ferret, Olivier, and Tannier, Xavier. 2017. Unsupervised Event Clustering and Aggregation from Newswire and Web Articles. Pages 62–67 of: Popescu, Octavian, and Strapparava, Carlo (eds.), *Proceedings of the 2017 EMNLP Workshop: Natural Language Processing Meets Journalism.* Copenhagen: Association for Computational Linguistics.

Rishes, Elena, Lukin, Stephanie M., Elson, David K., and Walker, Marilyn A. 2013. Generating Different Story Tellings from Semantic Representations of Narrative. Pages 192–204 of: Koenitz, Hartmut, Sezen, Tonguc Ibrahim, Ferri, Gabriele, et al. (eds.), *Interactive Storytelling: 6th International Conference, ICIDS 2013.* Springer International Publishing.

Rumelhart, David E. 1975. Notes on a Schema for Stories. Pages 211–236 of: *Representation and Understanding.* Elsevier.

Salton, G., and McGill, M.J. 1983. *Introduction to Modern Information Retrieval.* Computer Series. New York: McGraw-Hill.

Selivanov, Dmitriy, and Wang, Qing. 2016. text2vec: Modern Text Mining Framework for R. https://cran.r-project.org/web/packages/text2vec/index.html.

Soricut, Radu, and Marcu, Daniel. 2003. Sentence Level Discourse Parsing Using Syntactic and Lexical Information. Pages 228–235 of: Hearst, Marti A., and Ostendorf, Mari (eds.), *Proceedings of the 2003 Human Language Technology Conference of the North American Chapter of the Association for Computational Linguistics.* Association for Computational Linguistics.

Sporleder, Caroline, and Lapata, Mirella. 2005. Discourse Chunking and Its Application to Sentence Compression. Pages 257–264 of: *HLT/EMNLP 2005, Human Language Technology Conference and Conference on Empirical Methods in*

Natural Language Processing, Proceedings of the Conference, 6–8 October 2005, Vancouver, British Columbia, Canada.

Vossen, Piek, Caselli, Tommaso, and Segers, Roxane. 2021. A Narratology-Based Framework for Storyline Extraction. Pages 130–147 of: Caselli, Tommaso, Palmer, Martha, Hovy, Eduard, and Vossen, Piek (eds.), *Computational Analysis of Storylines: Making Sense of Events*. Cambridge University Press.

Yan, Xinru, Naik, Aakanksha, Jo, Yohan, and Rose, Carolyn. 2019. Using Functional Schemas to Understand Social Media Narratives. Pages 22–33 of: *Proceedings of the Second Workshop on Storytelling*.

Yang, Bishan, and Mitchell, Tom. 2016. Joint Extraction of Events and Entities within a Document Context. Pages 289–299 of: Knight, Kevin, Nenkova, Ani, and Rambow, Owen (eds.), *Proceedings of the 2016 Conference of the North American Chapter of the ACL: Human Language Technologies*. Association for Computational Linguistics.

Yarlott, W. Victor, Cornelio, Cristina, Gao, Tian, and Finlayson, Mark. 2018. Identifying the Discourse Function of News Article Paragraphs. Pages 25–33 of: Caselli, Tommaso, Miller, Ben, van Erp, Marieke, et al. (eds.), *Proceedings of the Workshop Events and Stories in the News 2018*. Santa Fe, NM: Association for Computational Linguistics.

Yarlott, W. Victor H., and Finlayson, Mark A. 2016. ProppML: A Complete Annotation Scheme for Proppian Morphologies. Pages 8:1–8:19 of: Miller, Ben, Lieto, Antonio, Ronfard, Rémi, Ware, Stephen G., and Finlayson, Mark A. (eds.), *7th Workshop on Computational Models of Narrative (CMN 2016)*. OpenAccess Series in Informatics (OASIcs), Vol. 53. Dagstuhl, Germany: Schloss Dagstuhl–Leibniz-Zentrum für Informatik.

Author Index